James Stuart Candlish

**The Christian salvation : lectures on the work of Christ, its appropriation and its issues**

James Stuart Candlish

**The Christian salvation : lectures on the work of Christ, its appropriation and its issues**

ISBN/EAN: 9783337263607

Printed in Europe, USA, Canada, Australia, Japan

Cover: Foto ©Lupo / pixelio.de

More available books at **www.hansebooks.com**

# THE
# CHRISTIAN SALVATION

LECTURES ON

## THE WORK OF CHRIST

ITS APPROPRIATION AND ITS ISSUES

BY THE LATE

JAMES S. CANDLISH, D.D.

PROFESSOR OF THEOLOGY, FREE CHURCH COLLEGE, GLASGOW

EDINBURGH
T. & T. CLARK, 38 GEORGE STREET
1899

# PREFATORY NOTE

Dr. Candlish was for twenty-five years Professor of Systematic Theology in the Free Church College, Glasgow, and when he died two years ago there was a widespread desire among those who knew him that the results of his lifelong labour in this department should not be lost to the world. The contents of this volume have been selected, in response to this desire, from a considerable mass of manuscript covering the whole field of theology. On most of the great topics Dr. Candlish had written again and again, in whole or in part; and while this made the work of selection somewhat more difficult, it gives a guarantee that though he did not himself prepare this volume for the press, it may be regarded as representing his mature mind on the subjects with which it deals. The Lectures on the "Work of Christ," which stand first, were apparently the last continuous piece of work which he did for his class. Unfortunately the closing lecture on this subject—that on the "Intercession of Christ"—could not be found when it was decided to begin printing; it was only discovered in time to be inserted at the end of the volume. The other lectures were chosen, partly because of their connection with the work of Christ, which it had been decided should be central, and determine the character of the volume; partly because the subjects of which they treat —the Church, the New Life, the Sacraments, the Last Things—are, for various reasons, of special interest at the present time; but partly also because they illustrate more completely than most that combination of the biblical, the historical, and the experimental, which was the characteristic of all Dr. Candlish's work.

JAMES DENNEY.

# CONTENTS

## THE WORK OF CHRIST

### THE FACTS AS PRESENTED IN THE GOSPELS

|  | PAGE |
|---|---|
| 1. CHRIST AS PROPHET | 1-4 |
| 2. CHRIST AS KING | 4-6 |
| 3. CHRIST AS PRIEST | 6-10 |
|     The Threefold Office of Christ | 10-12 |
|     The Priestly Office in Particular | 13 |
| I. ATONEMENT | 13 |
|     Meaning of Sacrifice | 14-21 |

### THE NEW TESTAMENT TEACHING ON THE ATONEMENT OF CHRIST

1. Statements of Christ . . 22-27
2. Teaching of the Apostles—
   (1) Paul's Conception of Christ's Death as Redemption from the Curse of the Law . . . . . 27-30
   (2) Paul's Conception of Christ's Death as a Death to Sin, in which we share . . . . . 30, 31
   (3) The Conception of Christ's Death in Hebrews, as giving us access to God . . . . 31-33
   (4) View indicated by John, of Christ as our Atonement through Communion . . . . . 33-35

### SYSTEMATIC CONSTRUCTION OF THE DOCTRINE OF ATONEMENT

| Classification of Theories | 37-40 |
|---|---|
| Theories of Moral Influence | 40-42 |
| Objective Theories | 42-49 |
| Mystical Theories | 49-53 |

II. INTERCESSION—
  1. Biblical Foundation of the Doctrine . 255-257
  2. Nature of Christ's Intercession . . 257-261
  3. Extent of Christ's Intercession . . 261-263

## DOCTRINE OF THE CHURCH

|     |                                              | PAGE    |
| --- | -------------------------------------------- | ------- |
| I.  | Roman Catholic Doctrine                      | 54–63   |
| II. | Erastian Doctrine                            | 63–66   |
| III.| Evangelical Doctrine                         | 66–71   |
|     | Relation of the Church to the Kingdom of God | 71–79   |
|     | The Notes of the Church                      | 79–82   |

## THE NEW LIFE

|     |                                                          |         |
| --- | -------------------------------------------------------- | ------- |
| I.  | Renewal                                                  | 83–92   |
|     | The work of the Holy Spirit                              | 87–89   |
|     | After Christ's likeness                                  | 89–91   |
|     | Conditioned by faith                                     | 91, 92  |
| II. | Sanctification—what it is                                | 93–100  |
| III.| Sanctification—the means of it, and responsibility for it| 101–110 |
| IV. | Sanctification—its degrees—                              |         |
|     |    A. Roman Catholic View                 | 110–118 |
|     |    B. Antinomian View                     | 118–125 |
|     |    C. Perfectionism                       | 126–133 |

## THE SACRAMENTS

|     |                                       |         |
| --- | ------------------------------------- | ------- |
| I.  | Introductory and Historical           | 134–140 |
| II. | Nature and Relations of the Sacraments| 140–143 |

### BAPTISM

| |                                                            |         |
|-| ---------------------------------------------------------- | ------- |
|1.| Its outward form                                          | 143–148 |
|2.| Its significance                                          | 148–150 |
|3.| Its efficacy                                              | 150–152 |
|  | Who are to be baptized?                                   | 153–169 |
|  | Baptism of infants justified                              | 154–161 |
|  | Principle on which the children of believers are baptized | 161–169 |
|  | Baptismal Regeneration                                    | 169–179 |

### THE LORD'S SUPPER

| |                                      |          |
|-| ------------------------------------ | -------- |
|1.| The external sign                   | 180–185  |
|2.| The significance of the Supper      | 185–187  |
|3.| Its efficacy—                       |          |
|  |   A. Roman Catholic Doctrine | 187–191 |
|  |   B. Lutheran Doctrine    | 191–194  |
|  |   C. Zwinglian Doctrine   | 194, 195 |
|  |   D. Reformed Doctrine    | 195–200  |
|  |     Christ's Presence in the Supper | 200, 201 |
|  |     Qualifications for Communion    | 202–204 |

## ESCHATOLOGY

PAGE

I. Meaning of Life and Death in the New Testament—
  1. In the teaching of Jesus . . . 205–210
  2. In the Epistle of James . . . 210, 211
  3. In the teaching of Paul . . 211–219
  4. In the Epistle to the Hebrews . 219, 220
  5. In the First Epistle of Peter . 220, 221
  6. In the Second Epistle of Peter 221, 222
  7. In the teaching of John . 222, 223

II. The Intermediate State—
  1. Wide difference between the godly and the ungodly . 223–228
  2. Conception of penal or purgatorial sufferings for the godly . 228–232

III. The Final States—
  General Scope of New Testament language . . 232–237
  1. Universalism . . . . 237–241
  2. Conditional Immortality . . . 241–243
  3. Mitigations of suffering . . . . 244–249
  Rewards and activities of the saints in heaven . 249–254

# THE CHRISTIAN SALVATION

## THE WORK OF CHRIST

### *THE FACTS AS PRESENTED IN THE GOSPELS*

IN considering the work of Jesus as our Saviour, it is the actual facts of His life as they are presented to us in the gospel records that we must study and endeavour to understand in their meaning and purpose.

### 1. CHRIST AS PROPHET

Now the most obvious aspect that the life-work of Jesus of Nazareth presented to the view of His contemporaries, was that of a prophet or messenger sent by God, like the prophets of ancient Israel, and His immediate forerunner John the Baptist. As such Jesus was recognised by all those who were in any degree favourable to Him at all,—by Nicodemus when He came to him by night (John 3²), by the blind beggar to whom our Lord gave sight (John 9¹⁷), and by the multitudes in Jerusalem on His triumphal entry into the city (Matt. 21¹¹). When His miracles were recognised as really wrought by divine power, this was the lowest inference that was drawn, and some who did not go so far as to acknowledge Him to be the Messiah, thought He might be John the Baptist or one of the old prophets risen from the dead (Matt. 16¹⁴). Our Saviour's office, then, is undoubtedly that of a prophet or teacher sent from God, though it is also much more: it includes other functions besides that of revealing God, and even as a revealer He is away, and give place to what is more perfect. The matter in which He did this most distinctly was the Jewish law of marriage. He said that the permission of divorce was not in accordance with the original and ideal relation as instituted by God at creation, but a temporary permission, owing to the hardness of men's hearts, and not to be allowed by the perfect law of God's kingdom (Mark $10^{2ff}$). Again, in His broad statement that nothing entering from without can defile a man, He virtually, as Mark notes, made all meats clean (Mark $7^{15-19}$), and so indicated that the whole law of clean and unclean food, though divinely appointed for a time, was yet merely positive, and from henceforth to pass away. This practically involved the abolition of the entire external distinction between Israel as the one holy nation and the Gentiles. Similarly, in His conversation with the Samaritan woman, He declared that the special sacredness of any one place of worship was to be done away, and that the only requirement for acceptance with God was to worship Him as the Father, in spirit and in truth (John $4^{23}$).

## 2. CHRIST AS KING

These were real alterations in the positive institutions of the Old Testament religion of which Jesus, as teaching with divine authority, gave sufficient hints, which were afterwards applied by His apostles. But while He thus developed and perfected the revelation given before, of which He Himself in His pre-incarnate state had been the Mediator, the great theme of His earthly ministry was the announcement of its fulfilment in the kingdom of God now come. In the parts of His teaching already mentioned, Jesus acted simply as the old prophets had done, but in proclaiming God's reign already come, in His person, He went beyond them all, and invited men to Himself in a way none of them had ever done. "Come unto Me all ye that labour and are heavy laden, and I will give you rest"; "How often would I have gathered you . . . and ye would not"; "If any man thirst, let him come unto Me and drink"; "Can the children of the bride-chamber fast while the bridegroom is with them?" These and similar statements show that Jesus was not merely a teacher of divine truth, but the founder of a new society, which He called the kingdom of God, in which men should obey the highest morality as God's will, and enjoy the truest blessedness in God's fellowship. This is what theologians mean by calling Him a king, or at least this is what there is reason to think He meant when before Pilate He did not deny that He was the King of the Jews, as He surely would have done had that been a mere figurative expression, like the paradox of the Stoics, that the wise man is a king. He cannot be supposed to have died for a mere metaphor: the kingship that He claimed must have been a reality, though it was so different from the kingdoms of this world that Pilate could not understand it. This is confirmed by the fact that the great theme of His preaching was the kingdom of God. That was the subject of His longest public discourse (Matt. 5–7), and of nearly all His parables (Matt. 13, etc.). The substance of His teaching was a description of this kingdom of God or of heaven, the way of entrance into it, the character, duties, blessings of its subjects, its progress in the world, and its final consummation. This kingdom, moreover, He connected in a special manner with His own person: by His advent it was brought near to men, and His work on earth was the establishment of it. Thus while He was a prophet, He was also the theme of His own teaching; He proclaimed Himself in a way no other teacher of religion had ever done. Moses said, "What are we that ye murmur against us? your murmurings are against the Lord" (Ex. 16⁷). John the Baptist said, "I am but a voice crying." Jesus said, "Come unto Me," "Follow Me," yet was most manifestly meek and lowly in heart.

While, therefore, the work of Jesus on earth was undoubtedly that of a prophet, it was something more. He must be regarded also as a king. While refusing to be made a king by the people, or set up an earthly reign such as they expected, He spoke as one having authority: He called men to follow Him, He formed them into a community of which He was head and lord, and which was not a mere sect or school of disciples, but a church or congregation, a religious society, that has proved world wide. A certain preparation or transition to this was provided by the condition of the people of Israel since the Babylonian exile and dispersion. Israel was no longer an independent nation or political community. Those of the Jews indeed who had returned to Palestine had a political organisation of their own, subject to the rule of the successive Empires of Persia, Syria, and Rome; but the Jews of the dispersion were not politically under the magistrates of Judea, but under the rulers of their respective places of abode. Yet they were united in religion and national feeling with their brethren in Judea, and wheresoever they dwelt; and they all felt themselves to be the covenant people of God. Theirs was a unity such as had not been seen in the world before, intermediate between the old one of nations and the spiritual one of the Christian Church. They looked for a restoration of their former political independence, but Jesus led His disciples away from that idea to the formation of a perfectly spiritual and therefore universal society. Yet this was to be so truly a continuation and development of the old kingdom of God, that He called it the new covenant, or simply the covenant: it was the perfecting of the true Israel's relation to God in a new and higher form.[1]

### 3. CHRIST AS PRIEST

In this society Jesus reigns as the Messiah sent of God, and ruling for Him. That He is recognised as king by multitudes, and that through Him many in all ages have been brought to recognise and obey the highest laws of holiness and love, are undoubted facts of history and experience. But what is the power by which He does this? It is not force or civil constraint: it is not superstitious fear or selfish hope of rewards in a future life. These means have

---

[1] In the report of Jesus' words at the Supper, Matthew (26$^{28}$) and Mark (14$^{24}$), according to the best authorities, give only "covenant." Luke (22$^{20}$) and Paul (1 Cor. 11$^{25}$) give "new covenant." The reference seems to be to Jeremiah (31$^{31ff.}$); but according to Old Testament usage the same transaction is sometimes called a covenant distinct from former ones, and sometimes the renewal of the one covenant that Jehovah had made with Abraham and confirmed at successive times following, with various modifications.

no doubt been employed by many of Christ's professing disciples as substitutes or aids to the advancement of Christianity, but this has been contrary to the spirit of their Master, and apart from them the genuine precepts of His teaching have been most really and actively obeyed. The motive on which Jesus relied, and which has proved the most powerful, has been love to Him. As it is put in *Ecce Homo*, Christ sought and accomplished the moral restoration of men from sin to holiness by bringing them, under the strongest motives of love and gratitude, to live a life of holiness.

Now what is this great boon that Christ has bestowed on men that brings them under a sense of infinite obligation, and has proved a motive power of sufficient strength to overcome selfish and worldly influences, and prompt to a life of godliness and disinterested love to men? It has had this power, we must remember, not only over those who lived at the time and in personal intercourse with the historical Jesus, but over those multitudes in all succeeding ages who have acknowledged Him as their Lord, and lived and died for Him. It cannot, therefore, be merely the personal human kindness and grace of His conduct towards them, wonderful as that manifestly was; it must be something that He has done equally for those who believe on Him through the testimony of His immediate disciples. They also are directly sensible of owing an infinite blessing to the Lord, giving Himself for them. That blessing cannot be merely moral renewal or conversion. That is indeed a great blessing which we owe to Jesus. But it is effected, as we have seen, through the means of the moral influence of gratitude awakened by a previous boon which must be distinct from itself. That previous boon includes the revelation of God's grace and love to sinners, but not as a mere theoretic teaching, but as an actual communication; and in the New Testament it is constantly represented as forgiveness of sins or reconciliation to God through the death of Christ for us.

This is what makes the influence of Jesus specifically different from that of any other benefactor or elevator of the race, and entitles Him to be regarded as a priest, not less really than as a prophet and a king. He not only reveals the character and will of God, and secures in His disciples loving obedience to that will, and likeness to that character, but reconciles men to God by giving them forgiveness for the sins that separated them from God, and for this end especially He laid down His life.

He claimed as the Son of Man power to forgive sins (Mark $2^{5\mathrm{ff.}}$), and said that His blood was shed on behalf of many unto remission of sins (Matt. $26^{28}$), that He was to give His flesh for the life of the world (John $6^{51}$), that He was to be lifted up on the cross that whosoever believeth in Him should not perish but have eternal life (John $3^{14}$), that He came to give His life a ransom for many (Matt. $20^{28}$).

His disciples, though, as we shall see, viewing His work in different aspects, all agree in the great fundamental belief that He lived and died that we might be forgiven and reconciled to God. Paul says, "He died for our sins" (1 Cor. $15^3$), "for us, that we might live together with Him" (1 Thess. $5^{10}$), "He was delivered for our trespasses and raised for our justification" (Rom. $4^{25}$), "we are reconciled to God by the death of His Son" (Rom. $5^{10}$). Peter says Christ "suffered for sins, the just on behalf of the unjust, that He might bring us to God" (1 Pet. $3^{18}$).

John says "our sins are forgiven us for His Name's sake" (1 John $2^{12}$).

Our Saviour is not indeed expressly called a priest either by Himself or by any of His disciples except the author of the Epistle to the Hebrews, but it is noteworthy that that writer founds his exposition of that office on a verse in a Psalm to which Jesus on a memorable occasion appealed as a Messianic one (Matt. $22^{41\mathrm{ff.}}$). The elaborate comparison of His work with that of the Levitical high priest is appropriate only for Jews and students of the Old Testament, but in the other epistles His death is frequently described as a sacrifice; and when Paul says He gave Himself for us as a sacrifice (Eph. $5^2$), he virtually describes Him as doing the work of a priest.

In the broad general sense of one who reconciles us to God, and through whom we are to draw near to God, there can be no doubt that the idea of Christ being a priest is a New Testament one, and has the sanction of our Saviour Himself, and it is one that completes and gives coherent meaning to the other functions that He performs. As prophet and founder of the kingdom of God, He acts as the representative of God towards men; but He is also described, and describes Himself, as acting for men towards God, and the only title by which such a function is known in the Bible, or indeed in literature generally, is that of a priest.

The simplest and most general definition of a priest, according to the Bible, would seem to be, one who brings men near to God in worship. This includes two things—

1. He draws near to God himself in worship. His is a religious function, his official actions are acts of divine service. This appears from the derivation of the names in various languages. The Hebrew כֹּהֵן signifies etymologically attendant, and so designates the priest simply as the attendant of God: ἱερεύς and *sacerdos* just express the sacred or religious nature of his functions. This aspect of the office is brought out in Num. 16⁵, where the privileges of the priest of Jehovah are said to be (*a*) that he is His, (*b*) that he is holy, (*c*) that he comes near to Him, all describing religious qualities and functions.

2. But a priest's work is also and more especially to lead others after and with him in his service to God. It is implied that the priest has, or obtains, special access to the Deity, and that others may not come near to worship without his services on their behalf. This is specially brought out in Heb. 5¹, where a priest is said to be appointed ὑπὲρ ἀνθρώπων τὰ πρὸς τὸν θεόν—on behalf of men, as to things toward God. The function, then, of bringing men to God, leading and encouraging them to worship and serve Him, gathering them together about His temple and in His presence, is essentially a priestly work; and that was what Jesus undertook and performed by His life and death: a life of obedience and holy service to God, and a death freely and willingly endured in submission to God's will and for His glory.

The great reason why the mediation of a priest is needed is, according to Old Testament ideas, God's holiness and man's unworthiness to come into His presence because of sin. Hence forgiveness is a chief blessing obtained through priestly services; and we have already seen that that is the benefit for which Jesus' disciples acknowledge their obligation to Him, as a constraining motive of gratitude. The ascription to Him, therefore, of the office of a priest is not a mere figure of speech based on incidental and unessential likenesses, but the assertion of a real parallelism in its deepest meaning, with a function that has been included in nearly all religions in substantially the same sense.

### The Threefold Office of Christ

The representation of the work of Christ under the form of the threefold function of a Prophet, Priest, or King is not absolutely necessary for the exhibition of the Scripture view of His work; and there have been evangelical divines who have rejected it as artificial and arbitrary, alleging that there are various other titles given to Him in Scripture, such as Shepherd, Leader, Friend, which are overlooked by the common division, and some of which are better fitted to exhibit His grace and love.

The customary division, however, has a good deal to recommend it. For one thing, the notion of office in general, as a function to which He was called and appointed by God, serves to bring out the important truth that the work of salvation is carried on according to the will of God. There is no separation between the Son and the Father; there is not more grace in Christ than in God; it is according to the will and appointment of His Father that He acts all through. Even though one part of His work is the obtaining the forgiveness of our sins, yet that is not done at His own hand, as if He came in to persuade the Father to be gracious to us. He has been appointed and sent for that very purpose. This is abundantly testified by the whole teaching and bearing of Jesus, and by many emphatic sayings; it is implied in His being called the Messiah, the Sent, the Servant of Jehovah.

The three functions of prophecy, priesthood, and kingship represent great historical agencies in the history of salvation, that formed the preparation for Christ, and they are altogether worthy to be ascribed to Him. They are not mere figures, but actual definite employments. Christ's work is not indeed exactly the same as that of the prophets, priests, and kings in Israel; more especially His priesthood differs from all others in being not ritual only but real: it is the substance of which the ancient priesthood was but a shadow. But He was foretold in all the three characters; and, as was anciently observed, the anointing which He received, and in virtue of which He is called Messiah or Christ, points to these three classes of persons.[1]

Further, these three functions correspond to three great wants of our sinful state. The world into which Christ came is in darkness through ignorance of God, and needs to be enlightened, and He came to reveal God, and so to be the light of the world. This is the function of a prophet. Again, the world is sinful, disobedient to God's will, and enslaved under the power of sin, needing to be brought back to allegiance to God and made obedient to His holy will. To effect this is the work of a king.

But further, the world is guilty, exposed to the holy anger and righteous condemnation of God, needing to be reconciled to God, forgiven and accepted in His sight; and to obtain this is the work of a priest.

It is to be observed that this division of the work of Christ is not a chronological one, but a relative one. We are not to conceive that in one part of His life He executed the office of a prophet, in another that of a priest, and in a third of a king.

All through and in the same works He executes them all,

---

[1] That He was predicted and expected as a king is most obvious and undoubted,—this was the sense generally attached to the name Messiah in Jesus' time,—but it is also clear that in prophecy the Saviour to come is represented as a revealer of truth (Isa. 42, 49, 61), and was expected as such even in Samaria (John 4²⁵); still more distinctly (John 6¹⁴). He is more rarely called a priest; but the name is found in Ps. 110, perhaps is given Him in Zech. 6¹³, and when it is said of the Servant of Jehovah that He pours out His soul to death as a guilt-offering and makes intercession for the transgressors, priestly functions are ascribed to Him (Isa. 53).

and they are just different aspects in which His work may be regarded. In His miracles, for instance, He was most obviously acting as a king, delivering men from evils, but He also taught important truths as a prophet, and by His toil and sympathy with suffering He was bearing our sicknesses as a priest. On the cross He was most conspicuously offering Himself as a sacrifice, but He was also making the perfect revelation of God's character, and drawing man to Him by the power of His love.

Perhaps the old form of representing the offices of Christ tended to separate them too much, though that was not the intention of it; and greater unity in our view of His work may be secured by adopting the view of some modern theologians, that the kingship is the chief of Christ's offices, and that the functions of a prophet and of a priest are implied in and subordinate to that. Jesus' life-task was the establishment of the kingdom of God, of which He, as Messiah, was to be the sovereign. Since it is a kingdom, His functions are regal; but since it is a kingdom of God, He has not merely to unite men among themselves, but to bring them to God: hence He must also have priestly functions.

The representation of Christ's death as a sacrifice is so frequent and emphatic in Scripture that it can hardly be denied to be a natural and suitable one, and nearly all theologians have made use of it. But if we use the notion of a sacrifice without that of a priest, we run great risk of contemplating only the passive aspect of Christ's suffering and death, and laying stress only on what He endured. But, as we have seen, He Himself and His apostles lay great stress on the fact that He was active in it all, giving Himself, laying down His life, offering Himself to God. Hence our conception of Christ as our sacrifice is not complete unless we think of Him not merely as one on whom suffering was laid, and who was put to death, but as giving Himself up to suffer and die, offering Himself as a sacrifice, *i.e.*, as a priest as well as a sacrifice.

### The Priestly Office in Particular

Since the principal functions of a priest's office in general are offering sacrifice and making intercession, the priestly work of our Saviour is naturally divided into two parts, Atonement and Intercession, the former of which He accomplished once for all in His life on earth, while the latter He is continually carrying on.

Atonement in its modern sense seems the best term to express the idea conveyed by the Greek ἱλασμός with its cognates, corresponding to the Hebrew כפר with its cognates, used to describe the action of sacrifices in the Old Testament, and applied to our Lord's work by Paul, John, and the writer to the Hebrews. Etymologically, the English word means rather to reconcile, to make two parties to be "at one," and so would correspond to another set of words in the original, —καταλλάσσω and its cognates,—which also express an important biblical idea. But in modern English usage it has long lost this original sense, and is always understood to mean, not the reconciliation itself, but the work by which it is effected or made possible. This notion is expressed in the English Bible by "propitiation," and by many theologians also by "expiation"; but as these terms seem to involve questionable theories, atonement is preferable, as simpler and yet quite definite enough. Reconciliation and redemption are also precious scriptural ideas applicable to the saving work of Christ for us which we must also consider, but they include more than comes under the priestly office, though, as we shall see, they are founded and rooted in that.

### I. ATONEMENT

Atonement may be most simply described as the work of a priest offering a sacrifice to obtain the forgiveness and favour of God for sinners; and this is an idea that is found in every form of religion, in all ages and in all races of men sometimes, indeed, in very cruel and immoral forms, and sometimes in very dim and faded outlines; but very clearly in the religion of Israel.

When we apply this conception to our Saviour, as the apostles did, following out the hints of their Master, we mean that the sacrifice He offered was Himself, His life, His blood. He gave Himself to God in His whole life on earth: He lived to do the will of His Father and finish His work: He pleased not Himself, nor came to be ministered to, but to minister, to be a servant, to seek and to save the lost. This was the course of His whole life; it was an unbroken career of self-denying service of men, in obedience to the will of God; and it was crowned by a free and willing giving-up of His life for the great cause for which He had lived. His blood, He said, was shed for the remission of sins; He was to be lifted up that men might not perish but have eternal life. This is the great blessed reality which the apostles and their followers had before their minds when they spoke of Christ offering Himself a sacrifice for us, and which we must ever keep in view as we seek to understand how the notion of an atoning sacrifice is applicable to it, and serves to explain its meaning.

### *Meaning of Sacrifice*

The conception of Christ's work for us as an atoning sacrifice enables us to compare the Christian doctrine of atonement with those of other religions, and to examine how far these were preparations for, or gropings after, the true way of a sinner's reconciliation to God. For in nearly all religions the rite of slaying animals as a part of divine worship, and a means of obtaining the favour of the Deity, has prevailed. The origin and meaning of this remarkable custom are matters of interest, and it may be of importance, on which different opinions have been held.

It has been maintained by many theologians that the rite of animal sacrifice owes its origin to a direct divine appointment after the Fall, whence it has been handed down by tradition, though with many corruptions, in all nations. This view is not indeed supported by any express statements of Scripture, but was deduced inferentially from its representations and the facts of the case.

Since it belongs to God to prescribe the way of a sinner's

approach to Him, and He is not pleased with any mere humanly-devised worship, His acceptance of the sacrifices of Abel, Noah, Job, etc., was thought to imply that He must have in some way directed this special form of worship.

Again, if it was a mere device of man's superstition, it would seem unworthy of God to give it such an important place in the religious institutions of Israel.

It was also argued that the notion of pleasing God by inflicting pain and death on one of His creatures is so little suggested by nature or reason, that its independent appearance in widely distant lands and peoples could only be accounted for by a positive divine appointment at the first.

On the other hand, there were some, even of the strictest regard for Scripture, who thought that these reasonings could not outweigh the silence of the sacred record on a subject of so great importance; and in view of modern researches in Comparative Religion and Biblical Criticism, and the caution which we should observe in making a literal use of the early portions of Scripture, it is more difficult than it once seemed to make out a direct divine origin of sacrifice, and it must be regarded as at best an obscure and doubtful point.

The narrative of the offerings of Cain and Abel (Gen $4^{1-7}$) belongs to the same source (J) as the account of the Fall and of the first promise, and may therefore be read in connection with the statement ($3^{21}$) that Jehovah made for Adam and his wife coats of skin. Whether or not, as some think, the animals whose skins were thus used were slain in sacrifice, the statement implies that the guilty shame caused by sin was covered through the death of innocent beasts; and when we are told that Abel came before God with slain lambs, the meaning seems plainly to be, that he acknowledged himself a sinner, deserving death, and trusted to the promise on which God had made man to hope. His worship was like that of the publican in Christ's parable, while Cain's, a mere expression of thanks, resembled that of the Pharisee; and if the ancient record is not so much a literal history as a picture like that, intended to show in the very beginning of history the contrast between the humble believer and the self-righteous, it would not be less worthy of God or less instruclive to us. In any case, the narrative shows that at the time it was written bloody sacrifices were regarded as more pleasing to God than were vegetable offerings.

Sacrifice was not prescribed to Israel as a new thing when they came out of Egypt : it had been offered by the patriarchs, and it was taken for granted that it would continue to be offered in the nation now freed to serve Jehovah. Directions were given as to what, and where, and how they were to sacrifice; and these, which exist in the earliest Codes, are in the later ones so elaborate, that it is impossible to believe that it was merely an ancient usage tolerated, like slavery or divorce, and we must conclude that it was accepted and sanctioned by God as a suitable form of worship for that time. The notion of sacrifice is also used implicitly by Jesus Himself and expressly by His apostles, as an illustration of His work and death for us. These facts are enough to show that the inquiry into the meaning of the rite is not one of mere curiosity, but of real importance as fitted to throw light on the nature of Christ's salvation.

Three main ideas have been connected with the rite of sacrifice by the nations that have used it—that of a gift to the Deity; that of the infliction of pain and death on a victim to avert the wrath of the Deity; and that of life-fellowship with the Deity.

The most general notion of sacrifice is that of presenting something to the Deity in token of the adoration of the heart. As the religious feeling naturally and spontaneously tends to express itself in words in the form of prayer, so when especially deep and lively it will seek further expression in gifts, and so sacrifice has been well described by Hengstenberg as an embodied prayer (*verkörpertes Gebet*). The analogy of sacrifice and prayer is a real one, and will be found of use to solve some of the difficulties in the doctrine of Christ's atonement.

Wherever men believe in a God from whom they receive blessings, the instinct of religion will prompt them to thank Him for His gifts, and to pray for a continuance and renewal of His favour, and to express these emotions in the outward symbolic form of gifts. What they would offer would naturally be things in which they found pleasure themselves, and the simplest and most elementary forms of these would be food and drink. These might be offered simply as symbols that they desired to please the Deity, without the notion that He was really nourished by them ; but since anthropomorphism has so largely pervaded the religions of mankind, the idea appears in the popular belief of many nations, even in that of Israel in early times, that the Deity really partook of the sacrifices offered, or of the savour that rolled up to heaven along with the smoke. (See Deut. 32$^{38}$, Ps. 50$^{13}$; Homer, *Iliad*, 1$^{317}$.)

In this stage of religious history the form of sacrifice would depend on that of the food of the people. If they were agricultural and their diet vegetable, their offerings would be of corn, wine, oil, meal, cakes, and the like ; while if they used animal food, the flesh of slain beasts would be an equally natural gift.

There was a view widely held by philosophers, and expressed by Plato, Aristotle, and others, that the earliest and purest form of religion admitted only unbloody sacrifices, and that the introduction of bloody sacrifices was a later corruption. This is not borne out, but contradicted, by historical and archaeological evidence ; but it seems to contain recollections of a period of religious reform, associated with the names of Pythagoras and others, and probably parallel to the Zoroastrian movement in the East, when an attempt was made to soften the barbarism and cruelty of older usages by substituting vegetable for animal sacrifices. Under this influence, in the early historical period in Greece, unbloody sacrifices come into the foreground, and it might be expected that with the advance of refinement they would supersede the old bloody ones. But this is not the case ; for in the later age, just before and after the time of Christ, there was a remarkable revival of the old rites of sacrificial expiation in their most horrid and revolting forms. This seems to show that besides the notion of gifts there was embodied in the animal sacrifices some other idea that lay very deep in the human heart.

The idea of sacrifices as gifts to the Deity prevailed especially in anthropomorphic religions, where the powers of nature were personified and worshipped in human forms.

Thus it appears in the ancient Vedic religion in India, where the oldest form of sacrifice was not piacular, but consisted in offerings of food to the gods, which were supposed to nourish them. Somewhat later, but still in Vedic times, animal sacrifices appear, and the idea of expiation is connected with them. There are also in the ancient documents of the Brahmanas strange legends about the gods themselves having offered sacrifice to the Supreme Being, and by it obtained immortality and heaven.

The primitive Aryan religion in India afterwards developed in two directions—to philosophic Pantheism on the one hand, and popular polytheistic idolatry on the other. In the latter the idea of expiation found expression in the grossest and most cruel forms of sacrifice; but through the influence of pantheistic Brahmanism these were mostly confined to the worship of particular deities (as Kali), or of lower tribes, and the religion generally prevalent treats sacrifices simply as acts of homage, and rejects the slaughter of animals and any idea of expiation.

In the Hellenic religion, also, sacrifices were mainly conceived as gifts, since here especially the deities were worshipped in human form and conceived as magnified men. They were thought to be persuaded by gifts to be favourable to their worshippers. But the idea of expiation for sin by its penalty being laid on a sacrificial victim is not absent from the Greek ritual, and there are in their mythology well-known legends of human sacrifices being offered to avert the wrath of Heaven.

Thus even in those religions where sacrifices are most distinctly and pre-eminently offered as gifts, the idea of expiation has always, to some extent, come in, though in some cases, by reason of the character of the theology, it has not obtained a lasting or general hold. This appears very distinctly in the custom of human sacrifices, which, unnatural and cruel though it is, seems not to have been entirely unknown in any branch of the human race. This cannot be traced in any way to the notion of a gift to the Deity; for though it would be natural to offer the flesh of such animals as men used for food, it is impossible to suppose that human flesh could ever have been offered for such a purpose; and where human victims have been sacrificed, it has been frequently declared to be to avert the wrath of the Deity from those who deserved to die.

This piacular idea of sacrifice appears especially in the Roman, Teutonic, and Celtic religions. The gods of the Romans were rather abstract moral ideas personified than deified men, and the ideas of law, judgment, and retribution were strongly impressed on their minds. In their history we continually read of appeasing the gods and averting their anger by sacrifices; and we meet with stories such as those of Curtius and the Decii devoting themselves to death and the lower powers for the safety and victory of their country.

Besides the notion of gifts and that of averting punishment by vicarious suffering, a third idea connected with sacrifice in ancient times is that of mystical communion with the deity worshipped. This has been brought out, especially among the Semitic races, by Professor W. Robertson Smith, and somewhat similar ideas have been traced in other peoples in rude stages of civilisation. They rest on those primitive beliefs that led to totemism, that the divine power which was worshipped in nature showed itself especially in certain forms of animal life, and that those tribes that belonged to a common stock were literally descended from and akin to the animals whose name they bore and whom they reverenced as divine. Dr. W. R. Smith's conclusion is expressed thus: "We may now take it as made out that throughout the Semitic field the fundamental idea of sacrifice is not that of a sacred tribute, but of communion between the god and his worshippers by joint participation in the living flesh and blood of a sacred victim."[1] The animal sacrificed was thought to be one in which the divine life dwelt, and the kinship, held to be actually physical, was renewed and strengthened from time to time by the physical partaking of the sacred life. When this crude notion of the kinship of gods, men, and animals ceased to be held and was forgotten, then, on the one hand, sacrifices became mere sacred

[1] *The Religion of the Semites*, p. 327.

feasts, in which a part was given to the deity, and men rejoiced before him; while, on the other hand, for special atoning purposes sacred animals were slaughtered, though no longer eaten, but burned or otherwise disposed of, and the blood sprinkled. While the earlier ideas prevailed, the animals sacrificed were not regarded as food offered to the deity, but rather as embodiments of the deity, and the rite was one of mystic communion. With this conception the practice of human sacrifices is more explicable than on the theory of gifts for food, because the divine nature might be conceived to be embodied in men as well as in animals. At a time when religion had the form of Animism, or worship of the soul, believed to be immanent in nature, kings and priests, usually the same, were regarded as incarnations of this divine power, and on their being in life and vigour depended the prosperity of the people. But just for that reason they were not allowed to die a natural death through gradual decay, but were killed by violence, that the divine life might pass in full vigour to their successors. Then, again, the death of the vegetation in winter and its revival in spring led to the idea of a periodic death and rising again of the deity, as seen in the legends of Adonis, Attis, Dionysos, Osiris, Proserpine, etc.; and the harvest ritual and customs of many even European countries point to the notion of the killing of the corn spirit when the corn is reaped, and its coming back to life in spring. An animal or human victim sometimes represented the corn spirit, and its flesh was either eaten or put into the ground along with the corn sown for the new crop. Afterwards, when anthropomorphic deities took the place in men's minds of nature powers, the animals that had been by old custom sacrificed as being the embodiments of these powers came to be regarded as being or representing things hostile to the now personified god, so that their death tended to appease the anger of those deities. And as in the progress of refinement animals came to be substituted for human victims, the idea arose that in all cases the animal offered took the place of a man at the altar.

That these ideas of mystic life-fellowship with the Deity,

and of the death and revival of the nature spirit, did exist in connection with sacrificial rites in many races seems undeniable, however strange and repulsive they seem to us. Whether they are the most ancient notions connected with bloody sacrifices, and those to which in all cases they can be traced back, does not appear equally certain: the facts have been brought to light comparatively recently, and the period is one of very great and obscure antiquity.

In the sacrificial ritual of Israel all the three ideas of gifts, of piacular suffering, and of life-communion are recognised and symbolised, yet each is guarded with rules that tend to prevent the abuses to which it is liable.

The idea of gifts is expressed by the simplest and most general term, corban, applied to all offerings in general, and by the presentation of all before Jehovah. But it was made plain that God was not to be imagined to partake of human food, by the prohibition of offering some things commonly used as food, such as leaven and honey (Lev. $2^{11}$), and, on the other hand, of eating with blood, which was reserved entirely for sacrificial use (Lev. $17^{10}$). Thus while the altar was the table of Jehovah, and the sacrifice on it His bread, a broad and firm distinction was made between its solemn service and a mere meal.

Again, the idea of expiation was expressed by the fact that for sins of ignorance pardon was not obtained without the shedding of the life-blood of a victim; but the abuses to which this idea often led were restrained by the absolute prohibition of human sacrifices; and that man might not think of God as a Being who delighted in suffering and death, they were taught that it was of His grace that He permitted them to draw near by sacrifice, and that He had given them the blood to be an atonement for their souls (Lev. $17^{11}$).

Once more, the idea of life-communion with the Deity was expressed in the sacrificial feast on the flesh of the victim: but all the disgusting and cruel practices of eating living flesh and blood were dissociated from it, and Israel was taught that their relation to Jehovah was not of a physical but of a moral nature.

## The New Testament Teaching on the Atonement of Christ

We have now to study, first, those sayings of Jesus Himself that speak of the purpose of His work and death, and then the fuller explanations given by His apostles, especially by Paul, John, and the writer to the Hebrews.

### 1. Statements of Christ

From a comparatively early period in His ministry Jesus gave indications that it would be closed by a violent death, so that there is reason to believe that He was aware of this from the first. But up to the time of Peter's confession, near Cæsarea Philippi, He gave only general and obscure hints (John $2^{19}$ $3^{14}$, Matt. $9^{15}$, Mark $2^{20}$, Luke $5^{35}$), though the urgency and haste with which He pursued His work of teaching might indicate a consciousness that it would be soon stopped by His opponents. After the disciples were firmly convinced that He was the expected Messiah, He at once declared plainly to them that He was to be rejected and slain by His people and raised up the third day (Matt. $16^{21}$). This would at once exclude all ideas of an earthly Messianic reign, such as even the Twelve might entertain, and also suggest that His death and resurrection were not merely incidents in His history, but essential parts of His work. Thereafter He several times repeated the announcement, giving more particulars each time, and declaring that there was a divine necessity in the things He was to suffer (Matt. $17^{22}$ $20^{17}$, Mark $10^{33}$).

Jesus presents His approaching suffering and death in various aspects. It is the consequence of His faithful witness to truth and righteousness and, above all, to the love of God, against the hard legalism and hypocrisy of the predominant parties in Israel, and so it was analogous to the persecution and martyrdom of the prophets of old. This He brought out in the parable of the wicked husbandmen (Matt. $21^{33-39}$), and in various other sayings. It is also an act of obedience to the will of God; for He gave Himself up to death freely and voluntarily, and in both these respects, and in the meekness and patience with which He suffered, He is an example to us all. These aspects of His approaching death Jesus could and did present as soon as He announced it at all; but since His disciples were so unwilling and slow to admit even the fact that He must be rejected and crucified, He could not fully explain to them the deeper reasons and the further purposes of these things. Yet He gave from time to time intimations that His death was no mere accident, but an essential part of His work, and when the crisis was close at hand He embodied its meaning in a solemn and significant rite.

Among His sayings to this effect are those in which He speaks of His sufferings as a baptism with which He has to be baptized (Luke 12[50]), and in which those who would share in His glory must take part (Matt. 20[22, 23], Mark 10[38, 39]). This must mean that He should be overwhelmed as by a flood, but should rise from it with new life; and in connection with this reference Matthew and Mark both report the memorable saying, "The Son of Man came not to be ministered unto, but to minister, and to give His life a ransom for many" (Matt. 20[28], Mark 10[45]). These words convey at least two weighty assertions—first, that His death was no mere passive endurance, but a deliberate action on His part, the crowning act of the purpose of His whole work. This is confirmed by sayings recorded in the Fourth Gospel: "the bread which I will give is My flesh, for the life of the world" (John 6[51]); and, "I lay down My life for the sheep"; "no one taketh it from Me, but I lay it down of Myself. I have authority to lay it down, and I have authority to take it again" (John 10[15-18]). These sayings plainly declare that His death was a voluntary self-sacrifice on His part for the sake of men; and that, attested by Matthew and Mark, implies also, second, that it was a vicarious act, the giving of a ransom instead of many. Jesus undoubtedly gave Himself up in His death to the will of God; and so, whether He alluded to the half-shekel of atonement money (Ex. 30[12, 16]) which He had just before been asked to pay (Matt. 17[24, 27]), or to the words of Psalm 49[7], He must have meant that He was to give up His life to God, not merely for the good of men but in their place.

Then, on the eve of His death, we find Jesus significantly associating it with the Passover (Matt. 26$^2$, and perhaps also Luke 22$^{15}$), and according to all our authorities instituting an ordinance, the Lord's Supper, specially in memory of His death, which shows what an important part of His life-work He held it to be. His body is represented by bread broken, His blood by wine poured out, and that is said to have been "for you," "for many." The blood is further said to be that of the covenant, or the new covenant, *i.e.* the perfect relation of peace with God foretold by the prophets, sometimes as the restoration of God's ancient covenant, sometimes as the establishment of a new one. Once more, the purpose of the blood-shedding is declared to be "unto the remission of sins," which was a chief blessing of the new covenant promised through Jeremiah (31$^{33, 34}$). Whether we can rely on the verbal accuracy of all these statements or not, the scope of the institution as a whole is plainly this, that Christ gave Himself up for us to a violent death, in order that thereby we might be brought into a new relation of covenant and peace with God.

There are also certain statements ascribed to Jesus in the Fourth Gospel quite akin to those in the Synoptics already cited, that should be kept in view in estimating His testimony about His death before it took place. In John 15$^{13}$ He says, when referring to His love to His disciples, "Greater love hath no man than this, that a man lay down his life for his friends." The preposition rendered here "for" ($\upsilon\pi\acute{\epsilon}\rho$) does not necessarily imply substitution, but it does not exclude it, and it suggests a direct purpose to benefit His friends, such as a mere martyrdom does not include. Again, in John 17$^{19}$ He says, "For their sakes I sanctify (or consecrate) Myself, that they also may be sanctified in truth." He refers undoubtedly to His leaving the world by death; and, as is shown by Deut. 15$^{19-21}$, His words mean, I give Myself a sacrifice on their behalf, as their representative, that they also may be consecrated as sacrifices to God.

From a consideration of all these testimonies of Jesus

taken together, it appears that He regarded His death as far more than merely a martyrdom, or the endurance of suffering unto blood, for His faithfulness to the truth of God against the world's opposition. It was not a mere suffering or catastrophe that ended His work: it was an integral part of His work itself, the crowning purpose for which He came, the fact in His earthly life that He designed to be most solemnly kept in remembrance by His disciples, a great act of obedience to His Father's will, which procured for men the greatest moral blessings, such as forgiveness and eternal life in covenant with God.

That these are true representations of what our Lord really taught, and not due merely to the working of the disciples' minds, putting inferences of their own into their Master's mouth, is confirmed by two considerations, one positive and another negative. On the one hand, they are ideas common to all the New Testament writers, however different and more extensive their further ideas are. All alike view Jesus as not merely an example and a martyr, but as a Saviour, and, with the exception of James, all speak of His death as accomplishing our redemption, while even he speaks of our sins being forgiven through prayer in the name of Jesus (James $5^{14f.}$), and of our being saved by faith in Him, when it is living and working. Whence could such an agreement in a view of our dependence on Jesus as a redeemer, which was then quite new and original in the world, have been derived, if not from hints and suggestions by Jesus Himself, just such as are recorded in the Gospels?

On the other hand, the teaching ascribed to Jesus is elementary as compared with the expositions given in several of the epistles, especially those of Paul and that to the Hebrews. No full explanation is given by Jesus of why He must die, or how His death is related to the sin of the world, or for what reason it obtains forgiveness for men. These questions inevitably arose, and the apostolic epistles, many of them written before the Gospels, contain various lines of thought that contribute to a rationale of the great fact. Now, if the reports of Christ's sayings had been coloured by later apostolic thought, we would have found some of these

Pauline or other ideas imported into them; and since this is not so, we are led to conclude that the Evangelists have given us faithful reports of what Jesus taught.

Yet while giving no full theological doctrine of His atonement, the sayings of Jesus at different times about His work and death have this amount of unity among themselves, that they together represent them under the notion of a sacrifice, which was then an actual and familiar form of worship not only among the Jews but in all nations. The term "ransom," the analogy to the Passover, the blood of the covenant, the idea of sanctifying Himself, all point in that direction, and lead us to think that this was the idea in Jesus' own mind, or the thing with which He wished His disciples to compare His work for men. This is confirmed by the fact that the conception of Christ's work as a sacrifice is common to those of the apostles who have each their own distinctive views in further explanation of it. Paul explains it by reference to the law and justice of God, and in other places to the mystical union of believers with Christ; the writer to the Hebrews, by the holiness of God as permitting access to Him only through blood: John dwells on our relation to Christ as our life; but they all alike, as also Peter, freely use sacrificial language in reference to the work and death of Christ. This appears as a commonplace of Christian belief, underlying all the various forms of thought on the subject, and not needing to be proved or justified, but assumed as an acknowledged truth. The most obvious and natural explanation of this is, that it was derived from Jesus' own teaching.

It should also be noticed that this is not a mere matter of opinion or belief, but represents a great historical fact in the progress of religion. Christian worship has been from the beginning destitute of outward sacrifices, and so formed a sharp contrast with the rituals to which its converts had been accustomed, whether in Judaism or in heathenism. Yet it did not effect this great change by means of any theory that struck against the idea of sacrifice, as Buddhism, for example, did. On the contrary, sacrificial ideas and language pervade all its earliest records. The view expounded in Hebrews, and tacitly assumed elsewhere, is not that outward sacrifice is a service unworthy of God or unauthorised by Him, but that, as practised in Israel at least, it was a significant service suitable to a former time, and foreshadowing the great work of salvation by the Servant of Jehovah, who made His soul an offering for sin. The remarkable transition from sacrificial cults to a religion in which the holy life and voluntary death of Jesus were recognised as the perfect and final sacrifice, was made by the first Christians almost without observation or opposition, and this great fact can best be explained by the view given in the Gospels that Jesus Himself led them to regard His work in that aspect.

## 2. TEACHING OF THE APOSTLES

While the apostles in their discourses and epistles contained in the New Testament nearly all repeat or assume the elementary teaching about Christ's atonement given in the sayings of the Master Himself, and confirmed by His history, that He gave Himself as a sacrifice for us in order to the forgiveness of our sins, some of them have been led, under the teaching of the Holy Spirit, to make further explanations of this great transaction, which show its relation to other truths of religion, and enable us to understand it better. This has been done most fully by Paul, to whom we owe the exposition of two distinct but complementary aspects of it; but further contributions to the doctrine have been made by the writer to the Hebrews, and by John; and all these deserve careful and distinct consideration.

### (1) *Paul's Conception of Christ's Death as Redemption from the Curse of the Law*

The idea of redemption in general by Christ's death on the cross is found also in the epistles of Peter, and is founded on our Lord's use of the term ransom, and the relation of His sacrifice to the Passover, and so may be regarded as part of the elementary, though as yet unexplained, teachings common to all Christians from the first. But Paul was led by his experience to give a fuller explanation of its meaning.

brought up under the law, he had a supreme regard for it as the expression of the will of God and the duty of man, requiring nothing short of perfect obedience, on pain of incurring God's curse or condemnation; and with all his efforts to obey, he could not satisfy his conscience, and felt ever in bondage under a law that condemned him. But when he saw that Jesus, who had died the cursed death of the cross, was the Son of God who freely gave Himself up to that death to save us, this was to him the redemption that his soul needed. Thus in Gal. $3^{10-14}$ he puts this in the form of an argument against seeking justification by the works of the law. As many as do so are under the curse, for the law's sentence is against all who do not render perfect obedience, and this no man can do. But Christ bought us out from this curse, becoming a curse for us by hanging on a tree. Here the idea of substitution is unmistakable. Christ's death comes in place of the curse due to us. But it is brought into connection with the further idea of the law. That cannot be broken to let transgressors free: it receives its due in the death of Christ, which, as he had said before ($2^{19-22}$), is in a true sense the death of the believer in and with Him. "I through the law died to the law," i.e. the law has slain me, and now I am free. It slew me when it slew Christ, for "I have been crucified with Christ." Christ's death on the cross, then, was a fulfilment of the law's sentence against sin: a maintenance of its inviolability, and homage done to it in place of the sentence due to us. Christ suffered on our behalf in order that we might be forgiven and blessed, while yet the law was not broken. It is no doubt the law of the old covenant as given to Israel that Paul has directly in view; but he cannot mean to say that only Jews needed to be redeemed, or were redeemed, by Christ. The law of Israel represents for him the divine law in general, and there is no way for anyone, whether Jew or Gentile, being freed from its curse but through Him who was made a curse for us. The whole argument of this epistle shows that the reason why Christ's death in our stead was necessary was that the law of God might be maintained and its claims met.

In the Epistle to the Romans Paul gives substantially the

same explanation, only in more general terms, with reference not merely to God's law, which might be conceived as a specially Jewish and positive institution, but to His justice, which is an essential attribute of His being, and His moral government of all men alike. He shows how all have incurred God's wrath by sin: the Jews by not having kept the law in which they boasted, and the Gentiles by transgressing the law of nature written in their hearts; how neither can be justified by works of law, but how both alike may be justified freely by God's grace, through the redemption that is in Christ Jesus, whom God has set forth as making atonement[1] in His blood, for a demonstration of His righteousness on account of the passing over of the sins of the past in forbearance, with a view to the demonstration of His righteousness in the present time,[2] that He might be just and the justifier of him who is of faith in Jesus (Rom. $3^{24-26}$). Here it is plainly taught that God's justice, in virtue of which He punishes sin, might seem to be called in question by His forbearance to sinners and His forgiveness of believers; but that by the shedding of Christ's blood, as an atoning sacrifice to redeem sinners, God is shown to be just in both of these acts of grace to sinners. This passage, which is the one in which Paul sets himself most expressly to explain how the work of Christ saves us, plainly teaches that the shedding of His blood as an atoning sacrifice and redemption for us showed the forgiveness of believers in Him to be consistent with the righteousness of God as the Judge of all the earth. In the light of this statement we can see what Paul means when he says repeatedly and in various forms, Christ died for our sins. He was delivered on account of our offences (Rom. $4^{25}$), *i.e.*, they were the reason why He suffered; He gave Himself about our sins (Gal. $1^4$), *i.e.*, they were the business or matter with which He had to do in His sacrifice; He died for our sins (1 Cor. $15^3$), *i.e.* on behalf of them that they might be

---

[1] It seems simplest and most natural to take ἱλαστήριον as an adjective, but the sense is not materially altered by either of the alternative views, a propitiatory sacrifice, or a propitiatory covering or mercy-seat sprinkled with blood.

[2] Hofmann's view that πρὸς τὴν ἔνδειξιν should be construed as depending on πάρεσιν is favoured by the force of the preposition and the article, and seems to avoid tautology better than any other.

forgiven: all these aspects are implied in the fuller explanations given to the Galatians and to the Romans, and all are founded on the memorable saying of Jesus, that His blood was shed on behalf of many unto the remission of sins. Another remarkable saying of Paul is that in 2 Cor. $5^{21}$: "Him who knew no sin, He made sin on our behalf, that we might be made the righteousness of God in Him." Here it cannot possibly be a moral change in Christ that is meant, but it points to our Saviour having been made the representative of sin on our behalf, just as in the Levitical law the special sacrifices for sin and guilt were called by the names "sin" and "guilt" themselves. The purpose stated, "that we might be made the righteousness of God in Him," points to our being accepted as righteous because by faith we are in Him, the Righteous One.

(2) *Paul's Conception of Christ's Death as a Death to Sin, in which we share*

Some of the passages already considered show that Paul was far from viewing our Lord's sacrifice as a thing entirely outside of us. If His death redeems us from the curse of the law, it is because we are crucified with Him (Gal. $2^{20}$, $3^{13}$); if He was made sin that we might be made the righteousness of God, this is done to us in Him (2 Cor. $5^{21}$). This is what, in the apostle's view, secures our holiness and prevents the doctrine of redemption from being an encouragement to sin. Hence he explains it most fully when he is meeting that objection in Rom. 6, 7, 8. He says of believers, we died with Christ, were buried with Him, rose with Him, live with Him; and this is in virtue of a union with Christ which, as He teaches elsewhere, is effected by the Spirit of God through faith on our part (Rom. $8^{9, 10}$, 1 Cor. $6^{15, 16}$, Gal. $2^{20}$, Eph. $3^{17}$, etc.). Christ's death is virtually ours; and as He is said to have died to sin once for all (Rom. $6^{10}$),—*i.e.* not only to have died by reason of sin, but in respect to sin, so that sin has no more any claim or power over Him,—so we are said to have died with Him to sin (Rom. $6^{7, 11}$), and to the law (Rom. $7^{4}$). This is explained to mean being justified from sin, on the ground that the law has dominion over a man only so long as he lives (Rom $7^{1.2}$). Christ's death, therefore, frees us from the law in the same way as our own death would have done had it been possible for us to have died and risen again as Christ did; it frees us because it is in a true sense our own death, since when we accept Him in faith as our sacrifice, we truly die with Him to our old life of sin and condemnation, and being raised with Him to a state of pardon and peace with God, are enabled and morally constrained to live a new life of obedience.

This view of Christ's death also underlies the statement in 2 Cor. $5^{15}$; and it implies a mystical oneness between Christ and His people, so that what He does for them He did first for Himself. It shows how His sacrifice secures our holiness as well as our forgiveness, and redeems us from all iniquity, and purifies us to Himself a people for His own possession, zealous of good works.

There is no inconsistency, as some have thought, between this view and that given in the earlier chapters of the Epistle to the Romans. Both are too fully and earnestly expounded to permit us to suppose that in either the apostle is merely adapting his teaching to current ideas; and though theologians have often been too narrowly logical to take in both, and have developed one-sidedly now one and now the other, Paul's mind was comprehensive enough to find reason for both, and to him they did not contradict but complement each other.

It is possible, and not very improbable, that the view of our mystically sharing Christ's death as a death to sin is implied in 1 Pet. $2^{21}$ $4^{1.2}$, though some doubt this, and it is indeed not so clearly expressed as to make the interpretation certain. But as this epistle shows the influence of some of Paul's late writings, a reference in these places to the ideas of Rom. 6 seems the most natural explanation of their striking and suggestive expressions.

(3) *The Conception of Christ's Death in Hebrews, as giving us Access to God*

The Epistle to the Hebrews was addressed to Jewish believers, who were tempted to become dissatisfied with

Christianity because of the lack of the ritual ordinances to which they had been accustomed. A religion without visible priest, altar, or sacrifice seemed to them poor and bare; and the inspired writer has in view those who not merely regretted the external splendour of the temple worship, but who had prized its priests and sacrifices because they had really helped to give them peace of conscience and access to the presence of God. To such he shows that in the person of Jesus Christ we have a high priest far greater than Moses, Aaron, or any of the Levitical priests—more powerful, more sympathetic, performing a higher service in a heavenly sanctuary,—and that all the Old Testament rites were of value only as they were types and figures of His work. In this exposition he does not go into minute and arbitrary allegorising after the manner of Philo, but seizes on the great and simple religious ideas on account of which his most earnest readers valued the ritual. The root-conception is the holiness of God, His absolute separation from all that is unlike His own pure and perfect goodness. His dwelling is the Holy of Holies, and the veil separates men, as sinful, from His presence: they dare not approach, and their conscience is burdened with a sense of unworthiness and pollution. The high priest could enter on their behalf, not without blood, and they might get assurance of forgiveness through sacrifice. But the sacred writer teaches them that Jesus by the sacrifice of Himself has entered into the real, holy presence of God, and by His doing so He has done as much, yea far more, for us than any animal sacrifices could do. He really purges our conscience (Heb. $9^{14}$) as they could only do in symbol; He gives us boldness to draw near to God, and consecrates us for His service. He does this by offering Himself to bear the sin of many, for the annulling of sin, through the sacrifice of Himself.

In this form of presentation we have not the legal and juridical ideas that occur in Paul's epistles, *e.g.*, righteousness, law, curse, justification, reconciliation, peace with God, but we have a parallel set of ideas that present the same realities from a subjective point of view, *e.g.*, the holy place, the separating veil, an evil conscience, sprinkling from an evil conscience, access to the holiest, service of God. We could translate most of the terms of the one series into corresponding terms of the other, and we see that their mutual relations are the same. There are also certain terms that are common to both forms of representation, such as sin, death, Christ's dying for our sins, forgiveness, etc., which occur in the teaching of Jesus Himself, and so belong to the common stock of New Testament theology, the fact of our redemption by Christ. In Paul's epistles and that to the Hebrews, explanations of the fact are given from different points of view, one more objective, juridical, and ethical; the other more subjective, typical, and religious;—the former viewing it in the light of God's moral law and government, the latter in that of the ordinances of worship and religious experience of men. Since both of these are real and important relations, the views founded on them are each legitimate, and neither contradicts nor excludes the other, for the great sacrifice of Calvary has not one only but many bearings on God and man and the universe.

(4) *View indicated by John, of Christ as our Atonement through Communion*

The statements on this subject contained in John's writings are hardly so many or so full as to entitle us to speak of an explanation or theory given by him, but they have such a distinct and unique character that they suggest a view of Christ's atoning work that deserves to be placed alongside of those already mentioned.

John has given expression to the highest conception of God as revealed in Christ by his great saying "God is love" (1 John $4^{8, 16}$); and while he also says "He is righteous" (*ib.* $1^9$ $2^{29}$), and "God is light" ($1^5$), he does not mean to assert different, far less opposing, attributes of the Divine Being, but rather to express the same great truth in these different ways. For righteousness is used by John, not in the sense of justice as of a moral ruler, but in the way that is frequent in the Old Testament, for the whole of moral goodness, and that in his view is summed up in love (see

1 John $3^{10-24}$). Again, the declaration "God is light" cannot be taken as indicating His holiness in distinction from His love, because it is expressly given as the sum of the revelation made by the Word of life being manifested. Light must be practically the same as love, and it is mostly in reference to the divine favour that the figure of light is used of God in the Old Testament. John does not ascribe separate attributes to God, but has one single conception of Him—love; but a love that is essentially true, pure, and righteous. God is revealed in this character in the sending of His Son into the world (1 John $4^{9, 10}$); hence this declaration is the message of the apostles ($1^5$). The world is in a state of sin, which is traced back ultimately to the devil ($3^8$), the evil one in whom the whole world lieth ($5^{19}$). Sin is essentially lawlessness; but the Son of God is sinless, and was manifested to destroy the works of the devil, to take away sins ($3^{5, 8}$). The expression "to take away sins" cannot, in view of the context, be limited to the expiation of their guilt, but must include the entire removal of them from those who are saved. In this connection John twice uses the sacrificial term "propitiation" ($2^2$ and $4^{10}$), in both cases applying it emphatically to the person of Christ rather than to any specific part of His work. But since it is the ground of His being our Advocate with the Father when we sin, the propitiation clearly has a God-ward aspect; and it is also said our sins are forgiven on account of His name ($2^{12}$). There is special reference to Christ's death when it is said "the blood of Jesus, God's Son, cleanseth us from all sin" ($1^7$); but the blood is viewed in $5^6$ not only as shed on the cross, but as belonging to that true human nature in which He came by His birth. John regards the whole person of Christ as our propitiation; and the way in which we obtain an interest in it is by personal life-communion with Him. His notion of salvation seems to rest on that discourse of Jesus in the synagogue of Capernaum, in which He speaks of giving His flesh for the life of the world, and says we must eat the flesh and drink the blood of the Son of Man.

The sacrificial reference seems to point to that form of offering in which the whole flesh of the victim was eaten by the worshippers in order to seal their union with the Deity, a rite of which the Passover was the chief instance retained in the worship of Israel; and John conceived Jesus as the true Passover, and has given a mystical and spiritual interpretation to what may have been in primitive times a very rude and barbarous rite.

Christ's death is also represented by John as being the great example of love and incentive to imitation on our part ($3^{16}$); but it would be wrong to think that he ascribes to it only a subjective moral influence, for he distinctly represents our Lord's whole life and character as the ground of our forgiveness and fellowship with God, though he has not afforded the means of giving a precise answer to the question why it was necessary that our Saviour should suffer and die.

### Systematic Construction of the Doctrine of Atonement

Such are the outlines of the materials that the New Testament supplies for a doctrine of the atonement of Christ. From them the Christian Church has framed statements of the fact, which is the essential object of her faith, and as such finds a place in her creeds as accepted by all believers; while theologians, in pursuance of their aim and duty to gain as full an understanding as possible of the meaning of the fact, have sought to construct an intellectual theory that, while true to Scripture, may fit into the systematic conception of Christianity as a whole.

It is implied in all the apostolic statements, and in the testimony of Jesus Himself, that His giving Himself up to suffering and death was on account of our sin, and on our behalf, and is the ground of our salvation: and this may be said to have been the testimony of the great body of the Christian Church in all ages, while various theories were current as to the mode of this great transaction. In the Nicene Creed it is said that our Lord became man on account of us men, and on account of our salvation, and that He was crucified on our behalf. The Athanasian Creed says that He suffered for us. Similar and not much more full are the statements contained in the more elaborate Confessions of the Roman, Eastern, and Protestant Churches, with the exception of the Socinian. Even the Westminster Assembly gives a very simple formula, going beyond the scriptural statements just mentioned only by adding the technical phrase " to satisfy divine justice," which, as we shall see, is of somewhat elastic meaning.

But while the Church has been anxious to express in her professions of faith the great fact of our salvation through Christ's death for us, without requiring all her members to agree in any intellectual explanation of the way of that salvation, theologians have legitimately and usefully endeavoured, by means of the biblical representations, to arrive at such an explanation. For this it is necessary to compare the various New Testament views, to consider how they are to be correlated, which are figurative and employ local or occasional allusions, and what great universal and perennial relations there are by means of which the reason of Christ's dying for our salvation can be understood.

In the pursuit of this great aim the Pauline conception of Redemption has been that most generally employed, and this not unnaturally or unreasonably, since it is very fully presented in the New Testament, and contains ideas of universal validity, and familiar especially to Roman minds. But at first it was often applied in erroneous ways; and even when that was not done, it was sometimes pressed in a narrow and one-sided manner, to the exclusion of the complementary views which the New Testament contains. This led to reactions, to attempts to base a theory of atonement entirely on moral or mystical ideas, and to various modified or intermediate views; but the result of the long and varying discussions seems to point to a view which shall do justice to all the biblical aspects of the truth as that in which theology shall ultimately acquiesce.

CLASSIFICATION OF THEORIES

It is not very easy to make a satisfactory classification of the various theories of the atonement that have been held in the Church, as may be seen from the very different arrangements of them by some of the ablest writers who have attempted it. This arises from the fact that every theory includes many points, and may agree with some in one point and with others in another; also that the same terms have often been used in different senses, and the true meaning of some theories has been disputed or misunderstood. But since it is useful, in order to get what is good out of various opinions, to have a correct idea of the mutual relations of these, we should endeavour to arrange them according to their natural affinities, making the most important differences the main lines of division.

Now the most essential question for determining the difference of views as to the death of Christ is, What was its object? to what was its efficacy directed? on whom or on what was it designed to have an effect? The answer may be either—

(a) Only towards the sinners who are saved by it (subjective or man-ward theories); or

(b) Also towards God's honour, law, government, or character (objective God-ward theories); or

(c) Towards something distinct both from God and man (objective dualistic theories).

The efficacy towards men is that of moral influence; towards God it is expressed by the term satisfaction; but besides these there is another view important enough to form another class:

(d) mystical theories, many of which are subjective, though not all.

The earliest attempt at an explanation of how Christ has redeemed us by His blood is found in the writings of Irenæus, and though it is not very clear or satisfactory, it is not so discordant with Scripture as has been supposed by some. He ascribed the necessity of redemption to the justice of God, but at the same time he regarded the bondage from which we are redeemed as a captivity to Satan; and thus gave occasion to an idea, that was adopted by many subsequent writers in the ancient Church, that Christ gave Himself a ransom to Satan, the Dualistic theory. But it is doubtful whether Irenæus really meant to assert this. He says, indeed, that Christ redeemed us by His own blood in a manner consonant to reason, giving Himself as a redemption for those who had been led into captivity by the apostasy which tyrannised over us; and, he continues, the Word of God did righteously turn against that apostasy and redeem from it His own property, not by violent means, but by means of persuasion (*suadela*). But it is not clear to whom this persuasion is meant to refer. If to the apostasy, then there is taught the view of a ransom to Satan: and that is Baur's opinion, who taught that in this connection Irenaeus was entangled with the Gnostic idea of a distinction between the God of righteousness, who was but an inferior Demiurge or world-framer, and the Supreme God of goodness and love. But Dorner and other equally competent scholars think that this is not clear, and that the persuasion of which Irenaeus speaks may have been meant in reference to men. This would give a different colour to his statement, which on any view must be regarded as ambiguous.

But whatever may have been Irenaeus' view, the notion of Christ's death being a ransom given to Satan was held by many of the ancient Fathers: for since our Lord is frequently said in Scripture to have delivered us from the power of Satan, and since His death is called a redemption or ransom, it seemed not unnatural to put these two things together and to regard Satan as the minister and executioner of divine justice, an aspect in which he is sometimes presented in Scripture. But it was impossible to carry out such a view as a serious explanation of the facts without running into notions altogether grotesque and unworthy of God, *e.g.*, that Satan overreached himself, thinking he could retain the Son of God in his power, or that, by unjustly putting to death the Sinless One, he lost his right of inflicting death on sinners. These strange ideas were current in the Church from an early time down to the eleventh century, though never to the exclusion of other and more scriptural views, which were expressed sometimes by the same writers. Often they were mere illustrations used for popular impression, and may be compared with the crude illustrations employed for the like purpose in modern times. But when the idea of a ransom to Satan is taken seriously, it is easy to see that it implies a dualistic theory, and is utterly inconsistent with our Lord's own words, who spoke indeed of meeting and overcoming the prince of this world, but never of yielding His life up to him, but always of giving it as an absolutely free act to His Father, doing His will and glorifying Him.

These dualistic theories should warn us of the danger of pressing too literally the conception of a ransom; for the doctrine of Christ's suffering being required by the claims of eternal justice has seemed to some critics to imply the existence of a law or power distinct from and even above God Himself. So Principal Simon[1] thinks that Dr. Dale's view, at least in its earlier form, implies an unconscious or crypto-dualism. It would perhaps do so if we did not always remember and make plain to ourselves that, when we speak of an eternal justice, we mean nothing distinct, still less separate, from God Himself. No modern theologian deliberately means to assert a view of redemption representing it as given to any other than to God, and any statements that seem to imply the existence of any power outside God to which a ransom is paid must be regarded as exaggerated consequences of extreme and one-sided applications of the biblical figure of redemption.

Of all the ancient Fathers, Athanasius gives the most satisfactory account of the reason and purpose of Christ's death. It was necessary, he says,[2] because of the truth of God, who had threatened death as the punishment of sin; and it was a vindication of God's truth in this, because Christ made Himself entirely one with us, so that His death is really, though mystically, ours also. While he has some fanciful ideas, these do not enter into his main statements; and he is entirely free from the notion of a ransom to Satan.

The theory of a ransom to Satan was conclusively refuted by Anselm in his *Cur Deus Homo*; for though repeated a little later by Bernard against Abelard, it passed thereafter into discredit and oblivion. In the same work Anselm propounded a positive explanation of the atonement more complete and systematic than had ever been given before, so that from this time the doctrine became a subject of direct discussion, and has

[1] *The Redemption of Man.*     [2] *On the Incarnation*, cap. 6, 7.

never since ceased to be so. In the same century, too, distinct expression was first given by Abelard to the purely subjective theory of the atonement, which has ever and again reappeared in various forms, and is still held by many.

In examining the merits of the different theories of the Atonement and the elements of truth contained in each, it will be convenient to begin with—

### THEORIES OF MORAL INFLUENCE

Under this name are included all those views that ascribe only a moral or subjective purpose and effect to our Lord's sufferings and death, or, in other words, which regard them as merely designed to have directly or indirectly a salutary influence on the minds and hearts of men, whereby they may be turned from sin to God. The peculiarity, and, as most Christians think, the error, of this view lies entirely in its assigning this as the only purpose of Christ's death: it has been regarded as seriously defective, not for what it asserts, but for what it denies. It is undoubtedly taught in Scripture, and proved by experience, that the sufferings that Jesus so meekly and patiently endured do tend to melt the hearts of those who contemplate them, to awaken in them love to Him, and to lead them to imitate His example of self-sacrificing love; and it follows that they must have been intended by God to have these effects, and so to contribute, by this moral influence, an important part in the work of our salvation. These truths have been universally admitted, though sometimes, perhaps, the assertion of the doctrine of redemption may have tended to throw them too much into the background. In reality, however, that doctrine, rightly understood, tends not to obscure but to bring out more clearly and affectingly the moral influence of the Cross of Christ.

The moral influence theory of the work of Christ has been very fully expounded and discussed ever since the rise of the Socinian theology in the sixteenth century, and it has assumed somewhat different forms in successive periods, bringing out all the various ways in which our Saviour's sufferings have a gracious effect on us. Abelard, holding the true Deity of Christ, laid chief stress on the fact that His suffering and death for sinners is a revelation of the love of God, and so fitted to win our love and gratitude and turn us from sin. The Socinians, believing our Lord to be a mere man exalted to supreme dominion as the reward of His work, held His work on earth to have been only that of a prophet revealing especially what they called the placability of God, *i.e.*, His readiness, in pure benevolence, to forgive sinners, on their repentance and amendment. In connection with this they ascribed three purposes to Christ's death—(1) As that of a martyr it sealed His testimony with His blood; (2) it gave an example of meekness and patience under suffering and wrong; (3) it makes Him capable, in His exaltation, of sympathising with us, and so more effectually helping us. The English Unitarians in the end of the eighteenth century discarded the old Socinian view of the exaltation of Christ, and hence could not ascribe to His sufferings the third of the purposes formerly asserted. But they retained the other two, and they added the idea that the death of Christ was necessary to His resurrection, and that was the great and only certain evidence of a future life.

In modern times the moral influence theory has been held by many who do not, like the Socinians, deny the Deity of Christ. By them Abelard's view of His sufferings as a manifestation of the love of God has again been brought into prominence, and the Socinian ideas of martyrdom, of example, and of sympathy, have been reproduced, often with more spiritual insight and depth of feeling, but without adding anything of essential importance to the earlier representations.

But after all that has been done to exhibit the various ways in which the death of Christ exercises a moral influence for good on man, the assertion that this was its only purpose must be judged to be at variance with the teaching of the New Testament. To reconcile it with the many and various statements which have been before cited, requires a mode of interpretation extremely forced and unnatural, such as the Socinian expositions in many cases are now acknowledged to be, or the supposition that the inspired writers were continually using the most far-fetched figurative language.

Another weighty objection is that the denial of all but a subjective purpose in the sufferings of our Saviour makes the chief reason assigned for them, the revelation of the love of God, an unintelligible and empty show. Love is indeed shown in the endurance of self-denial, toil, and suffering for the sake of others, if there is some independent necessity for such endurance, or if it secures some objective benefit for those for whom they are endured. But when it is denied that any such necessity existed, or any such benefit is attained, and the purpose of the endurance is only and simply the exhibition of love, the transaction is degraded to a level with the fantastic ideals of mediæval chivalry, in which men tried to show their love and devotion by exposing themselves to needless and useless hardships and dangers. If we would maintain a worthy view of God's love, as revealed in the Cross of Christ, we must believe that it was endured not merely to convince us of His love, but to save us from real and great evils from which we could not otherwise be delivered.

A third objection is, that all these theories consider only the subjective aspect of sin, and assume that if we are delivered from the love and power of it and turned to God, nothing more is needed for our salvation. But this is to ignore the bearing of sin on our relation to God, the reality of which is testified not only by Scripture but by conscience. There is a sense of guilt and its desert, and of something being done to make up for the wrong done in the past, the strength of which is testified by the universal prevalence of the rite of sacrifice for sin ; there are solemn testimonies of the holy and just anger of God against sinners, which show that this aspect of sin is a most real and serious one, and must be dealt with if our case is to be fully met and our consciences satisfied ; and the sacrifice of Himself which Christ offered is represented as doing this, besides its effect in changing our hearts and lives.

### OBJECTIVE THEORIES

Since all Dualistic theories of the atonement must be rejected as radically unchristian, and since those of mere moral influence, though containing important elements of truth in what they assert, are seriously defective by reason of their negations, it is proper to consider next those explanations of our Lord's sufferings and death which ascribe to them an objective God-ward purpose and effect, holding that they were designed not merely to exert an influence on men, but to have a bearing on God or something pertaining to God. This has been maintained by the great majority of Christian theologians, at least from the eleventh century onwards; but it has been put in various forms. The term that best designates this class of views as a whole is Satisfaction, taken in the general sense of the accomplishment of the divine requirements for the forgiveness and salvation of sinners, but the word has been somewhat variously understood, and has been discarded by some who do not essentially differ from those who use it. The chief point of difference is as to what is that divine requirement to which satisfaction is made.

The first form in which this view was systematically put was that expounded by Anselm, in his treatise *Cur Deus Homo*, on the necessity of the incarnation and death of the Son of God; and in it the requirement was taken to be a personal one, and the satisfaction to be made to the honour of God. Anselm regarded sin as not merely a violation of man's own nature tending to degrade and destroy himself, but as an offence against God—as being a robbing God of the honour due to Him from all His rational creatures. What these all owe to God is to honour Him by a loyal obedience to His will revealed to them as law. When they fail to do so, and follow their own will instead, they rob God of His honour; and so sin is to be regarded as a debt which has to be repaid, that God's honour may be restored. When God punishes sin He forcibly subjects the sinner to His will, and so recovers the honour of which the insubordination of the sinner has deprived Him. But God's honour may be restored in another way, namely, if there could be rendered to Him an honour as great as that of which man's sin has deprived Him. This can only be done by the Son of God, who is greater than all that is not God, giving Himself freely to die for sinners, and His self-sacrifice is a satisfaction according to the old sense of that term, *i.e.* not a penalty, but something offered and done instead of the penalty. Anselm always clearly distinguishes the two terms, and says that sin must be followed either by satisfaction or punishment. In his view, too, the redemptive element in Christ's work does not lie in His suffering simply as such, but in His freely undertaking an act of self-sacrifice to which He was not bound.

This theory contains certain important portions of truth which have been generally recognised. The general principle that the necessity of Christ's death lies in God, and the view of the duty of all to honour God, and the value that God sets on His honour, are founded on Scripture ; and the conception of sin as a debt is also a biblical one, but it is employed too exclusively by Anselm. Thus his explanation is open to the objection that as it is quite free to a creditor to remit a debt freely without either payment or satisfaction, it does not appear why God could not forgive the debt of sin by mere free grace ; and it is noticeable that, in the last resort, Anselm falls back on the consideration that it would not be fitting that sin and obedience should be treated by God in the same way. Again, while Anselm was right in emphasising the active element as a most essential one in Christ's sacrifice, his notion of it as a satisfaction for a debt led him to think only of the greatness of our Saviour as enabling Him to render to God an honour outweighing the dishonour done by man's sin : he failed to show any special connection between Him and those who are to be saved.

The chief general ideas in Anselm's theory have been accepted by the great body of scriptural theologians in later time, namely, that sin is to be viewed as an offence against God ; that the need of satisfaction lies in the claims of God which cannot be waived ; and that Christ, by His obedience unto death, has met these claims for us and made our forgiveness possible. Some even in our own time have thought that not only in these but in all its details his explanation is satisfactory ; but most have tacitly or openly modified some of the particulars of Anselm's view. The exclusive reference to the divine honour and the consequent conception of sin as simply a debt were open to the objections above indicated, and later theologians fell back on Anselm's ultimate suggestion, that sin and obedience must not be treated alike, and so substituted for the honour of God His justice, as that which needed to be satisfied. Again, the limitation of the satisfaction of Christ to what He was not bound to render was an inference from the debt theory, and fell with it as a needless subtlety. Later schoolmen did not hesitate to say that Christ bore the punishment of our sins; and the want in Anselm of an explanation of the connection between Christ and those who are redeemed was supplied by Bernard's saying: "the Head suffered for His own members," and afterwards more fully by the Reformers' doctrine of our union to Christ by faith.

Thus arose a second form of the theory of satisfaction, according to which it was made to the justice of God, understood in the legal sense as the principle of giving to each his due. In virtue of this, God cannot allow sin to go unpunished; but Christ, by His freely enduring sufferings and death, has borne the punishment that our sin deserved, and God has been pleased to accept this for us and to forgive us for His sake. This was the view prevalent at the Reformation both in the Roman Catholic and Protestant Churches, and afterwards elaborated by the scholastic theologians of the seventeenth century against the Socinian doctrine of mere moral influence. It lays chief stress on the passive aspect of our Lord's work as the endurance of the punishment of sin in our stead; and this is indeed a true and scriptural aspect of it, though there was a danger of going too far in asserting an exact identity between what Christ suffered and what sinners have to endure. Further, it makes this whole transaction not one of private right, as that between a creditor and debtors, but of public law. God, as the Judge of all, must do right, and He shows His grace as well as His justice in both providing and accepting a Substitute to bear the punishment of sinners. This was in substance, with various modifications, the doctrine of the great dogmatic writers of the seventeenth century. It retained the principal points of the Anselmic theory, but gave up some of its less satisfactory details: and it could be, and was, successfully defended against the Socinian objections that a debt may be forgiven without satisfaction, and that when payment is made there is no grace in forgiveness.

But certain other criticisms were not so completely answered. It was urged that Christ cannot be said to have endured the very punishment that we deserved, nor even a suffering equivalent to it, especially because His sufferings were only for a short season, while the doom of sin is eternal; and when it was replied that, in virtue of the infinite dignity of our Saviour as the Son of God, His brief endurance was equivalent as a vindication of divine justice to the eternal suffering of sinners, this could hardly avoid the appearance of bringing in a metaphysical idea to decide a moral question. Again, the question arose, and has become more pressing with the growth of enlightened humane jurisprudence, How can justice, in the strict distributive sense, be manifested by the punishment of the innocent for the guilty? It could indeed be answered negatively, that Jesus suffered with perfect willingness, so that no injustice was done to Him, and that the suffering of the holy Son of God is a fact undeniable on any theory; but in order to show positively how it satisfied God's justice, the theologians of that day had recourse to the analogy of practices such as the punishment of sureties and hostages, which the jurisprudence of their time approved, but which are condemned by more enlightened ages.

These considerations, while they do not overthrow the scriptural evidence for the doctrine of Christ's satisfaction, make it difficult in the present day to regard as satisfactory the strict juridical form of it without some modification or supplement. The sense of this led to a third form of this doctrine, which is known as the Governmental view, according to which the satisfaction of Christ is made not to the distributive justice of God, but to what was called public justice, which has for its aim the maintenance of the moral order of the universe. This theory is generally traced back to the treatise of Grotius, *de Satisfactione Christi*, 1617; but the view expounded there does not really differ essentially from the juridical one, though one point in it was afterwards developed into the Governmental theory. He defends the doctrine that Christ's suffering for our sin was a satisfaction to the justice of God, as the Supreme Moral Governor, and that He really bore the punishment of our sin in our place. Only he held that the end of punishment is not the abstract purpose of rendering to the evil-doer his due, but the maintenance of the moral order of the universe by preventing offences in future. The impossibility of sinners being pardoned without satisfaction arises from the danger of crime being encouraged with impunity and the government of God set at nought, which would be injurious to the highest interests of the moral universe. That this is one aim of punishment cannot fairly be denied. It is recognised in Scripture (Deut. 13$^{11}$ 19$^{20}$, Ps. 125$^3$), and must ever be a prominent consideration in human jurisprudence. But when this is held to be the only purpose of punishment, there is a tendency to alter the conception of justice and to regard it, not as the love of right for its own sake and the determination to give each his due, but merely a wise regard for the general virtue and happiness of the community. Grotius did not go so far as this; but it was maintained afterwards by Leibnitz and others, who resolved all God's moral attributes into benevolence, that justice is simply benevolence guided by wisdom. Then the sufferings of Christ came to be regarded as merely exemplary, intended to show God's hatred of sin and to deter men from it. This has a certain resemblance to the mere moral influence theory; but there is an important difference in this, that the impression made by these sufferings is held to be not only on the sinners who are forgiven, but on the whole moral universe; so that the effect of the atonement is really objective, and has regard ultimately to the government of God. This theory was adopted by many of the later Arminians, by the theologians of the so-called "Enlightenment" on the Continent, by the New School in America, and by many English divines. The chief objections to it are that it gives an unworthy representation of God's action in requiring the sacrifice of Christ, as having regard to the interests of the creatures rather than to His own character and glory; that it makes His purpose to be merely to produce a certain impression on the universe, and so tends to make the Cross of Christ a mere display, not an actual exercise of justice and mercy.

Still, though defective and open to grave objections, this

view is not really so great a deviation from the juridical doctrine as has been thought by many both of the opponents and supporters of the latter. It ascribes a truly objective efficacy to the sacrifice of Christ, and it avoids some of the difficulties of the strict juridical theory. Its supporters can use with all sincerity the common language of Scripture and of the Churches' Confessions as to the death of Christ in our stead and for our sins; and though their statements are somewhat less precise than those which adhere to the older form of doctrine, they convey the most important points in it. In a recent American document there is distinct evidence of this. In 1837 the Presbyterian Church in America divided into the Old and New Schools, on account of differences on the atonement and other doctrines. Several errors were charged against the New School, and to meet these they adopted a document called, from the place where it was drawn up, "The Auburn Declaration." In 1868, when a reunion of these Churches was contemplated, this declaration was approved by the Old School Assembly, as containing "all the fundamentals of the Calvinistic Creed," and on this basis the Churches were united in 1870. Its statement on the atonement is: "The sufferings of Christ were not symbolical, governmental, and instructive only, but were truly vicarious, i.e., a substitute for the punishment due to transgressors. And while Christ did not suffer the literal penalty of the law, including remorse of conscience and the pains of hell, he did offer a sacrifice which Infinite Wisdom saw to be a full equivalent. And by virtue of this atonement overtures of mercy are sincerely made to the race, and salvation secured to all who believe."[1] This is a very judicious and well-balanced statement, including elements of all the forms of the objective view of the atonement and avoiding the excesses of each. It asserts, with Anselm, the important fact of Christ's action in giving Himself a sacrifice, without limiting it, as Anselm did; it avoids the extreme assertion of many, who held the juridical view, that Christ suffered the very same penalty as sinners deserve; and it guards against the tendency of the governmental theory to make the Cross a mere unreal display.

[1] Auburn "Declaration," § 8, in Schaff's *Creeds of Christendom*, iii. p. 778.

Still it cannot but be felt that these are largely negative determinations; and it may be noticed that all these theories are founded entirely on two of the sets of statements by the apostles, Paul's doctrine of redemption, and the sacrificial explanations in the Epistle to the Hebrews, and have mainly proceeded on the plan of taking from Scripture the idea of righteousness, and interpreting this by various philosophic assumptions, while the series of statements about our union with Christ in His death have been overlooked or little used. To this appears to be due a certain hardness in all these forms of doctrine, as well as some of their theoretical difficulties, and a natural reaction against these led to the emphasising of the neglected elements of Pauline and Johannine teaching. When these were used as superseding or excluding the juridical element, one-sided mystical theories were the result; taken as supplementing that element, they point to the most satisfactory view that seems attainable.

### MYSTICAL THEORIES

The term "mystic" is a somewhat vague one, and may be fairly applied to views that have a very distinct quality in common, but in other respects are very different. The common element may be defined as the belief that there are things which are to be apprehended by feeling, and not either by sense or reason; more especially that the soul has a direct communion with God through the conscience and heart, and is not limited to sense and reason as its means of communication. This belief can be kept from degenerating into mere fancy, if it be held that the truths and relations thus directly apprehended should be verified by their results in experience; while if no such test is admitted, the door is open to baseless subjective imagination. The most spiritual theologians have always recognised a mystic element in Christianity; but when it was exaggerated to an unbridled extreme, a reaction set in, which sought to eliminate from theology everything that could not be proved by sense and reason. From this tendency the expositions of the atonement in the seventeenth and eighteenth centuries suffered; and Schleiermacher was led to propound what he called a mystical view, distinct alike from the Socinian, which he called the empirical, and that current in the Church, which he designated the magical. On the Socinian view, the relation of the forgiven sinner to Christ is merely that of one who has been influenced by His love and example; on the Church view, it seemed to be only that of one who has been brought, by a sovereign appointment of God, into a legal relation to Christ. Schleiermacher maintained that he is brought into a life-fellowship with Christ, the one man whose God-consciousness has been perfect and unbroken; that by this union with Christ we receive a new life, which shall ultimately be perfect; and that meanwhile God forgives and accepts us because Christ has thus guaranteed that we shall at last be freed from sin. But in his explanation of the suffering of Christ Schleiermacher assumes a real life-union of our Lord, not only with believers but with the whole human race. In it, as a whole, there is just as much suffering as sin, and by suffering the sin is wiped out. But this is only true of the whole, not of each individual. Jesus, however, being perfectly holy, introduced no new element of sin, while He bore a large part of the suffering due to the race, and so took away its sin. The recognition of the spiritual life-union between Christ and the believer is a true and valuable element in this theory; but still it is a merely subjective one. Christ saves us by guaranteeing that we shall be perfectly freed from sin, and no other obstacle to forgiveness is recognised except our own love of and proneness to sin. Schleiermacher's whole conception of sin is generally recognised as too subjective, and few of those who have followed his leading ideas have adopted all parts of his system. The views of C. J. Nitzsch, Rothe, and Dorner, while recognising a mystical element, are yet distinctly objective in their character. So also at bottom are those of von Hofmann and Ritschl, although they deviate from the Church doctrine by excluding all juridical and penal ideas.

In Britain the mystical view was advocated by S. T. Coleridge; and of his followers F. D. Maurice, Kingsley, and others pressed it to the exclusion of any God-ward effect of the atonement; while M'Leod Campbell and, in a modified way, Bushnell, retained, in principle, that idea. A mystical theory has also been connected with the view of E. Irving, that Christ assumed our sinful human nature, and by virtue of His own holiness kept it absolutely free from all personal sin, and thereby sanctified and made acceptable to God the whole of that nature.

The mystical theories in general include one important truth, that our relation to Christ as our Redeemer is not a mere moral or federal one, but a real spiritual union. But they are defective and misleading when, by asserting this of all men alike, they make it a thing not verifiable by its results, or when they represent redemption as merely a subjective change in us, and not also an alteration of our relation to God. In the latter case they are open to the objections against the theory of mere moral influence, though in some respects they are greatly more profound and spiritual.

But when the mystic element is not pushed to such extremes, and is accepted as supplementing and not superseding the idea of an objective bearing of the atonement on the requirements of God's character and law, it is a thing that has been recognised by the most spiritual Church teachers in various ages, as Athanasius, Bernard, Luther, Calvin, Jonathan Edwards; and it enables us to form a conception of Christ's work that is free from the one-sidedness of most other theories, and probably comes as near to doing justice to the whole teaching of revelation and enabling us to understand the great redemption as is possible.

According to the teaching of Christ and of His apostles, as contained in the New Testament, there is a union of Christ and His people which is vital and spiritual, and though not discernible by the senses or demonstrable by reasoning, yet really apprehended by the soul and verified by its fruits; and when this is recognised in connection with the atonement, along with the corresponding truth of Christ's spiritual oneness both with God and man in virtue of His incarnation, the defects of many theories of the atonement may be supplied, and a more satisfactory explanation approached.

Such recognition avoids the need of regarding Christ's substitution for sinners as a mere sovereign appointment of God, or covenant transaction between parties having no closer relation. No doubt the supreme authority of God must be acknowledged as the basis of the whole plan of redemption, and the notion of a covenant of grace is a scriptural one that brings out the free mutual consent of God and Christ and believers; but, besides these, there is in the mystical union of Christ with the race, and of believers with Christ, a moral reason for the substitution of the Saviour for sinners. He gives His life a ransom in their stead because He is their representative, and He is their representative because He has become the Son of Man. His tie to the race is a real and living one: He not only has taken the same nature, but has for them all the feelings of a brother. Thus though He does not share their sin, and cannot feel personal remorse of conscience or repentance, He does share in the shame and grief that a good man feels for the evil-doing of his family or of his country; and since He is at the same time one with God in His abhorrence of these sins, it is by no mere appointment or covenant that He bears the punishment of them, but is a natural consequence of His oneness both with God and man. Being truly human, He feels that nothing human is foreign to Him; and, being truly divine, the interests of the divine holiness are His also.

On the other hand, when believers are forgiven because of Christ's sacrifice of Himself for them, it is not as if His merit was ascribed to them by a mere legal fiction, for they are brought into such a vital union to Christ that His death is truly, though spiritually, theirs also. They accept His sacrifice as made on their behalf, acknowledging, in true penitence, that they have deserved all that He endured; and, entering with sympathy into the spirit in which He did so, they give glory to God by a heartfelt confession of sin, and faith in Jesus as the sin-bearer. These exercises of our souls cannot indeed merit forgiveness from God, but they make it suitable that Christ's obedience and sacrifice should be accepted for us. He has honoured and fulfilled that holy law of God that we had disobeyed; and though we cannot, by any acts of ours, so honour it, yet when we truly sympathise with Christ's work in doing so, it is fitting that it should be accepted on our behalf.

Again, the recognition of the mystical oneness of Christ with sinners enables us to give a more biblical explanation of that justice of God which is said to be satisfied or, in Paul's language, declared by the propitiation of Christ, than either the Anselmic notion of commutative justice, analogous to the payment of a debt, or the seventeenth century notion of distributive justice, rendering to each their due, or yet the governmental one of public justice, aiming at the prevention of offences. These are explanations largely coloured by the views of jurisprudence current in different ages; but the biblical idea of justice or righteousness is in most cases a more comprehensive one, not separated sharply from other moral qualities, such as godliness, kindness, mercy, faithfulness, truth, but including the whole of moral goodness and duty. As ascribed to God in His relation to men, this would mean His love and approval of all these moral qualities, with which must be associated His hatred and condemnation of all that is opposed to them. If sinners were pardoned and received into His favour by a mere amnesty, or on account of a repentance that is imperfect and itself mixed with sin, this attribute would not be manifested, nay, would not be exercised; it would be impossible to believe that it exists in God. But when the holy and sinless Son of God becomes the Son of Man, making common cause with the sinful race, and not only honours and obeys the law of God that they have broken, but, being Himself the Lawgiver, freely and lovingly bears, to the extent that a sinless one can, all the sufferings that are the expression of God's holy hatred of sin: and when those who accept Him as their representative and Lord are forgiven and blessed on account of this work that He has done for them: is not His righteousness, in the biblical sense, manifested and satisfied in a more perfect and glorious way than we could else conceive?

THOSE who are called by the Word and Spirit of God to union with Christ are represented in Scripture not merely as a number of individuals, each standing by himself, but as forming one entire body. It is true that the union by which they are connected with Christ is an individual one: each of the saved stands in direct and immediate relation to the Saviour. But when they are thus united to Him, they are also united one to another, and form a collective body of which He is the Head.

On this, as on many other subjects in religion, there are just three fundamentally different forms of doctrine, all others being modifications of one or other of these. The truth as it is in Jesus has always been opposed by two opposite kinds of error, which have assumed diverse names and aspects at different times, but against which the Church has always to be upon her guard. In the days of our Lord's earthly ministry there were the Pharisees on the one hand and the Sadducees on the other; in our day the Pharisees are represented by the Romanists and Romanising parties in Protestant Churches, the Sadducees by the Rationalists and Rationalising school; while equally distinct from both is the scriptural and evangelical faith.

### I. ROMAN CATHOLIC DOCTRINE

In order to bring out more distinctly what we hold to be the true view of the Church of Christ, I propose to explain, first, the Romish principle and doctrine on the subject, and then those of the Rationalists. The difference of these theories turns on the way in which the statements in Scripture in regard to the universal Church of Christ are understood and explained. For it cannot be denied that there is presented to our view in the New Testament one universal holy fellowship of men united to Christ, of which the most glorious things are spoken, and with which the most precious blessings are connected. In a word, the teaching of the ancient Creeds which express a belief of one holy Catholic Church is unquestionably founded on Scripture: the question is, what is the nature of that fellowship of which such things can be said, that "Church which is the body of Christ, the fulness of Him that filleth all in all"? More especially, differences of opinion have turned on the question, in what sense is the Church of Christ one?

The Romish mode of answering this question may be best explained by tracing briefly its actual rise and progress in the history of the Church.

The company of believers in Jesus, that met first in the upper chamber at Jerusalem, and was gradually increased by those who were added on the day of Pentecost and afterwards, might fairly be regarded as realising the idea of the one holy Church which is the body of Christ. There was in that society a real living fellowship with the risen Saviour; there were blessings enjoyed and hopes cherished in it to which the outer world were strangers: there was a holiness and mutual love that manifestly marked its members as somewhat different from others. As long as this society continued to be such that they could have common meetings and act as one body, no serious difficulty might be found in working out the idea of the Church.

But as in course of time the number of the disciples increased, and especially as they were scattered abroad and came to live in various and widely separated cities and lands, the question would needs occur: "How is this society now to maintain its unity? The Church, which is the body of Christ, must above all things be one as He is one; but we are many, and not merely many in one nation, as Israel of old, but many in all nations, scattered in handfuls here and there through all the world." The original idea of the unity of the Church was the common possession by all its members of the new life to God in Christ. This is the conception of the apostles and apostolic fathers, and is found as far down as Origen (*c. Cels.* vi. 48). Then arose the idea that unity in doctrine is also required, as appears in the conflict with the Gnostics, *e.g.* in Irenaeus and Tertullian; and then further, in order to maintain this unity in doctrine, the episcopal government of the Church was developed, the bishops being the custodiers of the genuine tradition of apostolic teaching; and so a unity of organisation came to be insisted on, and this ultimately superseded the two former and more vital kinds of union. The controversies of Cyprian against Novatian, and of Augustine against the Donatists, mark the triumphs of this principle. According to it, the way of maintaining a real unity in such circumstances was to fall back on the idea of one organisation and government. The Church, however greatly it may increase, and however widely it may spread, must still be one; there cannot be only one congregation or assembly: let then the various congregations be linked together in one organised system and under one government. Each congregation was one whole, because it was under one pastor and bench of bishops or elders; and all the congregations together made one whole, because all alike were under such bishops, who might meet together from time to time, as occasion called, in synods or councils. The development of the episcopal form of Church government was closely connected with the effort made in early times to maintain the unity of the Church, and to heal the schisms that were occasioned or threatened by the different tendencies among the disciples of Jesus. By this means the Church, even when spread through all the world, like the tree grown up from the little grain of mustard-seed, might yet be one, and all its members might feel themselves joined one to another as part of one great whole. This Catholic Church is represented as being one also in point of time, as being in all ages one and the same; and as its unity in point of space came to be regarded as consisting in its being under one system of government, so its oneness in time is held to consist in having been always under this government, which must be preserved in unbroken continuity from the foundation of the Church on through all the ages of its history.

Each of the Church's ministers must be able to trace his succession upwards as having been ordained by a bishop, and he again by one before him, and so on up to the apostles, who were chosen and ordained by Christ Himself. One government existing throughout all the world, and carried down uninterruptedly through all the ages, is the idea of the Church's unity that has widely prevailed throughout Christendom.

But when the unity of the Church was made to consist in oneness of government and organisation, it was soon felt that something more was needed than merely being under the same order of office-bearers. The idea of the uniting bond of the Church residing in the collective body of bishops or pastors, which Cyprian seems especially to have maintained, might suffice for a time, but could not satisfy long. As each congregation or group of congregations was held to be one because under one bishop, so the whole Church, if it was to be one in organisation, must be not merely under one sort of government but under one actual government. And as the unity of single congregations or districts had come to be sought not in councils or assemblies but in individual bishops, the wider unity of the Church must be maintained in the same way. Hence the bishops must be united under archbishops, and these again under metropolitans or patriarchs, and these again under one universal bishop, that of the world's capital, Rome, in whom the government of the whole Church was to be concentrated and its unity visibly manifested. Thus step by step there was developed the Popish idea of the Church, which is thus defined by Bellarmine: "Cœtus hominum ejusdem Christianæ fidei professione et eorundem sacramentorum communione colligatus sub regimine legitimorum pastorum ac praecipue unius Christi in terris vicarii"; no internal virtue being required to make one in some sense a member of the Church, which is as visible and palpable as the kingdom of France or the republic of Venice (*Eccles. milit.* c. 2).

To the Church as thus defined, Romanists ascribe all the glorious things spoken in Scripture of the City of God, regarding all the promises of perpetuity, guidance, and preservation given by Christ to the Church, as belonging to the external organism of which Rome is the head. It is believed to be the body of Christ, the family and kingdom of God, the bride, the Lamb's wife; in the Church and in it alone all saving blessings are held to be, and all who are outside of its pale are regarded as aliens from the commonwealth of Israel and strangers from the covenants of promise, without God and without hope in the world, while all who are within the pale are safe for eternity, being fellow-citizens with the saints and of the household of God. It follows from these principles, that as all spiritual blessings depend upon connection with an outward society, so they are communicated by outward means—by rites and ceremonies, by sacraments and ordinances; that the mere performance of certain works, as such, the simple reception of certain sacraments *ex opere operato*, bestows grace and salvation; and that the power to do this belongs to the outward organisation of the Church, and depends on her ministers being the lineal successors of the apostles and in communion with the Bishop of Rome. In a word, the Church as an external society is on this theory the divinely-appointed institution for conveying spiritual and eternal blessings to mankind; and it does so by a supernatural power, by means of outward rites and observances. Thus the whole of this system of religion hangs together with the theory of the Church: it is all one connected and consistent whole, and the idea of the Church as an external visible society is the centre and heart of it all. Now this is indeed a very magnificent and imposing idea—that of a body diffused through all the world, existing in every land and clime and in all ages, yet everywhere and always one and the same, acknowledging the same faith and observing the same divine worship under one vast hierarchical system, ascending by regular gradation from the parish priest in the remotest and obscurest corner of the world to the universal bishop and vicar of Christ, the earthly head of the whole body. It is an idea that has exercised an almost magical power over the minds and hearts of mankind, captivating their imagination and overpowering their reason. The palmy days of its supremacy were in the Middle Ages, but it still has to this day no small power of attraction and fascination to many.

For the view that is widely prevalent and officially expressed by what is known as the High Church or Ritualistic party is identical in principle with that of the Church of Rome, and differs from it only in not making actual communion with the whole Church and subordination to one outward government a necessity for salvation. In these respects it is simply less consistent and logical than Romanism, being in fact just an imperfect development of the vast idea of that system.

It agrees with the Romish theory in principle; for it makes the Church primarily and essentially an outward visible society, and this is the πρῶτον ψεῦδος, the root and germ, in theory and in history of the whole Popish doctrine. It is true many of the High Church party allow the distinction, which is essential to the maintenance of Protestantism, between the Church visible and invisible; but this is not sufficient to make out a radical difference from the Romish view. For some of the most eminent Romish divines admit the distinction, and even the formal deliverances of the Church of Rome involve a recognition of it. Indeed, in the light of modern discussions some such distinction cannot be avoided. But the mere recognition of an invisible Church is of very little avail when the first and chief place is given to the Church visible. As the distinction, when properly understood, is not of two different Churches, but rather of two aspects of one and the same Church, so everything depends upon which of the two is the primary and leading one, and the High Church view agrees thoroughly and formally with the Romish one in regarding the Church as in the first instance an outward society. This is clear from the fact that they regard an outward organisation as an essential mark of the Church. So thoroughly, indeed, do they subordinate the invisible to the visible Church, that they regard the former as entirely included within the latter. They acknowledge that there are some in the Church visible who are not members of the Church invisible, but they do not admit that any can belong to the Church invisible who are not included within the bounds of the visible Church. Thus the outward organism on which they insist, that of episcopal government with apostolic succession, is to them a mark and limit not only of the visible but of the invisible Church. Now the real and vital distinction between the Popish and Protestant views of the Church is well put in a few words by Möhler: "The difference between the Catholic and the Lutheran view of the Church can be reduced to a short, accurate, and definite expression. The Catholics teach that the visible Church is first, then comes the invisible: the former gives birth to the latter. On the other hand, the Lutherans say the reverse: from the invisible emerges the visible Church, and the former is the groundwork of the latter. In this apparently unimportant opposition a prodigious difference is avowed (*Symbolik*, § 48)." On this all-important point the adherents of the Ritualist or High Church party range themselves on the side of Rome.[1] Some of them deny that there is a Church invisible distinct from that which is visible: and even when they admit this, as some do, it is with them a mere empty statement which they are obliged to make and to have recourse to in argument, but which they practically leave out of sight in the application of their views. In a Catechism entitled *Theophilus Anglicanus*, by Dr. Wordsworth, afterwards Bishop of Lincoln, published with the sanction of his bishop and archbishop, we read as follows (p. 26):—"Q. If we desire to be saved, is it necessary that, if we are able, we should be members of the Christian Church?—A. It is. Q. How does this necessity appear?—A. From the nature of the case. Christ Himself has instituted a Society on earth in which men are to receive the means of grace and salvation, and has revealed no other way to this end; they, therefore, who will not enter and continue in this Society exclude themselves from participation in the privileges of the gospel." There you will observe that the author, though he has before admitted the distinction of the Church visible and invisible, speaks of the Church, that Church out of which is no salvation, as an outward visible society, thus simply adopting the fundamental principle of Romanism on this matter.

[1] See *Church Doctrine Bible Truth*, by Rev. M. F. Sadler, p. 42.

Agreeing thus in principle with the Church of Rome, the High Church party only differ from that Church in the extent to which they carry the principle. They think that the unity of the Church is sufficiently maintained by a uniform government by bishops, who may meet in particular or universal councils; whereas Romanists contend that the unity of the Church demands not merely a uniform but a sole government in the hands of one supreme universal bishop. Accordingly, Romanists maintain that none is in the Church of Christ who is not in communion with the Bishop of Rome; while the Anglicans hold that the separation between them and Rome does not cut off either party from the Catholic Church. Except this, it would be difficult to point out a single difference between the two views: and that the Romish is the natural development of the Anglican is evident both from history and reason. The High Anglicans occupy precisely the position that was taken up by Cyprian and other eminent Fathers of the third and fourth centuries at a time when the Romish theory was being developed; and their doctrine gave place, in the course of a few generations, to the full-blown system of Popery, which is the consistent logical issue of the first principle adopted by both in common.

There is evidence that Christ and His apostles instituted a government and order in the religious societies which they founded; but the thing that would have been most necessary were this view true—a system by which the several local communities should be bound into one organism—is precisely that on which they have given fewest and least definite instructions. The general principle of the Church being essentially an external organised society is indeed entirely at variance with Scripture. The Bible gives us views of the nature and attributes of the Church that are entirely inconsistent with this theory of it in either of its forms.

(1) It represents the Church as consisting of saints, of those who are sanctified or made holy by Christ Jesus, of believers in Him, or those who have saving faith. Nowhere are any persons addressed as being members of the Church without being also addressed as believers or holy brethren. Thus, to take one example out of a vast number, the Epistle to

the Ephesians,—in which so much is said about the Church, and in which the readers are reminded of their high privileges as in the Church which is Christ's body,—is addressed "to the saints which are at Ephesus and faithful in Christ Jesus." Now, it cannot be said of any external society as such, that all who are in it are godly and believing persons; hence it is a fundamental principle of the Romish theory that no internal or spiritual qualifications are needed to determine who are members of the true Church, but that it is a body consisting of all sorts of men, holy and wicked, believing and unbelieving, provided only they are united by a profession of faith and an organised government. In order to escape the force of these considerations, they who adopt this theory are obliged to modify the notion of holiness as a quality necessarily belonging to the Church, so as to make it mean not actual moral purity, but either a mere outward dedication to God, or a profession of obligation to holiness, or the power of the Church to make holy. It is only in such senses as these that the Church, on this view of it, can be said to be holy, not in the natural, proper, and ordinary sense of the term.

(2) Again, it is plain from Scripture that salvation is not exclusively confined to any one outward society, however sacred its character and extensive its precincts. "God is no respecter of persons, but in every nation he that feareth Him and worketh righteousness is accepted with Him." Against this great principle the whole theory of the Church as an outward organised society rebels, no less than Pharisaic Judaism of old, for it confines salvation and all spiritual blessings to one body, and declares that outside of its pale, however sound in belief, earnest in effort, and holy in life any one may be, there is for him no salvation or acceptance with God.

(3) Further, this system necessarily implies that spiritual blessings are conveyed through certain outward acts; while it is most clear, both from Scripture and observation, that this is not so. It is not by any mere external rite, as by magic, that grace and salvation are conveyed to men, but by inward, moral, and spiritual means.

If there be a Church all whose members are holy and heirs of salvation, it is clearly, as both Scripture and experience teach us, no external society whatever of which this can be said. To assert that there is, is to overturn the whole gospel of Christ and put another gospel in its place. This theory, then, of the One Holy Catholic Church must be abandoned and condemned as false.

## II. ERASTIANISM

When we find that the Romish theory of the Church is altogether baseless and unscriptural, the question naturally arises: What are we to put in its place? what is that body of which so much is said in Scripture? Some there are who think that there is no escape from the doctrine of the Church of Rome but by going to what may be regarded as an opposite extreme. Starting as before from the Church as it existed in apostolic times, as a little company of disciples of Christ, and following it as it spread and expanded to fill the world, they differ from the former view in not regarding one organised government as essential to the unity of the Church, and they also practically deny or explain away its unity. The Church is one no doubt, they will say, but it is one only as the whole human race is one. It is a number of people united by holding similar views about God and Christ, having the same principles, the same objects and aims, contending each in His own way against the same evils; and united by the sympathy that naturally arises from their having so much in common, but not one in any stricter or higher sense. Then, just as the human race, though in a certain sense one, having one common humanity and certain sentiments and feelings of universal sympathy, is not all one nation or empire, but divided into various States, each having its own political government, so the unity of the Church does not require one common government over all its members, but may be consistent with each part of it having its own distinct organisation. Further, as there are in the political world different sorts of government in different countries, according to the circumstances, or necessities, or likings of the people,—despotism in one, limited monarchy in another, aristocracy in a third, and democracy in a fourth,—so it naturally follows, according to this view, that it is free to the Church, at different times, and to every part of it in different places, to adopt any form of government or organisation that may seem most suited to the times or circumstances in which they are placed. Thus, it would be natural that the form of government of the Church in any particular country would be somewhat similar to the political system established there; and there is nothing in this view of the Church that would make it wrong to mould or modify its institutions in such a way. Still further, if the Church becomes so much assimilated to the body politic, and if the nation in which it is becomes largely pervaded with Christian ideas and feelings, it will come to be very difficult to preserve a distinct line of demarcation between Church and State. The idea of identifying or merging them into one will not be far off. They are societies of the same general nature, ruled by the same general principles, and having similar ends in view; they come to be regarded as one and the same: the Church is made to be but one particular aspect of the State, or department of its action; and just as the nation maintains an army for defence, and a legal and judicial body for the administration of justice, so it may maintain an ecclesiastical body for the promotion of religion. Then as the Church, on this view, is so flexible in its forms and modes of government, the State may take upon itself to control and direct it, to determine what shall be its creed and form of government, who shall be its ministers and members, and what shall be its line of action. The various parts of this view of the Church have not indeed been so completely combined and wrought into one systematic doctrine as those of the Romish theory, but they have been separately maintained by influential thinkers, and some of them at least combined into a unity.

The Erastian theory is so called from Thomas Erastus, a physician in Heidelberg, who first distinctly propounded it in the sixteenth century, although it was practically realised in the relation of the Oriental Church to the Empire, and hence is sometimes called Byzantine. It maintains that the power of discipline in the Church is a branch of the power of the State, and therefore ought to be directed and controlled by it; and those who in modern times have defended this theory have sometimes gone further, and held that not only is the power of the Church simply a part of that of the State, but that the Church itself is identical with the State, and ultimately destined to be absorbed into it or superseded by it. This is the view of Hegel, Rothe, and Strauss in Germany, and of Arnold, Coleridge, and Stanley in England. It is widely prevalent as a way of thinking and feeling, and often finds expression in current literature. It is the sort of theory on which the practical relations of Church and State are worked out by many minds in the present day; it harmonises well with some of the prevailing tendencies of modern thought, agreeing with the somewhat lofty notions of the day as to the excellence and perfectibility of human nature, and with the desire of freedom from the restraint of definite creeds and laws that characterises our time. Besides these attractions for many, it seems to not a few to be the only alternative to the Romish theory, and the only refuge against its arrogant claims.

Nevertheless, we do not hesitate to say that this idea of the Church is as unscriptural as the theory of the Church of Rome. It does not at all correspond to what is said of the Church in the New Testament. However we may explain it, it is not a mere heterogeneous mass of people that is suggested to our minds by the statements of Scripture, but a united living whole; it is not a body whose form and manner of being is variable according to the varying will of men or changes in human society, but one that is ever essentially the same; it is not a mere department of some larger and higher society, to whose laws and orders it is bound to submit, it is an independent body, divinely instituted and gifted with certain ordinances and a certain independent freedom and authority. It is a kingdom not of this world, and not destined to be swallowed up or lost in any worldly kingdom, for in the vision of the consummation of all things seen by John in Patmos, the Church is not seen to disappear from view or give place to the State as the kingdom of God: on the contrary, it appears in a more glorious form than ever, descending from God out of heaven as a bride adorned for her husband. The Church is represented in Scripture as the witness for God in the world, the pillar and ground of the truth; but according to this theory, it has no one certain faith, and proclaims no one uniform truth. In a word, this view of the Church is closely connected with an entire system of religion which underrates the importance of the knowledge and belief of the truth that God has revealed, and the necessity of a supernatural work of grace for the conversion and salvation of sinners. It is the consistent Church theory of the Rationalistic or Broad Church school, just as the former is that of the Romanist or High Church party. For the views that men take of the nature and attributes of the Church are determined to a large extent by the opinions they hold as to the whole scheme of divine truth and the way of salvation for sinners.

### III. Evangelical Doctrine

Hence it is to be expected that if there is, as we believe, a system of truth taught in the Bible different alike from Romanism and Rationalism, the system of Evangelical Protestantism, there will be also a view of the Church capable of being maintained and worked out in harmony with the evangelical system, and equally free from the errors of the two opposite extremes. It is sometimes apt to seem as if there were no alternative between them; and the adherents of both are ready to take advantage of this: the Romanist to urge upon men that if they would have any certainty for their faith and hope, if they would not be left to the endless doubts and shifting fancies of Rationalism, they must take refuge in the friendly bosom of the Church of Rome; and the freethinker, on the other hand, assuring them that, unless they would be the slaves of spiritual despotism, they must cast aside all authority, and be a creed and a law to themselves. But, nevertheless, there is a real, consistent, and defensible position that may be maintained between these two extremes; as on other questions of doctrine, so also on this of the nature of the Church.

The fundamental principle of Evangelical Protestantism is the recognition of the person and work of the Holy Spirit, especially as the Spirit of Christ, through whose agency Christ acts and works on the earth, even though He is now ascended up to heaven. This may be regarded as the key that solves much of the perplexity in which many controverted topics are involved by Romanism on the one hand and Rationalism on the other. Its application to this subject is direct and obvious.

The Church, says Paul, is the body of Christ (Eph. 1$^{23}$), and the one body (*ib.* 4$^4$); but how is it one body? Because it has one Spirit. "There is one body and one Spirit." It is so in the natural body, from which the image is taken; the body consists of many members,—bones and sinews, veins and arteries, and the like,—and it may be anatomised and divided into parts; it seems to be not one but many. Yet it is not a mere collection of particles of matter, however beautifully arranged: it is one living whole. Why? Because it is animated by one spirit. Let the living soul take its flight and leave the body lifeless, it is no more one: it is a mere heap of particles of dust, ready to mix with kindred dust. But let it be animated with the breath of life, and it is a living whole or unity. So, this figure indicates, and Scripture also teaches in plain language, the unity of the Church depends upon the Spirit: it is the unity of the Spirit. Now, it is observable in both of the theories we have been considering, the Romish and the Rationalistic, however different and opposite, that in both alike the work of the Spirit in this matter is ignored. The Broad Church theory, which makes the bond of union of the lowest possible kind, manifestly omits to take into account any special supernatural agency of the Spirit; and the High Church theory, though it may professedly acknowledge the Spirit's agency, yet naturally does away with it by regarding it as confined to a certain outward organisation, and acting through certain outward rites. Now, as long as we lose sight of the work of the Spirit we shall be unable to find any alternative between these two theories, unless it be some mere modification of one or other of them; but the moment we recognise and give its due place to that great work, we see the true idea of the one holy Catholic Church of which these are distortions and counterfeits. "Wherever the Church is, there is the Spirit," said Cyprian; and he added, "where the Spirit is, there is the Church"; but this was put second, and came to be very much left out of sight in the times that followed, when the Papal idea of the Church was gradually built up on the former half of the maxim. It would have been much better to have reversed the order and put in the forefront the motto, "Wherever the Spirit is, there is the Church," leaving to follow, as a subordinate inference, "Where the Church is, there is the Spirit."

The Church, says Paul, is the body of Christ (Eph. 1$^{23}$), and how it is so he explains in what follows. It is His fulness, *i.e.* that by which he is filled or made up—His complement, as it were, for the head is not complete without the body: the Church is in Christ. But, on the other hand, He is in the Church: it filleth Him; but He filleth it as well: He filleth all; and He filleth the Church, not in the sense of being in the whole body simply as a whole; for it is added, in all He filleth all, by being in all, in every one of the members, as the soul is in the body, all in the whole and all in every part.

The twofold bond of our individual union to Christ which is the result of effectual calling is the agency of the Spirit on God's part and the exercise of faith on our part, and this same twofold bond unites all believers to Christ and establishes the unity of His body, the Church.

That Church is one, because it is in all its members livingly connected with one Head by one Spirit: it is holy, because the Spirit that dwells in all its members is the Holy Spirit, who makes them all holy; it is Catholic, because it consists of the whole of those everywhere throughout the world who truly believe in Jesus. It is no mere external organised society, and yet no mere loose collection of individuals: it is the entire company of those who, in all places, acknowledge and trust and love the Lord Jesus as their Head and Elder Brother, and look up to God as their Father in Him. With this idea all the Protestant definitions of the Church harmonise: they differ somewhat in form, but agree in substance.

Whether we say, with the Westminster Standards, that it is the whole number of the elect, or, with Amesius, that it is *cœtus vocatorum*, or, with the Church of England, that it is *cœtus fidelium*, " a congregation of faithful men," etc. (Art. xix.), or, with the Lutheran Church, that it is the communion of saints—we recognise in all these forms of expression that the Holy Spirit, as applying Christ and His redemption to us, is the principle of the Church's unity. For effectual calling, faith and holiness are the effects and results of this work of the Spirit.

From this recognition of the Spirit as the bond of union in the body of Christ arises the distinction between the Church as it is invisible and as it is visible.

Primarily and in its own nature, the Church is invisible. Not that it does not consist of men and women who are outwardly seen, and who, for the most part, manifest their faith and love in their outward lives; but what makes them members of Christ and of His Church is not any outward profession or act of which men can judge, but the inward and secret state of their hearts, which the Lord alone can discern. " The Lord knoweth them that are His "; He alone searches the hearts and tries the reins of the children of men. But while He alone can tell with absolute certainty who are His, and the only complete assurance we can ever have of our being in Christ is the inward witness of the Spirit, yet as the hidden life of faith manifests itself by its fruits, and believers are commanded to profess their faith and unite with one another in worship, love, and good works, we cannot but recognise all who profess their faith and conform their profession by a consistent walk as brethren in the Lord, and those who do so form what we call the Church of Christ visible. (See *Confession of Faith*, chap. xxv.) These are not two Churches distinct from each other, as Romanists accuse us of believing: they are just two different aspects of one and the same Church: on the one hand, as it is seen and known by God only, who knows all hearts; and, on the other hand, as it is recognised by us, who can only judge after the outward appearance. Thus the distinction of the Church as visible and invisible arises solely from the imperfection of our discernment, and is really a different mode of viewing the same spiritual body. We know that there is, and ever shall be, a people of God on earth, elect according to the foreknowledge of God the Father, through sanctification of the Spirit unto obedience and sprinkling of the blood of Jesus Christ (1 Pet. 1²), and we are taught many great and precious truths about this true spiritual Church of Christ; we must accordingly often think and speak of it in this, its highest, sense. But at the same time there are duties that we are commanded to perform towards the people of God; and as we cannot certainly know who are such, we must perform them to those whom we judge, to the best of our ability, to be truly His, always remembering that our judgment is a fallible one, and may very probably be mistaken. The invisible Church is the ideal which, in the sight of God, is at the same time real; the visible Church is for us the concrete reality that represents the ideal. In the end the two will coincide, and all apparent duality that exists now in our view of the Church will be merged in absolute unity, when the ideal shall be realised, and the real raised to the purity and perfection of the ideal.

Sometimes the interest and contendings that men have for the Church are depreciated by the remark that, on Protestant principles, it is only the Church visible, not the Church invisible, the true body of Christ, that these concern: that, *e.g.*, the freedom for which our fathers contended and suffered is not the true spiritual freedom of the people of God, but only an outward ecclesiastical privilege, or that the union of separated bodies of Christians is not the true spiritual unity of the body of Christ. But when we bear in mind that the distinction of the Church invisible and visible is not one of two separate Churches, we may see that these representations are mistaken. The Church visible is the concrete body with which we have to do, and is not to be despised because it is not identical with the true Church. It is altogether delusive to fancy that we are showing regard to the purity, or freedom, or unity of the Church invisible, while we are caring nothing for these qualities in the Church as visible. On the contrary, it is our duty to aim at making the Church visible, as much as possible, like the Church invisible. It is no thanks to us that the Church invisible is one, holy and free: no sin or unfaithfulness of ours can affect it. But what is given to us to do is to endeavour, as far as in us lies, to secure that the Church visible have these excellences and blessings; these may be betrayed by us if we are careless and unfaithful, or maintained and promoted if we are diligent and faithful servants of the Lord.

It is ours to seek that the visible Church of Christ be as much as possible holy as the Church invisible is, that we and our fellow-disciples be living in faith and following after holiness. It is ours to maintain, at all costs and in the face of all opposition, the liberty of the Church visible, as the Jerusalem which is above is free, which is the mother of us all. It is ours to labour that the divisions in the Church visible may be healed, and that it may become more and more like the Church invisible in unity. It is ours to seek that it may be like it, too, in catholicity, embracing people of all nations in its limits, by seeking to spread the glorious gospel of Jesus Christ among all nations.

### RELATION OF THE CHURCH TO THE KINGDOM OF GOD

It may be proper to consider here the relation between the notion of the Church and that of the kingdom of God, both of which are important scriptural ideas. In former times these were apt to be confounded, and it was assumed that all that is said of the kingdom of God applied to the Church. In mediaeval times the visible Church was identified with the kingdom; and even in the Protestant Churches, when this error was corrected, the notion of the kingdom of God was too much ignored or lost sight of. In modern times the distinction has been observed and applied, though sometimes in a way that is exaggerated and dangerous. The idea of the kingdom of God has been used by some to supersede that of the Church invisible. It is said that this is the true distinction that ought to have been made by the Reformers, and that only confusion has sprung from the notion of a Church invisible.[1] That is held to involve a contradiction; for a Church, from its very nature, must be an organised society, whereas the members of the Church invisible are, from the nature of the case, incapable of being such.[2] The Church, therefore, is on this view essentially visible: an outward organisation subordinate and preparatory to the kingdom of God, which is the ideal spiritual body or holy fellowship to be realised at last. In reply to this, it may be said that the term ἐκκλησία does not necessarily denote an organised society, and that if the figure of a body suggests some organisation, it is not necessarily an outward one, but may be that formed by the different gifts and capacities of doing good given by Christ to each of His true disciples. This rejection of the idea of the Church invisible is connected on the one hand, as held by such men as Stahl, Delitzsch,[3] etc., with an exaggerated importance and authority assigned to the outward organised Church; and, on the other hand, as held by Rothe and others, it is associated with a merging of the Church in the State, and a maintenance of gross Erastianism. For as the Church is regarded as being primarily and essentially an outward organised body of this earth, and only connected with the kingdom of God as being an institution subordinate and preparatory to it, then either this external society is regarded as the divine institution for salvation, out of which none are saved, or else the outward Church is held to have no essential and necessary connection with salvation; and thus there is a plausible ground for holding that the external institution, like all others of that kind, must be subject to the supreme authority of the State, and that such State interference with the Church is no infringement of the authority of Christ, since it leaves the true spiritual fellowship of the kingdom of God intact.

Let us see, however, whether the distinction between the Church and the kingdom of God, as it is grounded on Scripture, does really lead to such conclusions. That there

---

[1] So Schweizer, quoted and approved by Krauss, *Unsichtbare Kirche*, pp. 119, 120.
[2] Rothe, quoted by Müller, *Dogm. Abh.* p. 286.
[3] *Ib.* pp. 282, 284.

is such a distinction must be admitted, and some features of it are obvious. Thus—

(1) There is an obvious difference in the formal character of the two names. The Church (ἐκκλησία) denotes, and can denote only, a group or company of persons; the kingdom of God or of heaven (βασιλεία τοῦ θεοῦ, τῶν οὐρανῶν), again, includes much more, and may denote something quite different. Its leading element is the idea of rule, lordship; and it may mean not only the persons who are ruled, but the authority or the exercise of the rule over them. It may denote the reign of God, or the sovereignty of God, as well as the subjects of His rule; and in fact in many, perhaps most, of the places where it occurs, it might better be rendered the reign of God than the kingdom.[1] This is denied by some on the ground that, though the phrase βασιλεία τοῦ θεοῦ would in itself be ambiguous, history had determined its meaning to be, not reign but kingdom. But I think the construction in some places shows that it must mean reign.

(2) Though both of the expressions are to be traced back to the Old Testament, and explained in the light of Old Testament ideas, they are founded on two different conceptions. That of the Church corresponds to the congregation (קהל) of Israel, so often mentioned in the history of the Exodus. The kingdom of God, again, corresponds to the idea of the theocracy, the rule of Jehovah over His people, and ultimately over all the earth. The former is the conception of a people gathered out from the rest of the world and brought into special covenant relation to Jehovah: the latter is that of a kingship of God, in which His will is to be done, and His name honoured at last by all. The congregation might continue to exist even when the Lord's enemies triumphed and cast off His authority;[2] the kingdom of God, however, was then fallen, and could only be looked and hoped for as a thing of the future, as in the book of Daniel, with which especially our Lord's teaching on this point is connected.

(3) The Church or congregation of the Lord denotes a purely religious association of persons, and describes them

[1] See Stanton, *Jewish and Christian Messiah*, p 217.
[2] See, *e.g.*, Ps. lxxiv.

simply by the relation in which they stand to Him. This is clearly at least the New Testament idea of the Church: its members are associated for worship, proclamation of the gospel, and mutual edification. But the kingdom of God includes in its functions and activities all that is comprised in the province of human kingdoms and human life generally. This is especially clear from the Old Testament descriptions of it, and it is not contradicted by anything in the New Testament. As J. Müller puts it,[1] "State, science, art, do not fall within the circle of Church life, the first not at all, the others only partially, and so that they must retain the independence of their principles. Yet they all belong to the kingdom of God, in so far as they have for their foundation the idea of the living God revealed in Christ. So far as they rest on that foundation they form, along with the Church, one great combination of persons, activities, services, under the one King, Christ."

In a word, the Church is a religious notion; the kingdom of God a moral one.

It is in accordance with this distinction that we find Jesus speaking very often and prominently of the kingdom of God, and only once or twice of the Church; while the apostles, especially Paul, speak much of the Church, and not so frequently of the kingdom of God. There was a Church in existence when our Lord came. The Jewish people was the congregation of God: they were not a kingdom; there was no theocracy or visible kingdom of God on the earth; there was an almost universal rebellion against God; the kingdoms of the world were in the hands of Satan. Jesus proclaimed that the reign of God was at hand, and called men to repent, *i.e.* to turn from their rebellion, to loyal obedience to God as their King. The spiritual kingdom of God needed to be founded, and men needed to be taught that it is a spiritual kingdom, and not a restoration of the outward kingdom, as under David or Solomon, or even of the theocracy, as in the days of Moses. They needed to be called and moved to yield themselves up to God, and obey and honour Him in all the spheres of their conduct. Hence the kingdom of God must

[1] *Dogmatische Abhandlungen*, p. 310.

form a large and prominent topic in our Lord's teaching. On the other hand, the Jewish Church was already in existence, and what it needed was simply to recognise Jesus as the promised Messiah. It was only when the great majority, and their official representatives, failed and refused to do so that Jesus reconstituted the Church in a new form, on the basis of the confession that Peter was the first to make: "Thou art the Christ," etc. As a separate body from the Jewish Church, though still claiming to be the true circumcision, the Christian Church came into existence after the ascension of our Lord, and hence, naturally, is more spoken of by the apostles than by Jesus Himself.

Further, the Church is the great means for promoting and extending the kingdom of God. To Peter, as the first of the living stones of which the Church is composed, Jesus promised the keys of the kingdom of heaven; the religious society is the means of securing the true moral order among mankind, because religion is the ground and condition of all true morality. If men are to be brought into right relations among themselves, they must first be brought into right relations to God. The Christian πολίτευμα is a holy temple.

But while the kingdom of God ought to be recognised as thus a distinct conception from the Church, I do not think that the recognition of it can enable us to dispense with the Reformation distinction of the Church invisible and visible. For—

(1) The Church is spoken of in Scripture in such terms as can only denote what is meant by the Church invisible, the body of true believers in Christ. These representations are especially to be found in the Epistles to the Ephesians and Colossians and the First to Timothy; and those who would entirely banish the idea of the Church invisible from Christianity are almost necessarily constrained to deny the Pauline authorship of these epistles, and regard them as belonging to the post-apostolic age, or at least as having less direct authority. This is a proceeding, however, which does violence to the true principles of criticism and historical evidence, though this is not the place to enter on the question. It must, however,

be admitted that if these books are part of the New Testament, the idea of the Church as invisible is unmistakably taught there. The Church is not limited to an outwardly organised society: it is the body of Christ, the whole of those for whom He gave Himself to redeem them, and whom He purifies and perfects by His Spirit. This body is from the nature of the case one not definable by men unless salvation is made to depend on outward rites.

(2) The same distinction of an outward and inward, a man-ward and God-ward aspect, is made in Scripture in regard to the kingdom of God. The parables of the wheat and tares (Matt. 13$^{24\text{-}30,\ 37\text{-}43}$) and of the draw net (ib. $^{47\text{-}50}$) are expressly said to illustrate the kingdom of heaven: the good seed are the children of the kingdom, i.e. in the true spiritual sense, in the eye of God. But they cannot be certainly separated from the tares until the end of the world, when they that offend are cast out of the kingdom in which they have hitherto been, i.e., the kingdom as it is outwardly in the sight of men. As, then, the Church is presented to us not only as visible but also as invisible, so, on the other hand, the kingdom of God is represented as not merely invisible but also visible. In fact, the distinction between visible and invisible is one not at all peculiar to the Church, but applicable to a great many other things, and, indeed, one that we cannot avoid applying to every object, in regard to which our judgment may possibly not correspond to the reality. It is simply the distinction between real and seeming or apparent. This is very clearly brought out by Jonathan Edwards in his *Inquiry Concerning the Qualifications for Communion*, pt. ii. sec. i.: "We find the word saint, when applied to men, used two ways in the New Testament. The word in some places is so used as to mean those who are real saints, who are converted and are truly gracious persons, as 1 Cor. 6$^2$, Eph. 1$^{18}$ 3$^{17,18}$, 2 Thess. 1$^{10}$, Rev. 5$^8$ 8$^4$ 11$^{18}$ 13$^{10}$ 14$^{12}$ 19$^8$. In other places the word is so used as to have respect not only to real saints but to such as were saints in visibility, appearance, and profession; and so were outwardly, as to what concerns their acceptance among men and their outward treatment and privileges, of the company of saints. So

the word is used in very many places, which it is needless to mention, as everyone acknowledges it.

"In like manner we find the word Christian used two ways: the word is used to express the same thing as a righteous man that shall be saved (1 Pet. $4^{16\text{-}18}$). Elsewhere it is so used as to take in all who were Christians by profession and outward appearance (Acts $11^{26}$). So there is a twofold use of the word disciples in the New Testament. There were disciples in name, profession, and appearance, and there were those whom Christ calls disciples indeed (John $8^{30,\,31}$, Luke $14^{25\text{-}27}$, John $15^{8}$). The same distinction is signified in the New Testament by those that live, being alive from the dead, and risen with Christ, and those who have a name to live . . .

"The distinction of real and visible does not only take place with regard to saintship or holiness, but with regard to innumerable other things. There is visible and real truth, visible and real honesty, visible and real money, visible and real gold, etc. etc. *Visible* and *real* are words that stand related one to another, as the words *real* and *seeming*, or *true* and *apparent*."[1]

There is one point omitted in this and many similar representations. The Church invisible is regarded as included within the visible, whereas in point of fact as there may be, and are, seeming believers who are not really such, so, conversely, there may be and are real believers who do not appear to be such. For aught we know, the membership of the invisible Church may be far more numerous than of the visible. I firmly believe that it is; though from the expressions often used, it is sometimes made to appear as if the opposite were the case. The limitation of the real Church invisible to the bounds of the visible has indeed been sometimes explicitly maintained in connection with the doctrine of the Lutherans, that the operation of the Spirit is always through the external call of the gospel. In accordance with this view, the Church is regarded not merely as the society of the saved, but as the institution for the salvation of the world; not only as the *cœtus* but as the *mater fidelium*.

[1] This quotation from Edwards is slightly abbreviated.

Now, there is no doubt that the Church has a function to discharge in the promotion of God's cause in the world and the gathering in of sinners to the Saviour, but it is simply that of witnessing for the truth, and it is no other than every one has who knows the gospel in any way. "The Spirit and the bride say come": there is the Church's work, but it is also the work of any and every one. "Let him that heareth say come." We must beware of regarding the Church as the institution for salvation in such a sense that men must come through it, or through any ordinances in it, to Christ. The true Protestant principle is that we come directly to Christ, and through Him enter into the fellowship of the Church; not as Romanists hold, come first to the Church, and only through the Church and its ordinances enter into fellowship with Christ.

The reason why it is of some use and importance to consider the doctrine of the Church after that of the believer's union to Christ, and before unfolding the benefits implied in communion with Him, is not at all that the Church is the institution through which these benefits are conveyed to the individual, but, on the one hand, that union to Christ is that which constitutes the totality of believers, His body; and, on the other hand, that that union of the whole body to Christ as the last Adam is the ground of their being regarded and dealt with by God as one, and so lays the basis of that imputation of Christ's righteousness to His people, which forms an essential part of the blessing of justification. By working out the conception of the Church as the body of Christ, the collective mass of those who are united to Him by the Spirit's work in Effectual Calling, we have gained a view of Christ as the Head of a new humanity, the second great representative of the human race. Over against the first man, Adam, and the race who are all in him, and in him all die, we can now contemplate Christ with a seed given to Him, a new race of mankind, the Church, which is spiritually united to Christ as the race is naturally to Adam.

By conversion wrought by the Holy Spirit a man ceases to be merely a *proto*-Adamite, as it has been called, and becomes a *deutero*-Adamite: he acquires a new head and representative; he ceases to be merely in Adam, he is now in Christ: not merely united to Him individually, but one of the great body of which He is the Head and Lord. Or, to express it otherwise, he passes from the Covenant of Works to that of Grace, in the former of which he was represented by Adam, in the latter by Christ.

### THE NOTES OF THE CHURCH

There is a topic commonly referred to by theologians in this connection, the Notes of the Church. By these are meant certain marks by which the true Church of Christ can be discerned from any other society or body claiming that name and honour. These, however, have a meaning and importance only on the Roman Catholic theory of the Church. If that Church, out of which is no salvation, be an external body, then obviously it is of the utmost importance to be able to discern what that body is, since from a comparatively early time there have been various separate communities calling themselves Christians, and each claiming the adhesion of believers. In order to meet this difficulty it has been held that there are certain outstanding marks, called *Notæ Ecclesiæ*, by which men may be enabled to recognise the true Church without requiring to verify every part of its essential definition. These notes have been variously enumerated. Bellarmine gives no less than fifteen, most of them of a very external and accidental character, beginning with the name Catholic and finishing with *infelix exitus adversariorum*, a mark which Rome has done her best to realise. But more generally the Notes of the Church have been enumerated by Roman and Anglican writers as four, founded on the epithets given to the Church in the ancient Creeds, "one Catholic Apostolic Church" (*Symb. Nic.*), "the holy Catholic Church" (*Symb. Apost.*). The notes thus indicated are Unity, Holiness, Catholicity, Apostolicity. The true Church is recognised by its being (1) a single external body; (2) holy, in the sense of being consecrated to God, for in any more inward sense the Romish doctrine cannot recognise holiness as an attribute of the Church; (3) catholic, as embracing Christians in all lands:

and (4) apostolic, either as holding the doctrines of the apostles, or as having unbroken apostolic succession in her ministers. An example of the application made of these marks, especially the last two, is to be found in J. H. Newman's *Apologia*, where he describes how at one stage of his history he hesitated between the claims of the Anglican Church, as possessing the note of apostolicity, and those of the Roman Church, as having that of catholicity. Protestants generally admit that the qualities denoted by these names do really belong to the Church as invisible, but that they are of an inward and spiritual nature, and so not fitted to be marks of an external society: that it is only in their spiritual sense that they belong essentially to the Church; and that in the external significance that Romanists attach to them, they do not always and exclusively belong to the true Church, and therefore can be no marks of it. It is not difficult to make out that the unity, holiness, catholicity and apostolicity ascribed in Scripture to the Church are not external and recognisable qualities, but of a spiritual nature, and that no such outward notes as can mark out one outward society as the Church are recognised in the New Testament.

Since the Notes of the Church had become a customary theological topic, the Reformers and most Protestant theologians thought it necessary, or at least undertook, to show not only that those alleged by Romanists are not really such, but also what are the true Notes of the Church, *i.e.* as visible, for to it they apply. And they were very generally agreed that they consisted of three—

(1) The preaching of the word, or the gospel of Jesus Christ.

(2) The administration of the sacraments; to which Calvin added—

(3) The exercise of ecclesiastical discipline.

Many of the Reformed Confessions include a statement of the Notes of the Church—the Augsburg Confession, The Thirty-nine Articles, mentioning (1) and (2); the Belgic and Old Scottish Confessions, adding also (3).

Less importance is attached to them in later Confessions: in the Helvetica Posterior they are only slightly alluded to, and

(1) alone is expressly mentioned; and in the Westminster Standards they are not referred to at all.

Dr. Bannerman holds that instead of extending the number to three, or even two, only the first—the preaching of the word of God—should be reckoned as a note of the Church.

And this indicates that really this whole idea has not that meaning and importance in Protestant theology that it has in the Catholic system. The necessity and use of such marks arises from the assumption that we have to single out one outward body, and must have certain palpable marks by which to distinguish it, these marks being not the essential qualities of the Church, but certain signs more easily recognisable. But if, on the Protestant view, salvation does not depend on our being connected with any outward body, but on our being united to Christ by faith, there is no need of such arbitrary marks; and what distinguishes the Church is not any such appointed marks, but simply its own essential nature. So when Protestants speak of Notes of the Church, they are really simply giving its definition, or at least its differentia, and not, as Romanists profess to be, describing some divinely-appointed tokens by which it is to be recognised. If we know what the Church is, we do not need a separate doctrine of the Notes of the Church, nor has such a doctrine any substantial meaning for us. The differentia of the Church may be said to be faith in Jesus Christ, the effect and end of Effectual Calling. Of the Church as invisible, the differentia or mark is real living faith in the heart, as known to God; of the Church as visible, the mark is professed faith, showing itself to men by word and deed. The first of the Protestant Notes of the Church, the preaching of the gospel, may be said to be in substance just the profession of faith; and so it is not so much a separate mark or note, but the very definition of the Church as visible. It is only in this sense that it can be safely taken as a note of the Church at all. Regarded as the teaching of pure doctrine, it is apt to degenerate into an external mark after all, as it has done in the Lutheran Church, where it has sometimes been held that all who do not hold certain definite doctrines are outside of the Church. To tie down the Church of Christ to one particular set of doctrines is an error of the same kind as to tie it down to one particular form of government. When the pure preaching of the gospel is made the chief, or only, mark of the Church, the only scriptural meaning to be attached to that is the expression of living faith in Christ; that is what makes a man a Christian, and a community a Christian Church, not the belief of any system of doctrines.

# THE NEW LIFE

## I. RENEWAL

THE blessings of salvation may all be summed up in the biblical conception of communion with Christ flowing from union to Him. When we investigate them, from the subjective point of view of the awakened and converted soul, by inquiring what are the religious needs that such a soul feels, and what there is in Christ to supply these needs, we see that when one is brought, by the gracious work of the Holy Spirit, to right feelings and desires, a primary and most urgent need that he feels, is the removal of guilt, and that in a way consistent with the justice of God. This is met by the free forgiveness and acceptance of the ungodly through faith in Christ, to whom, as the Lord's righteous servant, we are united so as to have communion with Him in His righteousness. This is the Pauline and Protestant doctrine of justification by grace, on account of Christ our righteousness, received by faith.

But the sense of guilt is not the only feeling of the quickened soul, nor is forgiveness the only blessing needed, and felt to be needed. We are sometimes represented as holding that when God justifies a sinner, He only changes his state and not his character;[1] but that is not our opinion: for though we maintain that to justify is not to make a man righteous, but to pronounce him such, yet we assert, with equal emphasis, that justification is never without regeneration and renewal. If it were, the wants of our souls would be very imperfectly met. For when the soul is really turned to God, there is a sense of the pollution and hatefulness of sin, as well as of its guilt and ill-desert, and of the need of

[1] This is stated and met very explicitly by Bishop Davenant, *De Justitia*.

being inwardly cleansed, so as to be made morally pure and good. The blessing by which this need of the soul is met is that of renewal, or, as it has been generally called by theologians, Sanctification. The latter term, in its biblical use, has a special shade of meaning which I shall explain by and by; but before doing so, it will be proper to consider the more general idea of moral renewal ($\dot{a}\nu\alpha\kappa\alpha\acute{\iota}\nu\omega\sigma\iota\varsigma$, Rom. 12²) as an essential part of the Christian salvation.

That this is needed, even after the great change wrought in the soul by Effectual Calling, may be seen by a consideration of the facts of the case. The new birth of the Spirit imparts to the soul a taste and desire for what is spiritually good, and a real and earnest hatred of sin and love of God, which becomes from thenceforth the ruling principle in the soul. This seems to be the nearest description we can give of the new life, "the seed of God" (1 John 3⁹), "that which is born of the Spirit" (John 3⁶), spoken of in Scripture. It is a principle of godliness, that seeks and desires what is according to God's character and law, and hates and strives against whatever is opposed to that.[1] The possession of this implies that the bias and bent of the soul is turned from being inclined to self and sin, to being inclined to God and goodness. This is the change implied in conversion, the result of regeneration. It is a radical and very great change. But it does not imply that the soul is at once made perfectly good in all its acts and feelings.

For there are temptations and tendencies to sin that are not removed by this great change. The deepest and most powerful cause of sin is no doubt removed—the selfish and worldly inclination of the natural heart. But there are other causes of sin that are not affected by the removal of that one, and that therefore remain even when that is gone. Thus there are temptations, arising from the fact that there are around us a multitude of objects and occurrences that tend to arouse in us desires and passions in themselves neither good nor evil, but such as in many cases cannot be lawfully

---

[1] This is most distinctly brought out in Charnock's *Discourses on Regeneration* (*Works*, iii. pp. 96, 105), and in Edwards, *On the Religious Affections*, Part III. § vii.

gratified, and so may lead to sin. In this way even a perfectly holy being may be tempted, as our Saviour was, and an innocent being, not fortified by habitual goodness, may fall before temptation. Besides these, there are in our case tendencies to sin, consisting of habits contracted by repeated acts, or peculiar dispositions that may be even stronger than habits. It is obvious that the impartation of a real and strong hatred of sin and love of goodness will not of itself remove these temptations and tendencies. A habitual drunkard, *e.g.*, may be truly converted, so that he now hates the excess he once delighted in. This change will make him desire and strive to be free from it. But it will not make the wine less pleasant to his senses, nor will it at once destroy the tendency that has been engendered by a course of indulgence. Now what is notoriously true in this case is equally true in general of all kinds of temptations and tendencies to sin.

Thus the change that results in conversion does not make the soul perfectly holy, or remove all habits or possibilities of sin. On the contrary, since it awakens a new-born hatred of sin and love to God, and shows in their true colours what sin and godliness are, it brings the soul into a state of distress and grief on account of its own sinfulness. The mind and conscience are enlightened to see what sin is; and many acts and states and feelings are seen to be deeply sinful that did not seem to be so at all before; the new love of holiness impels the believer to strive against these things, and to seek to have done with them; but he finds that temptation still has an influence upon him, and habit is still a power within him, so that he cannot avoid sin or live the pure life he desires to live.

Thus it is just when a man is born again that he most feels his need of renewal. Unconverted men are usually very little concerned about their moral character—at least about the state of their hearts. They generally think that they are good enough, and, if only some allowance were made, could stand God's judgment. But the work of the Holy Spirit in conversion dispels such fancies; and so it frequently happens that, when one is really converted, so far from being entirely freed from sin, he never saw or felt sin to be so powerful in him as since he began to hate and oppose it.

This is the account that Paul gives of his own experience in Rom. 7, and it corresponds with the experience of believers in all ages. In that passage the apostle declares that the law, or ruling principle, of his mind (νοῦς) is in accordance with what is right, for he delights in the law of God after the inner man; but there is a law of sin in his members, or his flesh, warring against it (Rom. 7$^{23}$). This exactly corresponds with the description that I have just drawn, from the nature of the case. The mind is the centre of our being, as appears from its being described as the inner man, and that has been renewed and turned to God; but the members, *i.e.* the various senses and faculties, have still their natural relation to external things, which give rise to desires that may be inordinate and sinful, and are not yet entirely under the control of the renewed mind. Hence Paul says: "the motions of sins . . . did work in our members . . ." (Rom. 7$^{5}$), and commands us to "mortify our members" (Col. 3$^{5}$), *i.e.* to put to death or extirpate those desires and passions, working through our senses, that lead to sin. Hence, too, Christians are warned against worldly lusts and carnal lusts, which need to be denied and avoided.

This view of the state of the regenerate soul, to which we are led by Scripture as well as by sound psychological observation, is entirely opposed to the Roman Catholic doctrine, that in regeneration all that is of the nature of sin is removed from the soul, so that it is thenceforth perfectly able to keep all the commandments of God. Romanists are led to this position by confounding justification and sanctification, and understanding the texts that speak of the entire taking away of sin not as denoting the absolute removal of guilt by a free and full forgiveness, but as including an entire removal of sinfulness. This is the only scriptural ground alleged for their doctrine, and it involves a wrong interpretation of these passages. On the other hand, in order to reconcile their position with the statements of Paul and the experience of Christians as to indwelling sin, they are obliged to maintain that the concupiscence (ἐπιθυμία) or lust of the flesh, which the apostle expressly calls sin, is not in the regenerate really of the nature of sin. This assertion is so inconsistent with the view of the law of God given by our Saviour, as requiring holiness of heart as well as of life, and violated even by impure desires, that it must be rejected, and with it must fall the doctrine that requires it as a support. The scriptural view is that of Protestants: that while the sins of believers are entirely forgiven in justification, and while we are delivered from the dominion of sin by regeneration, there is still corruption remaining in the regenerate soul which needs to be overcome and removed.

But Scripture also teaches that God does renew and make inherently righteous the souls of His people, and that this is one of the blessings of Christ's redemption. There is the great promise of the New Covenant, Jer. 31$^{33}$, quoted in Heb. 8, " I will put My law in their inward parts, and write it in their hearts"; the still more distinct statement in Ezek. 36$^{27}$, where, after saying "A new heart will I give you" (which specially points to regeneration), the Lord proceeds, "and I will put My Spirit within you, and cause you to walk in My statutes"—which describes a continual process of renewal. So Paul, in Rom. 8$^2$, ascribes his deliverance from the law of sin and death in his members to the law of the Spirit of Life in Christ Jesus, and to the indwelling of the Spirit of God and of Christ. So, too, in Phil. 2$^{12, 13}$, urging believers to work out their own salvation, he adds, "it is God that worketh in you both to will and to do." Peter prays in full assurance that the God of all grace would make perfect, stablish, strengthen, settle those whom He has called (1 Pet. 5$^{10}$); and John speaks of Christians as not only born of God, but also having His Spirit given to them and dwelling in them.

It thus appears that besides the great work of Effectual Calling, which is the beginning of the new life, there is a continuous work of the Spirit by which that life is carried on to perfection, and this may be taken as the first point in the doctrine of renewal or sanctification, that it is the work of the Holy Spirit. Our progressive deliverance from sinfulness is ascribed to the Holy Spirit dwelling in us. But in what sense, it may be asked, can this be? Since the Spirit is a divine person, He is present everywhere, and His agency sustains all creatures in life and being. It cannot be in this sense that His presence is the cause of moral renewal. But as the Spirit is said to come upon men when He begins to work in a special way on the soul, whether by gifts of wisdom, knowledge, and utterance, or by new moral and religious emotions and volitions, so when He continues to exercise such special influence, it may be said that the Holy Spirit abides upon or dwells in men. Thus as the beginning of our new life is effected by the Holy Spirit inwardly drawing us to Christ by the presentation of His grace and love, and so moving us to turn from sin to God, so the increase and perfecting of our new character is due to the Spirit continuing to exert His gracious influence, awakening holy desires and aspirations.

This work, like that of regeneration, is one of which we are not directly conscious, since it is exerted in those depths of our nature that lie beneath our consciousness; but its reality is known by its fruits; and as the inward work of regeneration shows itself in the experience of conversion, so the continual work of the Spirit in our renewal appears in the continuance of that turning from sin to God that is the essence of conversion. Hence exhortations to turn from sin and put it away are frequently addressed in Scripture to those who are truly the children of God, or are recognised as such; and hence, too, even those who may have no distinct memory of a first turning to God, may have real experience of this in the continual need they feel of self-denial and repentance and struggles against remaining tendencies to sin. As in the natural world the original creative act of divine power is followed up by the same power preserving all things, so it is here. The new creation of spiritual life, or life to God, must be followed up by the continual work of the same divine Spirit maintaining and developing that life.

This leads us to a second point in regard to the work of moral renewal. As it is wrought by the same Spirit through whose agency we are born again, so it is done in the same way —through the presentation to the soul of Jesus Christ our

Saviour. We are not renewed by a magical process or by one of mere power, but by one that deals with us as rational and free agents, i.e. by a calling of God in which Christ is presented to us, and we are invited and persuaded to accept Him and become one with Him. Thus the work of renewal is carried on in close connection with the person of Christ. The Spirit that dwells and works in the believer is the same that dwelt and wrought in Christ and secured His perfect purity in a world of sin and temptation. He was conceived by the power of the Holy Spirit; He grew and waxed strong in spirit; He was anointed with the Spirit for His saving work, to preach glad tidings and to heal those oppressed of evil. Now, having thus in His human nature received the Holy Spirit, He baptizes with the Spirit, and promises the Spirit as living water to all who, being athirst, will come to Him and receive Him by faith. Thus our renewal as well as our justification depends on our union and communion with Christ; and as in justification we are partakers with Him in His righteousness and acceptance with God, so in our renewal we are partakers with Him in the Holy Spirit, as the author of all moral goodness and purity.

Then the result of this is, that the character that is formed in us by this work of the Spirit is after the pattern of Christ's, and destined to become perfectly like His. He has left us an example that we should walk in His steps; the mind that was in Christ is also to be formed in us; we are to walk in love as He has loved us. This is the special type of Christian holiness—it is Christlikeness. It is like His in this, that it is attained through struggle and suffering. He, though Son of God, learned obedience by the things that He suffered, and so must we. We have a common experience as well as a common character. His course involved a birth, a temptation, a work, a suffering, a death, a resurrection, and a glorification; and in all these experiences we are called to share in a moral and spiritual way: we must be born again, we are tempted as He was, we suffer with Him that we may be glorified together, we die with Him that we may also live with Him. More especially, our moral progress is described as being conformed to the image of His death: dying with

Him to sin, that we may rise with Him to newness of life. The death of Christ was in its moral aspect the result and climax of His striving against sin, resisting unto blood. He might have "saved His life," and lived in comfort and happiness, had He tolerated sin, or held back from the work of taking it away, to which He was called. But just because He did not thus please Himself or consult for His own comfort, but made it His supreme and constant purpose to contend against sin and save sinners, He endured persecution, contradiction of sinners against Himself, and finally the death of the cross. That was the consequence of His faithfulness in reproving sin and resisting temptation.

Now we are moved and enabled by the Holy Spirit to imitate Christ in this, to take up the cross and to follow Him; we are called to put away from us all that is evil; and since evil dwells in us, that implies that we put away our very selves—deny or renounce ourselves, and suffer our old self to be crucified with Christ. Thus our self-renunciation and fight against the sin that dwells within us are analogous to our Lord's self-denial and suffering for sin. By the working of the same Spirit that dwelt in Christ, we are enabled to follow Him in this. This is one way in which we are said to be crucified with Christ, dead with Him to sin.

One way, I say, because there is another sense that these expressions bear, in which we must first of all make them our own: that of accepting by faith the sufferings of Christ as endured for us, and so entering into them, by believing, appropriation, and trust, that we see our sin cancelled by His blood, and so receive God's full and free forgiveness and deliverance from condemnation. It is in this sense that Christians are called to reckon themselves dead unto sin by the body of Christ, or with Christ, *i.e.* freed from the guilt and curse of sin because one with Him who died unto sin once. But this legal or ideal dying with Christ by faith is to be followed up by a moral dying with Him—mortifying our members, crucifying the flesh with its affections and lusts. Thus we are not only ideally but really conformed to Christ's death, and know the fellowship of His sufferings.

But we could not do so unless we were at the same

time made partakers with Him in His resurrection also—risen with Him, as well as dead with Him. For even in His own case it was the resurrection and the glory that was to follow that sustained Him, and enabled Him to resist unto blood striving against sin. It was for the joy that was set before Him that He endured the cross. He never announced His death without at the same time predicting His rising again; and when His soul was troubled, and He was fain to pray to be saved from the hour of darkness, He was sustained by the thought that by His dying He should bear much fruit, and His Father's name be glorified. In like manner, it is Christ's resurrection, and the pledge that gives of the favour and approval of God even now and His glory hereafter, that sustains the believer in the work of self-denial and mortifying the flesh. He is called to this as not only dead with Christ but risen with Him—risen to a new life in the favour and fellowship of God and joyful hope of His glory. This fellowship with Christ as the risen Saviour makes the believer's life, though it is one of painful struggle against sin, at the same time one of joy, hope, prayer, and heavenly aspiration. As risen with Christ, we are called to seek the things which are above.

Thus thoroughly is our renewal a communion with Christ,—communion with Him in the indwelling of the Holy Spirit, which is its cause, in the holiness of heart and life which results from that, and in the experience by which that blessed result is attained, a painful death to sin and a joyful life to God.

Hence we may see also a third point: that our renewal is by faith as well as our justification. For faith is that by which, on our part, we are united to Christ; and this union is the ground of our renewal, as well as of our forgiveness. As it is by coming to Christ by faith that we are justified, so it is by abiding in Him that we are renewed. Only faith does its work somewhat differently in relation to the two blessings. We are justified by faith, as it is a giving up of all righteousness of our own, and simply relying on Christ as our righteousness; we are renewed by faith, as it works by love and produces as its fruit all Christian virtues. In this respect we are called to be fellow-workers with God, to work out our own salvation with fear and trembling, since it is God who worketh in us both to will and to do of His good pleasure. It is only in regeneration, or the very beginning of the new life, that we must exclude all synergistic theories that would divide the work between God and man; but when the new life has been implanted, it is scriptural and true to say we are συνεργοὶ τῷ θεῷ (1 Cor. 3⁹). We are no longer merely acted upon, but ourselves also active. Hence our own efforts and works have a place in our renewal that they have not in justification. We are commanded to cleanse ourselves and perfect holiness, while at the same time it is God who cleanses and sanctifies us. This work, however, is all to be carried on in faith. Faith in Christ as our righteousness must be the foundation of it; for it is only in so far as we lay hold of Him, and receive in Him the complete forgiveness and acceptance which He freely offers, that we can have any heart to obey God's law as it ought to be obeyed. Faith in Christ also as continually aiding us by His Spirit must go along with the work of renewal.

The mistake is sometimes made of supposing that though for our forgiveness and deliverance from the guilt of sin we must look to Christ alone, for our deliverance from its power we must trust to our own efforts and resolutions. That is contrary to what the Bible everywhere teaches about our renewal. We must trust in Christ to make us conformed to the image of God. Holiness as well as forgiveness is by faith. Only as holiness must be wrought in us and not merely given to us, the mode of faith's action is somewhat different in the two cases. When we trust in Christ for forgiveness, we simply take God's word that our sins are forgiven; when we trust Him for holiness, we are not to believe that we are holy, but that God is giving us power to become holy, and if this trust is sincere it will at once lead to the appropriate action. We are justified by faith resting on Christ as our righteousness, we are renewed by faith acting in Christ as our strength.

## II. Sanctification—What it is

While sanctification has been commonly distinguished by theologians from regeneration, there is a very close connection between these divine works which must not be lost sight of. Any adequate conception of regeneration must lead to the inference that it implies, if it does not at once accomplish, an entire change in the character of those who are its subjects. Accordingly, sanctification, being simply the complete renewal of the soul in conformity to the character and law of God, must be a necessary consequence of regeneration, and indeed just its full development. Thus, in a true sense, sanctification may be said to be included in regeneration; and this aspect of it is of great importance as determining the nature of the divine operation in this work, and the way in which we are to co-operate in it. This is a thoroughly scriptural view, as appears from the fact that there are many words and phrases in the Bible about which it is not easy to say for certain whether they describe the initial work of regeneration or the subsequent process of sanctification, *e.g.*, to create a clean heart and renew a right spirit, to put off the old man and to put on the new.

This relation of these two divine works is most expressly brought out by John, in a weighty paragraph of his First Epistle, chap. 3[4-9]. The statements here made, that everyone that abideth in Christ sinneth not (v.[6]), and that he that is born of God cannot sin (v.[9]), have created much perplexity to interpreters, because they seem in their obvious sense to be at variance with experience, and even to contradict what the apostle writes in the very same epistle with equal emphasis and solemnity (1[8, 10]).

Hence some have endeavoured to limit the meaning of sin as here used, and that in various ways: Roman Catholics interpreting it of what they call mortal as distinct from venial sin, others limiting it to known and wilful sin, and others again, like Beza, rendering ἁμαρτίαν οὐ ποιεῖ, *peccato non dat operam*; Luther, *persistere in peccato*.

But it is now generally admitted by the best interpreters that all these explanations are arbitrary and unfounded, and that the true solution of the difficulty is to be found in the principle indicated in general by Augustine and Jerome: that the apostle is speaking of the new life in its ideal perfection. Everyone that abideth in Christ doth not sin, *i.e.* so long as he abides in Him, while he does so, and because he does so. But now this abiding in Christ is a permanent thing; it is not a matter of arbitrary and fluctuating choice, that one may do to-day and cease to do to-morrow: it springs from seeing and knowing Him, and is the natural and certain result of that. Therefore John adds, "he that sinneth hath not seen Him nor known Him." The perfects in this clause are noteworthy, denoting a past experience continued into the present—hath not and doth not. His sinning shows that he doth not now see or know the sinless Saviour, and so that he never has done so in such a way as to keep him from this sin. So again (v.[9]), everyone that hath been begotten of God, in so far as he is really so, doth not sin and cannot sin.[1] In the fullest actual sense this is true of the children of God in the final state of perfection in glory, when we shall be like God, for we shall see Him as He is (v.[2]). But in principle that is due to that birth of God which is realised even now, and implants an abiding seed of God in the soul.

The truth that we may gather from this passage is in brief this: that sin is inconsistent in principle with the spiritual life imparted by regeneration. This has at once an aspect of warning and of encouragement. It warns us most solemnly that he who would be a child of God must be an uncompromising foe of sin, and wage an internecine war with it, as that which, as Owen puts it, will kill him if he does not kill it. On the other hand, it affords a blessed encouragement to everyone who is really and earnestly desirous to be holy, and to avoid sin now and always, to be assured that his being born of God will assuredly secure this end, and that if he abide in Christ he will not sin.

Sanctification is thus the complement of regeneration in

---

[1] Calvin's comment is: "Dicit non peccare qui ex Deo sunt geniti. Nunc videndum est an Deus momento uno nos regeneret. Atqui constat sic inchoari in nobis regenerationem ut ad mortem usque veteris hominis reliquiae maneant."

such a sense that as long as it is not perfect, and sin remains in the soul, the new life imparted in regeneration must be held to be imperfect also, i.e., the soul is not thoroughly pervaded with the principle of spiritual life. The seed of God is there, but it has not yet grown to its full development, or assimilated to itself all that it is ultimately destined to do; the leaven has been hid in the meal, but it has not yet leavened the whole lump. This organic connection between regeneration and complete sanctification contributes to the explanation of the fact that in the New Testament the latter is often spoken of as a thing already accomplished in Christians. They are spoken of as already holy ($\mathring{a}\gamma\iota o\iota$), as having been sanctified ($\mathring{\eta}\gamma\iota a\sigma\mu\acute{\epsilon}\nu o\iota$, $\mathring{\eta}\gamma\iota\acute{a}\sigma\theta\eta\tau\epsilon$, 1 Cor. $1^2$ $6^{11}$), and Christ is said to have been made to them sanctification (1 Cor. $1^{30}$, Eph. $5^{26}$), though in other passages this is spoken of as a thing to be aimed at (1 Thess. $4^3$), a thing prayed for and promised (ib. $5^{23}$), and believers are $\mathring{a}\gamma\iota a\zeta\acute{o}\mu\epsilon\nu o\iota$ (Heb. $2^{11}$).

But there is another explanation of these assertions of believers being already holy, which is the more important because it throws light on the biblical representation of what holiness is, and how it is to be attained. Holiness, in modern religious language, has come to denote simply moral excellence in relation to God. When contrasted with righteousness, it describes the fulfilment of the duties man owes to God, as distinguished from those to his fellow-man; while, more comprehensively, it may describe both classes of morality, always conveying the idea of their being done as to God. Hence sanctification is commonly conceived and defined simply as moral renewal—the removal of sinful habits and tendencies, and the impartation and strengthening of those that are morally good in accordance with God's character and in obedience to His law. Now it is true that all this is involved in the words used in the New Testament, and that it forms a most important and characteristic element in the ideas represented by them. But it is also the case that this is not the whole of what they contain, and that there is another element that gives a peculiar aspect to their meaning.

The English word "holy" represents two different words in the original languages of Scripture which are distinct in meaning and never interchanged, ἅγιος and ὅσιος in Greek corresponding to קדוש and חָסִיד in Hebrew. ὅσιος is much more akin to our word holy in meaning, for it signifies pious, godly; it is always applied to persons in a moral sense, describing a particular virtue often mentioned along with others. ἅγιος, on the other hand, is a much more comprehensive term, and is never used as a particular description along with others, but always in a general sense. It is also not limited to persons, but frequently used of places and things, as the temple, the altar, the sacrifice, etc. Now it is from ἅγιος that the verb ἁγιάζω and the noun ἁγιασμός are derived, whence the term sanctification. It is quite certain that the notion of moral excellence did not originally belong to the word ἅγιος in Greek, and it is somewhat uncertain that it belonged even to the corresponding קדוש in Hebrew. Anyhow, the word ἅγιος in classical Greek is never applied to deity; and when used of men, it does not denote moral excellence, but means sacred, set apart or dedicated to the deity, and so venerable. It is thought to be derived from ἅζομαι, to reverence, and is frequently applied to inanimate things. ἱερὸν ἅγιον is a peculiarly venerable or sacred temple. The meaning of the word and its derivatives in the New Testament is, however, to be determined by its relation to קדוש for which it is used as an equivalent in the New Testament. That Hebrew word, also, is often used of lifeless things, as the temple, the altar, etc.; and when used of men, has frequently no reference to moral qualities at all, e.g. Ps. 106[16]. But it is the peculiarity of Old Testament language in this connection, that the word is very often applied to God, and used of Him with such emphasis as to be almost a proper name.

There is some doubt as to what is the radical idea of the word. It seems to be allied with חדש, new, and to denote literally that which is new. Some [1] think that from that it comes to mean clean, and that its other significations are derived from that sense; [2] others, that it denotes separated from common things; others,[3] again, give it the sense of bright,

[1] So Campbell, On Gospels; Hupfeld, On Psalms.
[2] So Hofmann, Schriftbeweis.
[3] So Cremer, Biblico-Theological Lexicon; Delitzsch (on Isa. 6) combines both.

splendid. Whatever be the precise shade of meaning in the first application of the word to God, it is clear that it does not denote one particular attribute of His character, but the general aspect of it as a whole—the sum of all His excellences, either as absolutely separate from all else or as infinitely bright and glorious. The former view, especially, explains the many places where the holiness of God is described as an awful aspect of His being,—" holy and reverend is His name," —but the latter, while not inconsistent with these, accounts better for that other set of passages in which God's holiness is praised as the salvation of His people and as their joy and song. On this view creatures are called holy not merely in the sense of being separated from common use, but as partaking in the glory of God, either as instruments by which His purpose of grace and redemption is carried on, or as receiving the blessings of that work.

In accordance with this primary idea of the adjective is that of the derivative verb sanctify. It is used either in a declarative or in a real sense. In the former way, that which is already holy is sanctified: and so we pray that God's name may be sanctified, and are commanded to sanctify the Lord in our hearts, *i.e.* to declare and manifest His holiness, to treat Him and His name as holy, with due reverence and awe. In the real sense, again, that which is unholy is sanctified, *i.e.* separated from common uses, and brought into such a relation to God as to partake of His holiness. This separation, again, may be either merely formal and external, as when lifeless things are consecrated to God, *e.g.* buildings, altars, vessels, sacrifices, etc.; or it may be inward and spiritual, when intelligent moral agents are the objects of it, and then it implies devotion of spirit and entire dedication to God. Israel was a holy nation in so far as the Lord had brought them into a special relation to Himself, taking them to be a peculiar possession and a kingdom of priests (Ex. 19$^{4-6}$), and the tribe of Levi and the sons of Aaron, who especially represented the people in the priestly privilege and work, were preeminently holy. But all the people were commanded to be holy because Jehovah their God is holy (Lev. 19$^2$), and He sanctifies them (Lev. 20$^{7,\ 8}$ 21$^8$). This holiness, however, in the Jewish dispensation consisted largely, if not entirely, in outward things—separation from other nations and from bodily pollution. In the New Testament Christ's people are the spiritual Israel, the royal priesthood, and as such are ἅγιοι, ἡγιασμένοι. The name, as applied to them, has a moral and spiritual import: it denotes not a mere outward ceremonial separation from the world and consecration to God, but one that is real and true, in the heart, and not in outward things. This is indeed the secret of moral purity and perfection. Still the word, as such, does not directly and immediately denote moral excellence, but rather nearness to God and fellowship with him. Christians are κλητοὶ ἅγιοι not so much because they are morally pure, but because they are brought near to God. But it is the very revelation made in the New Testament on this subject: that the pure in heart shall see God, and without holiness no man shall see the Lord. Hence Christian virtue, as delineated in the New Testament, has this peculiar character, that it is a means of drawing near to God, an act of approach and worship. It is not merely a duty discharged to Him: it is the exercise of a religious privilege and performance of a religious service, the offering of a living sacrifice. From this point of view we can understand the direct connection in which sanctification is placed with the sacrifice of Christ, especially in the Epistle to the Hebrews ($9^{14}$ $10^{10,\ 14,\ 29}$).

Without the atonement of Christ as a satisfaction to divine justice we could not have drawn near to God, nor could He accept any service or worship from us. Hence sacrifice is the indispensable preliminary to holy service: it was by sacrifice that all the persons and things dedicated to God in the Old Testament were separated and made holy. The sacrifice of Christ, as it is perfect and all-sufficient, entirely removes the obstacle of sin, and makes those who accept it by faith capable of drawing near to God; indeed it brings them near—they are sanctified and holy, *i.e.* their conscience is purged from dead works, sins that deserve death, that they may serve the living God with the spiritual service of new obedience. It is not quite satisfactory to say that the sanctification which is described as complete at once and effected directly by the death of Christ, is something different from what is meant by the theological use of the term; it is indeed a different view of the blessing, but it does really describe the same thing, and we ought to enlarge and enrich the theological conception of sanctification so as to include this scriptural aspect of it. Now, the idea of holiness as a spiritual service or worship of God enables us to do this. The object of all real worship is to see God's power and glory (Ps. 63), to behold the beauty of the Lord, and to inquire in His temple (Ps. 27). The beatific vision, often described by old writers as the highest good of man, is a true and scriptural idea. But holiness is very closely connected with that as its condition, and the pursuit and practice of holiness is the way by which we come to see God: it is to be followed with that in view as the desired and longed-for good.

Now the sight of God, though in its full perfection a thing to be enjoyed only in the future, is yet in degree realised by believers in this life. For in the life and work of Christ, who is the image of the invisible God, we do behold, as in a glass, the glory of the Lord. We do this, however, only by faith when we draw near to God by the new and living way which Christ hath consecrated for us; and in proportion to the strength and purity of our faith is the clearness of our vision of God. It is important to remember, as a general principle of practical Christianity, that there is no spiritual blessing promised in the future life that is not in some measure realised even here. This appears from the fact that all spiritual blessings are bestowed in Christ. The highest promise and hope that He gives to His disciples is to be with Him where He is, to share the love the Father has to Him and the glory He has given Him (John $17^{22,\ 24,\ 26}$). But the very principle of the gospel is, that we receive Christ even now, at once and as a free gift; and therefore we have in Him already the right of access to God and of all the blessings of heaven. We cannot receive Him at all without really embracing all these, and in principle renouncing all that is opposed to them; we cannot draw near to God even here if we regard any iniquity in our heart: and so if we are really Christ's, we may be said to be already holy, sanctified, and brought near to God, although we need to have the life of Christ made perfect in us before we can realise that nearness as a matter of actual experience. We are therefore commanded to follow after holiness as that which is necessary for our seeing God, for which we are admitted into His presence, on the ground of the work of Christ for us taking away the guilt of sin from our conscience; we are made fit for His presence, and actually brought into it, by the work of the Spirit in us removing the love of sin from our heart and the power of it over our will.

It is because we are already reconciled to God by Christ, and partakers of a new spiritual life in Him, that we are able thus to go on unto perfection. See Phil. $3^8$ $^{16}$. It is well said by Hofmann,[1] "that the peculiarity of Christian conduct consists in this, that the Christian acts as that which he is in order to become that more and more." He is dead to sin by the body of Christ; he is called to mortify his members upon the earth that he may be so more and more fully; he is risen with Christ, and he is called to set his affections on things above that he may have his treasure and his heart more and more in heaven, where Christ is; he has put off the old man, with his deeds, and therefore is called to renounce his practices; he has put on the new man, and is called to put on the Lord Jesus Christ, and make no provision for the flesh to fulfil the lusts thereof. He lives by the Spirit, and is called to walk by the Spirit, that his life may be ever more vigorous and healthy. The process of sanctification is not the acquiring by good deeds of a character entirely foreign to the believer: it is the working out by the obedience of faith of a character already implanted in germ in the work of regeneration. Even in the state of innocence man was not called to acquire by obedience a character that did not belong to him, but only to develop, under God's training, the inborn germ of original righteousness to its perfection in confirmed holiness; and still more, in the new creation, is there given at the outset the principle and root of the final perfection to be realised in glory.

[1] *Theologische Ethik*, p. 91.

## III. Sanctification—Its Means

The process of sanctification carried on in the believer's soul is, as we have seen, the work of the Spirit of God developing and maturing the new life implanted in Regeneration. In this respect it is a process of which he who is its subject is not directly conscious, and towards which he does not put forth direct and conscious efforts. But it is a work carried on according to the nature of man as an intelligent and voluntary agent; and so it is not merely an unconscious development, but a process in which the active energies of the soul are called into conscious and purposeful exercise. These two aspects of sanctification are worthy of closer attention. Both are clearly recognised in Scripture; for in one series of passages believers are represented as growing, being transformed into the image of God as by a vital and unconscious process; in others they are called to work out their own salvation—to become holy, to perfect holiness as by direct and conscious efforts.

1. The process, so far as it is unconscious, consists in the gradual development of the new principle of spiritual life; the Holy Spirit gains more and more possession of the soul, and moulds it into conformity with the character of Christ. The means by which this is effected is contemplation of the glorious and holy character of Christ as the image of God. This is brought out in 2 Cor. $3^{18}$, the passage that most distinctly exhibits the principle of this process: and the same thing is indicated in 1 John $3^2$, where the final and perfect result of the process is described: "We shall be like Him, for we shall see Him as He is"; and in proportion as we see Him, even now, we become like Him. This is in accordance with the general law of our moral nature, that when we habitually contemplate any character with admiration, sympathy, and love, we acquire ourselves qualities similar to those which we admire in our ideal. The working of this principle is seen in the unconscious influence that persons of strong and decided character exert over their friends and admirers, producing in them, in greater or less degree, the same character as they have themselves. The Spirit of God,

in sanctifying the soul of man, makes use of this general principle of human nature, since He works not against nature but rather in its favour. But being divine and having access to the inmost chamber of the soul, the Holy Spirit can act far more powerfully, and produce a more thorough and inward change, than that general law of itself could do. Now, it is one of the conditions of a healthy development of character by means of personal influence that it be unconscious, and not the effect of direct and intentional imitation. One may indeed deliberately choose to bring himself within the influence of some great and good personality, by whom he hopes to be moulded in character in a good direction, but if he were to make it his deliberate purpose to imitate him in all that he did, the likelihood would be that he would copy mere external and accidental circumstances, and perhaps defects, instead of learning and overtaking the leading principles that guide all the life and give its character of excellence to his friend's example. In order to this latter result, it is generally best to let the character and personality that we admire work unconsciously on our own, and our conscious effort will be simply to enter into and maintain friendly relations and converse with him. So it is also in this part of the process of sanctification. The believer's direct aim should be simply to live in fellowship with the Father and His Son Jesus Christ, and to allow the perceived beauty of holiness to exert its natural transforming influence. In this connection we may see the use and appropriateness of the means of grace, for these are just the instrumentalities by which the soul's fellowship with God is maintained, and the right and diligent use of them tends in this way to lead to conformity to His image. Here we have—

1. The word of God, which in various places is described as a means of sanctification. John $17^{17}$ has indeed been interpreted with some variety in details by different expositors; but even if ἐν τῇ ἀληθείᾳ be taken in the fullest and most literal sense as denoting not the means but the sphere or element in which the sanctification is to be carried on, there can be little doubt that that sphere or element is mentioned and emphasised by the following clause, just because their abiding in it is really the means of their sanctification. The

word of God, as the truth, is in fact the means of sanctification; but it is so as a light that not merely comes into contact with them externally, but envelops them and forms the atmosphere in which they live. Acts $20^{32}$ expresses still more directly the sanctifying power of the word. So also Eph. $5^{26}$, where ἐν ῥήματι seems most naturally to mean the word of the gospel; and even if it be not grammatically connected with ἁγιάσῃ, but rather with καθαρίσας, yet the spirit of the passage plainly warrants our regarding the word as the means of the subsequent sanctification, as well as of the initial purification denoted by the latter word. The same truth is also expressed in various forms in Jas. $1^{21, 25}$, 1 Pet. $2^2$.

The word of God is the permanent and fullest revelation of His character and work, and it is through it alone that we have an intelligent acquaintance with Him. In it we learn to know His character, just as by living with a man and hearing his conversation we come to know what manner of man he is; and just as the character of a great and good man, becoming known to us, moulds and influences ours to conformity with it, so the careful and reverent study of the word, in which God makes Himself known in Christ, is a most important and precious means of our sanctification.

2. Prayer is also a means towards the same end. In this exercise we are speaking to God, as in the study of the word we are hearing Him speak to us. Now this has the effect of maintaining the personal character of our relation to God. The mere study of the word may degenerate into a contemplation of abstract truth and duty; and that, however intently it may be carried on, can never have the power of personal intercourse. The mere record in a book of a perfect and attractive character will not exercise that powerful assimilating influence that the living man himself can have. Now the combination of prayer with the use of the word helps to secure that in the Christian life there shall be real personal intercourse with a living God and Saviour. We are to be studying the word with the assured belief that its truths are not merely great realities or revelations to men of old, but messages from God to ourselves here and now—messages

to which we may respond in prayer, and which may be sent to us as answers to our prayers. To keep up a real fellowship with God—a mutual speaking and hearing between Him and the soul—is one of the great difficulties of the Christian life. But such a correspondence fixed with heaven is surely not only a noble anchor to the soul in times of trouble, but a most precious means of growth and progress in holiness. It is not merely that prayer expressly made for holiness will be answered, but that prayer in general, the habit of praying —of conversing with God and asking of Him the things we need from time to time, whatever they may be—is a means of promoting our nearness and likeness to Him. This use and effect of prayer is indicated in various passages of Scripture. Jesus says, Luke $22^{46}$, "Rise and pray, lest ye enter into temptation"; where the meaning seems to be not, as in ver. 40, that this should be the contents of their prayer, the thing prayed for, but that by praying habitually they would be kept from the danger of entering into temptation. In Eph. $6^{18}$ prayer is described as a part of the Christian's armour against the enemies of his soul; in 1 Thess. $5^{17}$ it occurs as one of a series of injunctions closely connected with the prayer or promise of perfect sanctification in ver. 23; and a similar and more explicit mention of its relation to this occurs in Jude 20.

3. A third means of grace available in this connection is to be found in the Sacraments, in which the two former may be said to coalesce. In the word God speaks to us; in prayer we speak to God; in the sacraments there is mutual communication, sealed by outward symbols. In the right use of them the word of God and prayer are implied: there must be a devout listening to the revelation, which is symbolised and sealed in the sacramental rite, and also a pouring out of the heart to God in thanksgiving, prayer, and vows. Thus, therefore, the observance of these ordinances works in the same way as the word of God and prayer in promoting and expressing our fellowship with God, and so bringing us more under the transforming influence of His holy character as revealed in Christ. So the observance of the sacraments is described as one of the means by which the spiritual life of

the first disciples was manifested and promoted (Acts 2$^{42-46}$), and from these passages and others it appears that the social character of Christian worship has an important bearing on its efficacy as a means of sanctification. While Christianity is a personal concern, and much of the believer's spiritual history and exercise lies wholly between himself and God, it is also a social religion, and includes duties and privileges that are to be discharged and enjoyed in common with others; and the hearing of the word and prayer along with the brethren in the assembly of God's people is an important means of grace.

Of all these means of grace, it will be observed that faith is the condition and means by which they become effectual towards sanctification. The word will not profit unless it be received in faith; prayer, to be a means of grace, must be the prayer of faith; and the sacraments can only be rightly used in the exercise of faith.

II. But while to a large extent the process of sanctification is unconscious, and one in which the believer only indirectly acts with deliberate purpose, there is another and most important relation in which direct and conscious effort is possible and called for. Besides the series of passages in which the work is described as a progressive growth, like that of the seed growing up secretly, so that he that sowed it knoweth not how it grows, and only tends it by watching and watering, there are others in which Christians are exhorted to mould and frame their own characters to the pattern of holiness. Such are 2 Cor. 7$^1$, Phil. 2$^{12}$, 1 Pet. 1$^{14\ 15}$, 1 John 3$^3$.

We are not merely to be growing into conformity with the image of Christ by the unconscious influence of fellowship with Him, we are also to be purposely and designedly copying Him, and seeking to acquire a character like His. This direct and conscious purpose of imitating Christ can only with safety be applied to the general features and principles of His character, not to the details of His manner of life and actions. For in these respects there is an endless difference in the way in which holiness will show itself in different persons, times, and circumstances, and the attempt to imitate the Saviour in the external particulars of His life is a mistaken one, and sure to lead to great abuses and evils. In a certain period of the Church's history this mistake had much prevalence and destroyed much good. The idea of bringing back the Church, and especially her ministers, to an imitation of Christ was one that animated to a large extent the better minds in the twelfth and following centuries, and those who lamented, and desired to reform, the corruption of the times.[1] But, unhappily, they looked to an imitation of Christ in the particular form of His life on earth, and so their well-meant efforts failed to do permanent good, and were even productive of much harm. A life like that of Christ in His public ministry could not be led by all, but only by those who could separate themselves from the ordinary affairs of life; and so there was necessarily established a distinction of two classes of Christians, and the imitation of Christ reserved wholly for the higher and more select. Hence, also, this movement fell in with and strengthened the monastic ideas and practices of the times, and only led to a new development and temporary improvement of them by the institution of the two great mendicant orders.

The only safe imitation of Christ is that which is in the spirit and not in the letter. We are indeed taught that He has left us an example, that we should walk in His steps; but this is to be done not by copying His outward actions, but by having the same mind in us that was in Him—"walking in love as He has loved us, etc." In this sense alone can Christ be a universal example, to be followed not merely by a few who can renounce the world and give themselves to the direct service of God, but by all, even those most engrossed in the duties of this life. It is for this, as well as other reasons, that our being conformed to Christ's character must be to so large an extent unconscious and without direct effort.

For this reason, also, in our conscious efforts at the ideal set before us, we must discover and consider the principle of Christ's life on earth which underlies all the varied actions that He did. That principle we shall find to be childlike obedience to the law and will of God. This we find indicated both by His own sayings (Luke 2$^{49}$, Matt. 3$^{15}$,

[1] Such were Arnold of Brescia, the Abbot Joachim, etc.

John 4$^{34}$) and by the statements of the apostles (Rom. 5$^{19}$, Phil. 2$^8$, Eph. 5$^2$, Heb. 5$^8$).

It is in this that we are to be followers of Christ, and so we are taught expressly that it is by obedience that we are to mould our characters in accordance with the holy pattern set before us (Phil. 2$^{12}$, 1 Pet. 1$^{14}$).

Hence the importance that the law of God still has for believers. It is not superseded either by the principle of love and gratitude as a motive to holiness, nor by the life and character of Jesus as an example of it. Even with both of these we still need an express and authoritative declaration of the path of duty to guide our efforts after holiness. We are to obey, however, in a spirit of freedom, not of bondage; it is as obedient children that we fashion ourselves after the Holy One who has called us.

The process, as thus carried on, is in accordance with the principles of our constitution. The great law of habit implies that the performance of actions of any particular kind tends to form a character of that kind. The acts become more easy by repetition, and there is induced also an inclination to do them, and this process may serve not only to form a character, that had been neutral or indifferent, into a special type, but even to overcome an opposite tendency, that had produced a difficulty and dislike for the actions of obedience. This is the case with the soul in the process of sanctification. There are evil habits and tendencies to be eradicated as well as good ones to be cultivated; but in the course of time, by the help of God's Spirit, this may and will be accomplished. The Spirit is operative here in the way of animating and enabling the soul to each successive act of obedience, by which the whole character is gradually transformed.

There comes in here the use of various subordinate exercises, of which it may be useful to speak.

1. Self-discipline and mortification of sin. The need of this arises from the fact of the corruption of human nature remaining even in the regenerate. "The flesh lusteth against the Spirit . . . and they that are Christ's have crucified the flesh, with its affections and lusts." We are exhorted to mortify our members which are on the earth, and assured that if we,

through the Spirit, mortify the deeds of the body we shall live. It must be borne in mind here that it is not the body as such that is to be mortified, but the deeds of the body—sinful inclinations, the flesh, with its affections and lusts. It has been a great and far-reaching mistake in this matter to think that sin inheres in the body as such, and is to be eradicated by crushing and deadening all the bodily instincts and affections. This has led to the system of asceticism, with all its severities and extravagances—a system which held possession of a great part of the Church from a time soon after the apostolic age till the Reformation, but which not only led to the gravest abuses and corruptions, but proved utterly incompetent even to secure the end it sought.[1] It proceeds tacitly or avowedly on the Gnostic principle of the essential evil of matter, and assumes that men are to be made holy and heavenly by means of getting rid of what pertains to the body. The soul is held to be purified by every way of subduing and reducing the body; and restraint, want, and suffering are imposed, as being in themselves means of sanctification. But this is, as Owen[2] puts it, to attack the natural man, not the old man—the body which is good as a creature of God, not the body of sin. And the effect is that the extreme and unnatural rigour put upon the bodily nature tends, by undue repression, to provoke to excess even those animal passions against which the system is especially devised. Thus under the most stern outward asceticism there have often been burning inwardly the most violent lusts, and evil imaginations have taken in the breast of hermits the form of Satanic temptations. At the same time, as there are many forms of sin not at all affected by such bodily rigour, it allows such vices as pride, envy, cruelty, etc., to flourish unchecked. Thus there was produced by this system, even at best, only a false and spurious kind of holiness, that by its distortion of moral principles did incalculable mischief in the world.

But there is a true and legitimate self-discipline recognised and recommended in Scripture. Jesus says, "If thine eye offend thee, etc." (Matt. $5^{29}$), and calls on His disciples to

---

[1] See Isaac Taylor's *Ancient Christianity*.
[2] See Owen on *Mortification of Sin*.

deny themselves if they would follow Him. Paul summons Timothy to endure hardness (2 Tim. 2³), and says of himself, "I bring under my body and keep it in subjection, etc." (1 Cor. 9²⁷). But the principle of this discipline is not, that the infliction of suffering on the body of itself promotes holiness, but that when any tendency of our nature, be it bodily or spiritual, becomes a stumbling-block and would lead us to sin, it is to be repressed, at whatever cost of suffering or loss. This self-discipline aims its blows at sin, not at the body as such; it does not prescribe irrational and unnatural restraints or austerities merely for the sake of suffering; it denies the legitimate indulgence of any natural desire only when there is good reason for it in the fact that it would be dangerous to ourselves or others; and it strikes at sin of all kinds impartially, and not merely at those sins that proceed from sensuality. Thus it is a reasonable, safe, and proper means of cleansing ourselves from all filthiness of the flesh and of the spirit, and perfecting holiness in the fear of God.

2. Another means to that end is the resisting and overcoming of temptation. Temptation, when rightly met, is a school and discipline of virtue. Were it not fitted to be so, we should not understand how it could be appointed or permitted by God for innocent or for forgiven creatures. It was by means of temptation that man was to have risen at first from the state of *posse non peccare* to that of *non posse peccare*, and it is by means of it, among other things, that renewed men are to be made perfect in holiness. Even when they yield to temptation, God makes the very falls of His people means of teaching them humility, watchfulness, and self-denial, and so, indirectly, of promoting their sanctification. But the way in which He would have them to use this is not by yielding, but by resisting and overcoming the temptation. For this end watchfulness is specially needed, and often inculcated by our Lord and His apostles. We ought to have our eyes open to the dangers that beset us: to learn from self-examination and memory of our former falls from what side we are liable to temptation, and how we are apt to fail in duty, and sin against God; and to use such means of avoiding temptation, or fortifying ourselves against it, as we find to be necessary and suitable.

We have many means of defence; and Paul's description of the whole armour of God shows what these are, and how we are to use them (Eph. 6).

3. Once more, the right use of affliction is a means of sanctification. This is a truth taught and illustrated in many places of Scripture, especially Rom. 5³, 2 Cor. 4¹⁷,¹⁸, Heb. 12⁴⁻¹¹, 1 Pet. 1⁶,⁹. Here the Christian has the duty to perform of humble, patient submission to the will of God; and in this, very specially, He has a pattern in Jesus. Without a right use of it affliction will have no sanctifying effect—it may even lead to the very opposite result. But it is designed by God, to try, to exercise, and to perfect the virtues of His people; and He makes it effectual for these ends. The way to use affliction aright, so that it may have this effect, may be learned by considering the two errors against which we are warned in Heb. 12⁵.

One is thinking lightly of it—steeling our souls against it and not allowing it to impress us. This is the extreme to which strong natures are prone, and others too when the affliction is but slight. In this way we are apt to lose any good effect that it might have had, and was designed to have; for in order to have any effect at all, it must be felt.

The opposite extreme is, fainting or losing heart entirely under affliction, which is the fault of weak natures, and of all under heavy affliction. In this case the soul is so utterly overborne that it loses all faith and hope, and sinks into sullen or hopeless despair.

Now the remedy against both evils is the same—a recognition that affliction is sent in love and for a gracious end.

## IV. Sanctification—Its Degrees

### A. Roman Catholic View

The chief doctrinal questions about sanctification have reference to its perfection in this life. All Christians believe that it is to be brought to perfection at last when the children of God shall be holy and without blemish before Him. This is the intended goal of the work of our renewal. There is a sense, too, in which it may be said to be complete at once and from the outset; it extends to the whole of our nature and affects all its parts. It is not a change merely in the intellect, leaving the emotions and affections as they were, nor a change merely of the feelings, leaving conscience and will unaffected. If any man is in Christ, he is a new creature—our old man is crucified with Christ. Inasmuch as man's nature is a unity, the radical change of heart affects all the powers and faculties, and is seen in the new and harmonious working of them all. There are new perceptions of truth in the intellect, new convictions of truth and duty in the conscience, new affections towards God and Christ in the heart, and a new inclination and purpose in the will. The entireness of the change in this sense is asserted in the Westminster Confession (chap. xiii. 2), while at the same time it is declared to be imperfect in degree. This is a real and clear distinction, which has been expressed by saying that the believer's renewal has a perfection of parts (*perfectio partium*) but not perfection of degrees (*perfectio graduum*). The illustration usually given from the natural life is suitable and simple. A new-born babe may be said, in one view, to be perfect, because he has all the parts and limbs of a man: but in another view is not at all perfect, because not one of them has reached its full size. So it is with the new spiritual life: being a birth from God, it is complete and entire; but being only a birth, it is at first immature in all its parts, and gradually grows to perfection.

This view, which is in harmony with Scripture and spiritual experience, has been denied in various ways, and more especially in two forms that are found in very opposite sections of Christendom. It has been denied by the Church of Rome in a legal way, and by some extreme Protestants in an antinomian way.

The Roman Catholics hold that the change effected by regeneration, which they identify with baptism, is so entire that all that is truly sin is removed from the soul; a view based on nothing stronger than a misapplication of certain Scripture statements, and opposed to the experience of Christians. We have now to observe the consequences which they draw from this position in connection with sanctification, more especially their doctrine of good works. Holding that nothing really sinful remains in the regenerate, they maintain that they can perfectly fulfil the law of God, and that they are required to do so as the condition of the continued enjoyment of God's favour and final salvation. Thus they are anew under law to work for the reward.

The Council of Trent declares,[1] "that nothing is wanting to the justified that they should be held fully to have satisfied the divine law in proportion to the state of this life";[2] and Bellarmine discusses the subject more fully under the title, *de Justitia Operum*.

His first position under that head is that good works are necessary to the justified for salvation. This Protestants do not deny, though they have generally thought it needful to guard against legalism by saying that they are necessary, not in the way of merit for acquiring a right to final glory, but as commanded duties and indispensable means to prepare us for glory.

Bellarmine's second position is that justified men can fulfil the law of God, not indeed by the mere power of free will, but by the aid of the grace of God and the spirit of faith and love infused in justification. Similarly, Möhler states it as a reason why the forgiveness of post-baptismal sins is more difficult than of those committed before baptism, that the baptized have received power to fulfil the law of God, and therefore the guilt of their sins is greater. According to the Church of Rome all sins committed before baptism are forgiven in that sacrament, for the efficacy of which it is only required that the receiver do not put an obstacle in the way of it. For sins after baptism the sacrament of penance (*pœnitentia*) is provided, and for that is needed contrition of heart, confession to a priest, and satisfaction by works of penance. The absolution given in this sacrament, however, is not so complete as that in baptism: for while the eternal punishment due to sin is taken away, its temporal punishment remains to be borne, either by sufferings in this life or in purgatory after death.

This we believe to be an entirely unscriptural system; and the doctrine alleged as a reason for it, that the regenerate

[1] Sess. vi. can. xvi.      [2] Pro hujus vitæ statu.

are able perfectly to fulfil God's law, we think is also unfounded. The inspired writers all confess frailties and failures in duty, and this has been the experience and acknowledgment of earnest Christians in all ages. This is so plain, that Roman Catholics are obliged to prop up their doctrine by a distinction between what they call venial and mortal sins. The Council of Trent[1] admits that "even the most just and holy men fall sometimes into certain light and daily sins which are also called venial," but adds that they may entirely avoid what they call mortal sins.

The distinction, as stated by Thomas Aquinas,[2] is that those sins in which the soul is disordered to the extent of aversion from God are mortal, while those in which it is disordered, yet not made averse to God, are only venial; and that only the former deserve death, while the latter deserve only temporal punishment. But to this it may be replied, that if God be absolutely holy, any disorder that is really moral must turn the soul away from Him, so that the distinction is as destitute of ground in reason as in Scripture, where the wages of sin, absolutely, and not merely of a certain kind of sin, is declared to be death.

But Roman Catholics further maintain, in the language of Bellarmine's third position on the righteousness of works, that "the works of the righteous are simply and absolutely righteous, and also in a sense perfect, though not in such a sense that they might not be more so, and though they may be mingled with venial sins"; and the Council of Trent[3] pronounced an anathema against those "who say that in every good work a righteous man sins at least venially, or, which is more intolerable, mortally, and therefore deserves eternal punishment, and is not condemned only because God does not impute them for condemnation." This is an exaggerated and offensive statement of the Protestant doctrine, and is palpably incorrect, because it ascribes to them the distinction of venial and mortal sins, which they entirely reject. The real view of Protestants on this point is fairly and judiciously stated in the *Confession of Faith*, chap. xv. sec. 5. It is not

[1] *Conc. Trid.* Sess. vi. can. xi.   [2] Prima Secundae, Qu. lxxii. art. 5.
[3] Sess. vi. can. xxv.

alleged that when a child of God performs an act of obedience to His law, that is to be designated as merely or properly a sin; it is not denied that it is really and in the main good; it is only maintained that even in the best of such actions the motive is not purely and entirely that perfect love to God and holiness that we ought to have, nor is the action done with that whole-hearted decision and completeness of moral excellence that it ought to have, and therefore is in some respect defective as judged by the supreme standard of absolute holiness. No Christian who earnestly examines himself can fail to be aware that when he inquires closely into his best actions he will find them proceeding in part from doubtful or mixed motives, and that in many ways they might and should have been better.

Even Bellarmine is fain to admit this, so that the controversy very much resolves itself into the question of the absolute perfection of God's law and the guilt of what Roman Catholics call venial sins. It is only by lowering the standard of moral perfection that they are able to maintain their doctrine of the perfect righteousness of the works of the regenerate.

These doctrines, however, do not completely exhibit the extent to which Roman Catholics exaggerate human power and goodness, and encourage men to trust in their own works. For Bellarmine's fourth proposition under this head is, that by good works men are really justified, not, indeed, by the first justification, by which from unjust they are made just, but by the second, whereby from just they are made more just; and he asserts further, when he comes to speak of the merit of works, that the good works of the justified, being perfect and free from sin, truly merit the reward of eternal life, and may be trusted to for that purpose, if pride be avoided; though, he adds, in a sort of hesitating way, that it is safer to trust to the merit of Christ.[1] There has indeed been some difference

---

[1] Amesius' remark on this is shrewd and pertinent: "It has happened here to Bellarmine as to Balaam, who, when brought to curse, after great and various preparation, and seeking many enchantments, was constrained by God to bless Israel. In like manner Bellarmine, after spending all efforts through several whole books in defending human merits by every kind of sophism, here suddenly changed in the end, takes away all use of merits, and has recourse to grace alone" (*Bellarminus Enervatus*, Tom. iv. Disput. 42).

of opinion in the Roman Catholic Church as to the kind of merit to be ascribed to the good works of believers ; whether it is merit in the strict legal sense of condignity as it is called (*meritum de condigno*), or only of that lower kind called merit of congruity (*meritum de congruo*), *i.e.*, that it is fitting God should reward them. But since it is generally held by Romanists that merit of this lower kind belongs even to faith and other graces preparatory to justification, the more consistent Roman Catholic view of the works of Christians is that which ascribes to them merit in the strict legal sense. This is Bellarmine's opinion, and it is almost a necessary consequence of the doctrine that they can perfectly fulfil the law.

Some plausibility is obtained for this position from those passages of Scripture that speak of eternal life as a reward, if these are insisted upon alone and apart from the teaching of revelation as a whole. But Christ and His apostles frequently and emphatically teach us that, so far from having any claim to reward from God, we always need to implore His mercy to pardon our shortcomings and sins. And reward does not necessarily imply legal desert or claim as of right ; it may be, and often is, given of grace and bounty, as when a father encourages the imperfect efforts of his children to do well and please him by gifts and praises. So our heavenly Father deals with us. He has held out to us the blessings of His house as rewards for our obedience and faithfulness ; but this is of His own abounding grace, so that when He crowns us it is not in mere justice, but in loving-kindness and tender mercy (Ps. 103). Though eternal life is the reward of the Christian's course, it is not the less the free gift of God. It is utterly erroneous, therefore, to argue that because life is offered to us as a reward, therefore we may or must work out a title of legal right to it ; and it is needless and wrong on the other side to shrink, as some have been apt to do, from the Bible statements about rewards as if they tended to encourage a legal view. They are intended to stimulate and encourage us to self-denial and perseverance ; and to obey for the sake of the reward of God's favour and fear of His displeasure is no proof of a legal or servile frame of mind.

Finally, the top stone is put to the Roman Catholic

edifice of human righteousness and merit by the doctrine of works of supererogation. This teaches that believers can, not only do all that the law of God requires, but even perform more good works than are absolutely necessary for their own salvation, and so lay up a store of superabundant merit. The explanation given of this is, that besides the absolute commands of God, there are in the gospel what are called evangelical counsels, or counsels of perfection (*consilia evangelica, s. perfectionis*), things not commanded but recommended (*non mandata, sed commendata*), which may be disregarded without sin, but which, if accepted and obeyed, give a higher degree of perfection and merit. There are usually reckoned to be three such counsels, which form the three vows of the monastic life—(1) Voluntary poverty, (2) celibacy, and (3) regular obedience.

For (1) there is alleged our Lord's word to the rich young ruler: "If thou wouldst be perfect, go sell all that thou hast, and give to the poor," etc. (Matt. $19^{21}$); for (2) the statements of Paul in 1 Cor. $7^{7, 8, 26, 32}$, in which a preference is given in certain circumstances to celibacy over marriage; for (3) there are only general precepts of obedience to those who are over us in the Lord. But none of these passages really support the Roman Catholic doctrine. Christ's words to the rich youth were not spoken in answer to a question how he might be more perfect than others, but how he should obtain eternal life; and they were manifestly intended to test his earnestness, and to show him that he had not, as he thought, kept the commandments at all; the preference that Paul expresses for celibacy is not on the ground of any superior merit, nor does he hint at its having that; and the precepts of submission to our spiritual superiors are addressed as binding duties to all, and do not imply a blind and absolute obedience.

It is quite true that there are, and are recognised in Scripture, things morally indifferent, in themselves neither good nor evil, in regard to which Christians may exercise liberty, and for which one is not to condemn or despise another. Paul enlarges on this subject in Rom. 14 and 1 Cor. 7–9. But the meaning is not that we may choose at our own will to omit what in our position and circumstances would be a morally good deed; but simply that there are acts and courses of conduct which, when viewed in general and apart from circumstances, cannot be pronounced either good or evil, so that no universal rule can be laid down, but each Christian must be guided by a consideration of what is expedient in his particular case. But that very expediency is a rule that he is bound to follow, though another whose circumstances are not the same may be free and required to take a different course. The act in the abstract is indifferent, but when it presents itself to each one in the concrete, clothed in all the circumstances of time, place, person, relations, etc., it may present a distinct alternative between good and evil, or good and less good. Moral obligation and moral excellence go together. If there is no obligation in duty to any action, there can be no moral goodness in it; if there be real moral goodness, we are bound in conscience to do it. "To him that knoweth to do good and doeth it not, to him it is sin." God's law requires love with our whole heart, and calls us to be perfect as our Father in heaven is perfect. The idea of being able to go beyond that law and do more than our duty, is the most daring perversion of the principles of Bible teaching and sound ethics.

It is only fair to remark, that the Church of Rome is not formally committed to the doctrine of works of supererogation, since it is not expressly taught in her symbolic books; but she must be held as really responsible for it, since it is maintained by her most eminent divines, and forms the basis of her common and avowed practice of granting indulgences. In virtue of the communion of saints it is held that all the works of supererogation done by believers are available, not only for themselves, but for the whole Church, and form a treasury of merit which is under the control of the Pope as head of the Church, and which he applies in the way of granting indulgences by which men are exempted from the penances or temporal inflictions due to their sins.

Such is the monstrous system of human ability and merit that Romanists have built up, perverting the gospel of Christ, and leading men to self-righteousness and trust in their own goodness, lowering the standard of the divine law, extenuating the evil and guilt of sin, and fostering the pride and self-confidence of the human heart. The amazing audacity of some of these tenets is only equalled by the plausibility of others, and the ingenuity with which the whole system has been constructed and engrafted on the gospel of God's grace. When they are charged with substituting a scheme of salvation by works for the gospel way of salvation by grace, they have a ready answer, that all these propositions about the possibility, merit, and reward of works apply not to the unregenerate, but only to the justified who have been renewed by God's free grace, and that all the power and goodness they have are to be ascribed, ultimately, not to themselves, but to the Holy Spirit freely given them of God. Thus they are able in theory to escape the charge of Pelagianism, and to condemn that as a heresy. But the practical effect of their system is the same as if they avowed Pelagian opinions. For they hold that Regeneration is invariably effected in Baptism by the mere outward act in all who do not put an obstacle in the way, and therefore certainly in all who are baptized in infancy. Hence as that is the case with all born within the pale of the visible Church, Romanism in effect teaches them that they can and may obtain a title to heaven by their own works of obedience to the law of God, and it matters little that theoretically their power to do so is ascribed to a work of God alleged to have taken place, but of which they may see no fruit or evidence.

### B. ANTINOMIAN VIEW

The degree of sanctification attained at once by believers has also been exaggerated in another form, the very opposite in some respects of the Roman Catholic, which turns Christianity into a legal system. The opposite extreme to this is antinomianism, or the assertion that Christians are no longer under the law at all; and the notion of sanctification being perfect at once has been used to support that doctrine. In the sixteenth century the doctrine of the Reformers, that sinners are forgiven of God's free grace without any works of their own, and accepted as righteous in God's sight, was pushed by many to the conclusion that there was no sin in the believer, and that he did not need to concern himself about obedience to the divine law. No matter what he was in himself, God looked on him only in Christ, and could see no sin in him. He who is born of God does not sin: that is, said some, whatever he may do, though it might be sinful in other men is no sin in him whom God has accepted in Christ. By some this was combined with pantheistic ideas which subverted the foundation of morality: God's power was held to be the cause of all things, and by regeneration men were thought to be restored to a paradisaic state of knowing no distinction of good and evil. These extreme forms of immoral antinomianism were analogous to the views of the fanatical teachers in the Apostolic Age, against whom Paul gives warning in his later Epistles, and who are described in Jude and 2 Peter.

This licentious abuse of the notion that Christians are perfectly sanctified and free from the law has been universally discredited and discarded, but these positions are still held by some in connection with earnest efforts after true and high holiness. Those who are called Plymouth Brethren often speak of believers' sanctification as complete and perfect from the first, though they do not mean thereby to assert absolute sinlessness. On the contrary, they admit that the old nature still remains in the regenerate, though it is dead and may be kept entirely inactive. They seem to take in a literal and almost material sense Paul's representation of the old man and the new, the flesh and the spirit, as if they were two distinct entities or substances, so that the old nature may be said to be dead to God and to faith, and needing only to be kept in the place of death while we live in the energy of the new nature.

But as we cannot suppose that in regeneration any new substance or faculty is added to the soul, the new nature that is then imparted must be conceived as a disposition or principle moving us to use all our natural faculties for God, and no longer for self or the world. The old nature is therefore not a substance, but the disposition or tendency to live for self and sin; and that remains as long as it is active; when it can be said to be entirely dead, it has ceased to exist. Of this old nature Paul says two things— first, it has been crucified with Christ, believers have put it off; but, second, they have still to contend against it, and to be ever putting it off.

The former is spoken of as a thing done at once and once for all, and is connected with our being made one with Christ in His death: it means that the selfish tendency that determined our life and conduct before has received a deathblow; it is nailed to the cross, but it is not yet entirely dead; it remains and struggles against our better self, but it no longer reigns; and it shall not have dominion over us, unless by our unbelief or backsliding we allow it to do so. This is a truth that has often been practically forgotten, and it is this I believe that the Plymouthites desire to bring out by speaking of the old nature being dead and a new one bestowed. But we must not forget the other side of the matter which Paul also brings out, that we have still to strive against the tendency to sin remaining in us; and this is not a something that is separate from us, but belongs to our own very selves. The old man is the believer himself, and as long as this old man exists the new man is not yet perfect. These brethren seem to think that in regeneration we receive an entire and perfectly holy nature, which ought to expel and exclude the old nature; but that it is, as it were, ever coming back, and our business is simply to keep it out. But the matter is not quite so simple as that. The old and the new nature are not things but characters, and the new nature is not perfect till it has expelled the old and occupied its place. The conception that the new nature is perfect even while the old may coexist with it, leads to the conclusion that it may be a sufficient rule and guide to the Christian, and that being led by the Spirit he is no longer under the law in any sense. Sometimes it is asserted by those of this school that the law is so severe that it can only condemn us, and sometimes that the believer is called to walk by a much higher standard than the law, that of the new nature within him. Thus this view of entire sanctification is connected with a very different and opposite doctrine as to the Christian's relation to the law from that of the Church of Rome. Roman Catholics hold that believers when reconciled to God are again put under the law, and required to obey it as the condition of their continuing to enjoy God's favour and inheriting eternal life. Plymouthites, on the contrary, say that they are freed from the law entirely, even as a rule of life. Now, though their views are confused and erroneous, we can understand and to some extent sympathise with the motives that have led many good men to entertain them. They have been animated by a desire to connect the blessing of sanctification as well as that of justification directly with Christ, and not to consider it, as is too often practically done, merely as a work carried on by a different agency only indirectly connected with Christ. Hence they have come to regard it as a gift bestowed through Christ, complete and perfect, which we receive, just like justification, at once by faith in Christ. Into this notion they may have been led also in part by the biblical use of sanctification in the sense of consecration, which is effected directly through the sacrifice of Christ, and is the beginning of progressive renewal.

Then they have tried to help out this notion, and reconcile it with the teaching of Scripture and experience as to the sins of believers, by conceiving of the old and the new nature as distinct substances in us.

This is a much less dangerous and unscriptural way of propping up an assertion of perfect sanctification than the Roman Catholic one of extenuating the claims of the law and the evil of sin. But it involves a fanciful and unreal view of human nature, and cannot satisfy any clear thinker. Nor is there any need to have recourse to any such theory in order to bring out the connection of sanctification with Christ. This, as we have seen, can be done in a more sound and satisfactory way by recognising this blessing as the work of the same Spirit that dwelt and wrought in Christ, dwelling also in us when we receive Christ by faith, and producing in us the same mind and character as was in Jesus.

In regard to the relation of believers to the law, the question is, in what sense are they free from it? For there are passages that speak of them as not under law but under grace (Rom. 6¹⁴), dead to the law (*ib.* 7⁴), delivered from the law (*ib.* 7⁶), and elsewhere in Paul's writings; while in other places the law is described as still an authority to which Christians ought to have regard. Jesus said, " Think not I am come to destroy the law," etc. (Matt. 5¹⁷): and Peter, James, and John inculcate obedience to the law on their readers. Nay, even Paul himself does the same in the very Epistles in which he speaks of believers being free from law. The difference, therefore, cannot be traced to an opposition between Paul and the primitive Christian teaching, but there must be a way of reconciling it.

How this is so we may see if we distinguish the various elements contained in the complex idea of law. There is, first, the simplest and probably most original one of divine instruction as to duty. That is the root meaning of Heb. תּוֹרָה, *i.e.* teaching. In this view of it the law of God simply sets before us what is morally good, and He would have us to do and to be. This is what has been called the matter or contents of the law; it is an exhibition of the moral character of God so far as that can be imitated by us. But a mere exhibition of this would lack the legislative form of precept which necessarily flows from the supreme authority of God, and imposes obligation on man. Hence a second element in law is that of command, requiring conformity to the pattern of moral goodness as a binding duty. The contents of the law are put in the form of imperatives, Thou shalt, Thou shalt not, uttered by the authority of God. But, further, a third element is added when the law is clothed with sanctions of rewards and punishments, so that it says not only Thou shalt, but The man that doeth these things shall live in them, The soul that sinneth shall die. In this form the law has the character of a covenant prescribing to men the terms of their acceptance with God, offering rewards for obedience, and threatening punishment for transgression. Once more, fourth, when the law has been broken, it not only threatens death as a contingency that will follow on a possible transgression, but pronounces it as a doom already incurred—the element of curse or condemnation is added to the law, and it must now be regarded not only as teaching, commanding, and governing, but as condemning the sinner, and handing him over to punishment.

These would seem to be natural and necessary distinctions in the ideas connected with the conception of law, and they are recognised in Scripture. Now, by means of them we can reconcile and reduce to a simple and harmonious system the apparently opposite statements of the New Testament that have caused theological controversy. As we are speaking here of deliverance from the law, it is natural to begin with the last of the four elements that we have distinguished as belonging to it, the condemnation or curse which it pronounces on sinners. From that, all Christians recognise that we are freed by Christ. "Christ has redeemed us from the curse of the law" (Gal. 3$^{13}$). "There is no condemnation to them that are in Christ Jesus" (Rom. 8$^1$). This is the blessing implied in forgiveness and justification in the Protestant sense. But according to Paul's teaching, we cannot be free from the curse of the law unless we are free from the law also as a covenant prescribing the terms of our acceptance with God. "For," he says, "as many as are of the works of the law are under a curse" (Gal. 3$^{10}$). By being of the law, or of works, the apostle means seeking God's favour and blessing by obedience to the law; and his position is that we cannot be free from the curse if we are still under the law as a covenant. Hence we must say that believers are free from the law also in the third of the four aspects mentioned above, as prescribing the terms of our acceptance with God. This is what Paul means when he says, "Ye are not under law, but under grace" (Rom. 6$^{14}$): *i.e.* not merely free from condemnation, but no longer in a legal relation of servants working for wages, but in one of free favour as friends and sons of God. This is virtually contradicted by the Roman Catholic doctrine of good works, which makes believers to be free indeed from the condemnation of the law, but still required to obey it as a ground of enjoying God's favour, and liable to proper punishment, and not merely to chastisement, when they transgress. Against this view Protestants object, and hold that according to Scripture believers are freed from the law not only in its condemning sentence but in its covenant form, and in a relation of grace to God in which rewards are promised not of legal right but of His fatherly love, and sins are visited not with judicial penalty but with paternal chastisement.

But our freedom from the law in these respects has been obtained not by any abrogation of it or violence done to its requirements, but by the redemption of Christ, in which He has fully obeyed and honoured the law, and borne its curse for us. Hence it does not imply that we are freed from the duty of obeying the law in the prior aspects of it as the command of God, and as the exhibition of the ideal of moral goodness. It is on these points that the Antinomian controversy turns.

In the Lutheran Church it took the form of a discussion on what was called the third use of the law (*de tertio usu legis*). It was admitted that the law had, first, the purpose and use of restraining the open outbreaking of sin in unrenewed men. In this it acted as a bridle (*Zügel*); and, second, that of convincing of sin, and so being our schoolmaster to Christ. In this it was said to be a mirror (*Spiegel*) in which the sinner was made to see himself to be guilty and helpless. But some would acknowledge no other use of the law than these, under the gospel, hence no use at all for believers. The majority, however, asserted in the *Formula Concordiae* a third use of the law as a rule (*Regel*) for the believer. Those who deny this manifestly make a very sharp and broad distinction between the Old and the New Testament, and cannot recognise any continuity between the two. Hence they could not see the force of the evidence that has convinced other Protestants of the right of the children of believing parents to be baptized; and that view of the law is generally held along with Baptist opinions. Hence, too, they were led to exaggerate the spirituality of the New Testament Church, though it must be allowed that their views enabled them to get free from the Old Testament doctrine of persecution sooner than other Protestants.

The more extreme Antinomians denied altogether that Christians are under law in any sense, even as an exhibition of moral goodness; but this is plainly unscriptural and immoral. In this aspect the law is unchangeable. It is impossible that right and wrong can ever cease to be distinct or can be changed. The eternal verities of moral relations are immutable; it must ever be right to love God above all and our neighbour as ourselves, and wrong to be unloving.

The more temperate Antinomianism of the Quakers, Plymouthists, and others does not deny that we are under the law as a revelation of duty, and thus admits it to be binding in the first sense as to the matter or contents of it, but denies that we are under its commanding authority. It appears to them that the new nature that is imparted in regeneration should be sufficient as a guide and rule to the child of God, and that the force of an external command is needless. But, in view of the imperfect degree of our sanctification, that is a rash conclusion, and there are various uses that the law of God can serve even to a renewed man.

But even apart from and beyond these uses which the law has while we are here imperfect in holiness, there is a ground for its perpetual authority as a rule of life that is eternal and unchangeable, and which shows that the law of God shall be gloriously obeyed by saints and angels in the state of perfect holiness. It is for ever suitable to the relation that subsists between God and His holy and perfect creatures, that their goodness should still bear the character of obedience: "His servants shall serve Him." Yet the obedience that perfected saints render, and in some good measure that of believers on earth too, is not like that which unrenewed men give, extorted by fear against their will, or yielded in a mercenary spirit for hope of reward: it is spontaneous and free, springing from love, and performed with a hearty delight in all God's precepts. It is a service of freedom because a service of love; they walk at liberty because they seek God's precepts. In this gracious and glorious way the eternal law of God is ever honoured and obeyed in heaven. Let us cultivate such a frame of mind, and seek thus to obey it here on earth, so shall it be to us a law of liberty, a royal law, the law of our King who loved us and bought us with His blood.

## c. PERFECTIONISM

Besides the extreme exaggerations of the degree of sanctification which hold it to be perfect at once, whether in connection with legal or Antinomian views, there remains to be considered a less extreme form of opinion in the same direction known by the name of Perfectionism, held by Wesleyans and by some Presbyterians in America, where it has been called the Oberlin doctrine, from the College in the United States in which its advocates taught.

They do not agree with the general opinion of the Reformed Churches, that sanctification is always imperfect in degree in this life, but hold that perfection can be and sometimes is attained here. There are, indeed, some places where the word perfect is applied in the Bible to men in this life, but in none of them does it certainly denote absolute sinlessness. τέλειος in the New Testament is sometimes opposed to νήπιος, meaning of full age, in contrast with infants or immature (Heb. $5^{13, 14}$, 1 Cor. $2^6$ $3^{1, 2}$, Phil. $3^{15}$). Again, perfect is frequently used to describe entire sincerity and uprightness in serving God, in reference to men who are shown by the same record in which such testimonies occur to be not without sin. So in the case of Noah, Job, Zacharias.

In all the men of God whose lives are narrated with any fulness, we can see faults and sins, or we have their confessions of sins even to the end; as Paul (Phil. 3), John (1 John $1^{8, 10}$).

Nor can any certain evidence of perfection being attained in this life be drawn from the experience of Christians, which rather bears out the view that sanctification is always imperfect up to the end of our earthly course.

The description given of the Christian life is one in which the flesh wars against the spirit, and we have continual need to guard against temptation; and the fact that in the prayer that Jesus taught His disciples there is a petition for forgiveness of our sins point in the same direction.

The arguments by which Wesleyans and others support the possibility of perfect sanctification in this life are mostly drawn from the promises, the prayers, and the precepts of perfection contained in Scripture. The former two may be taken together, as the principle involved in them is precisely the same; the precepts must be dealt with separately.

God has in many places promised to sanctify us perfectly, and He has taught us to desire and pray for this; and we find inspired men praying for perfect holiness for themselves and others. Must it not, then, be a thing possible? Will not God fulfil these promises and answer these prayers? Yes, we reply, undoubtedly He will. But does it follow that He will do so during our life here? That is not specified in any of the promises or prayers, and we have no right to add any such definition to them. We believe that they shall all be perfectly fulfilled at last; and in several places our being made perfect and blameless is expressly connected with the presence of Christ, when He shall come again at the end of the age. We believe also that so far as God is concerned there is no reason why the promises of perfect sanctification should not be fulfilled even now, except our own sin and unbelief, and that therefore there is a sense in which it is true that a believer may be rid of sin, *i.e.*, if only he would resist it as he ought in the strength of the Lord. Our doctrine on this subject does not imply that we are to regard our sinning in future as a necessity, far less that we should have any complacency or acquiescence in it, or make provision for the flesh. On the contrary, we are to depart from iniquity, to hate every evil way. "These things write I unto you," says John, "that ye sin not": that is to be our honest effort and earnest hope; and we are to believe assuredly that God is able and willing through Christ to enable us to do that at once and from henceforth, if only we were earnest and trustful enough. There is no natural impossibility, no necessary barrier, between us and perfection; the only thing that stands in the way is the sinfulness and unbelief of our own hearts; and since we find from experience that we do come short in all things, and know that the people of God have always complained of sin to the end of their days, we do not think as a matter of fact that we shall be perfectly sanctified in this life. But though this is so there is nothing to prevent us striving, praying, and even hoping to be made perfect before death, though we cannot hope for this with that assured confidence with which we look for what God has absolutely promised. For though He has promised our perfect sanctification, He has not assured us of it at any definite time; and the more we know of the power of indwelling sin, the more will we see the obstacles to be overcome. We have some hope of ultimate success, and we are to act on the principle that if we can believe, all things are possible to him that believeth.

It is to be observed that our doctrine on this subject is, strictly speaking, a proposition about the past and present, not, as Perfectionists represent it, about the future. It is not revealed, as an article of faith, that all Christians, or I in particular, shall certainly sin in the future; but that all men, even believers, do actually fail of perfection, and transgress God's law. As to the future, we know that we ought to keep all God's commandments, and that God by His Spirit, given through Christ, would enable us to do this, so that there is nothing but our own evil heart of unbelief to hinder us doing it both now and always. No doubt our doctrine as to the present, of the imperfection and sinfulness of the best of saints, implies a general conviction that what is true now will also be true, as a present statement, a day, or a year, or a generation hence. Still we do not definitely believe we shall have any definite sin in the future; to do so would be really to consent to it. We know in some measure wherein we have sinned and failed in the past; but we are not required to believe that we shall fail or sin in the same way in the future. Nay, we are not permitted to believe that: we are to purpose and resolve that we shall not sin, and very specially not as we have sinned before; and we are to be assured that this is possible to us by God's grace, though from what we know of the perfection of God's law and the evil of our own hearts we believe that we shall still have to acknowledge, as we do now, that if we say we have no sin we deceive ourselves.

This is the explanation and use of the promises and prayers for perfection.

In regard to the precepts to be perfect and the like, they

cannot be made to prove the possibility of actually attaining perfection here, save on the principle that moral ability is the measure of duty, and that no command can be given to men which their own evil hearts prevent them from obeying. Now this is a principle that cannot be proved, and that is of the most dangerous tendency. It cannot be shown by any process of sound reasoning that anything more than natural ability is necessary to make a creature a responsible subject of law. Any physical impotence or outward constraint which makes it impossible for a man to obey even if he would, is inconsistent with responsibility and precept. But that is not the sort of impossibility we believe to attach to the believer's perfectly keeping God's law. Like the inability of sinners in general, it is of a moral kind, consisting in his own remaining inclination to sin, and disinclination to self-denial and unworldliness. Now this cannot be held to be inconsistent with the command to be perfect, without sanctioning a principle that would have a very wide sweep, and destroy the authority of God's law over sinners in general. If men cannot be commanded to do what is morally impossible for them, then sinners cannot be commanded to repent and believe on Christ; and all the precepts of God must be modified to suit the depraved condition of man. Herein lies the danger of this doctrine of Perfectionism. It is generally defended on principles which imply that the standard of the divine law is lowered in order that it may be within the power of men to obey it, and it naturally tends to foster that lax notion which teaches men to measure their duty by their attainments, not by the unchanging law of God.

Thus Arminians and Wesleyans, while maintaining that believers may and sometimes do attain in this life perfection, yet admit that this is not complete conformity to the law of God as given to man at first, but to that new law which, they conceive, Christ has given in the gospel. Hence they distinguish Christian or evangelical perfection from legal or sinless perfection. They hold that the lowering of the standard by which we are to be judged is due to the mediation and atonement of Christ, and that our ability to attain to even that modified standard, Christian perfection, is due to the work of the Holy Spirit in us. But there is no hint in Scripture of such a new and modified law. Christ Himself uniformly vindicated and republished the law of God as unchanging and eternal, and both He and His apostles made our ideal of duty higher than it had ever been represented before. The notion of a new or modified law is evidently only a corollary drawn from certain other positions adopted to support them; and it may be shown that the doctrines which seem to lead to it are distorted representations of truths which when rightly put lead to no such inference. Thus the idea that Christ has obtained for us a lower standard of judgment is just a wrong way of putting the truth that the good works of believers, though in themselves imperfect and stained with sin, are accepted for Christ's sake. This is taught in Scripture and recognised by Reformed theologians, and it explains how our works are well-pleasing in God's sight without requiring us to assume either that they are entirely sinless, or that the law has been relaxed for Christ's sake. That this is all that is really contended for by Wesleyans appears from this, that they admit that ultimately in glory the saints shall reach a higher degree and kind of perfection than what they call Christian perfection, and hold to be attainable in this life.

The Oberlin form of the doctrine is open to graver objection; for its advocates hold that the law of God is modified according to the moral power and circumstances of those who are under it, and that as a matter of simple equity, ability is the measure of duty. Thus the lowering of the standard of perfection is not held to be due at all to the grace of God in Christ, but to be a mere necessary act of justice. This, if logically carried out, would go far to exclude grace in any proper sense from God's dealings with men; while, at the same time, it makes the standard of moral law dangerously lax and variable.

There is, however, one consideration alleged by Wesleyans in favour of their view with greater plausibility, an examination of which may be useful. It is argued by Richard Watson, that as it is an axiom of Christian doctrine that without holiness no man shall see the Lord, if perfect sanctification be not attainable in this life, then either there must be some process of purification in the future life, or there must be something in death that delivers us from sin; and as neither of these alternatives is admitted, he infers that sanctification must be possible before death.

This argument is ingenious and plausible, but not solid. In the first place, it assumes that the seeing the Lord for which sanctification is required is at death, whereas there is reason to believe that the relevant passages of Scripture refer to the second coming of Christ. Further, the New Testament does recognise the power of sin in believers as connected in such a way with the body that deliverance from it and from the world of sense would have a very distinct effect in freeing us from the remains of sin. But, besides, it proceeds on the tacit assumption that the reason why God's work of sanctifying our souls is a gradual and long one, is that it must necessarily be so, and that He uses the means by which it is accomplished because He could not effect it without them. This alone gives force to the argument that if perfect sanctification is never accomplished before the end of this life, it must be effected either by death or by some purification after death. But the assumption is neither self-evident nor true. God uses means here as in general, not because He could not accomplish His ends without them (for He is almighty), but because there are good reasons why He should. In this matter more particularly there is no uniform proportion observable between the amount of moral renewal and the time during which it is carried on. We see some who have been early brought to Christ and never have been outwardly habitual sinners, spared for forty, fifty, or sixty years, growing in grace and confessing themselves not yet perfect; while others converted after half a lifetime of vice are taken earlier from the world. There are many mysteries in God's providence, and doubtless many reasons why some are spared so much longer than others. We can only very imperfectly tell from the outward life what the inward growth of the soul is, and we know that the teaching of the Spirit in a few days may sometimes be more powerful in moulding the character than years of less vivid impression. But whatever may be the reason why the sanctification of the soul is sometimes spread over a long life, we may be sure it is not this, that God could not accomplish it sooner.

He could make His people perfect at once were He pleased to do so, but we can see various good ends served by His using means and making the process a gradual one. The faculties of the Christian are called into exercise, and by that exercise are strengthened and developed; opportunity is given for the exercise and cultivation of some grace which would not be called into play in a perfect state; and believers are led to know themselves better, and to feel more deeply their frailty and dependence on God's grace, which is also magnified.

Now in the same way we can see reasons why this process should last all our life here. For one thing, a character of perfect holiness, would most fittingly be placed in a world of perfect happiness. For one who is justified and made perfect in holiness, suffering can serve no purpose. It cannot be penal, for he is forgiven; it cannot be a chastisement or a means of discipline if he is perfect. But in the present world, according to God's dispensation, there can be no perfect happiness; it is not, therefore, the suitable place for perfect holiness. Again, is it not fitting that as long as we are in this tabernacle we should be specially exercised in that humility which arises from the imperfections of our nature and character when these are viewed in a right spirit? It would not be suitable that in this vale of tears, where Christ is so much dishonoured and His cause so much opposed, His saints should have the triumphant happiness of being free from all sin. Further, would there not be a danger if some of the people of God were really perfect in this life that they would be regarded with idolatrous reverence by the others? We know what abuses and superstitions have actually crept into the Church from reverence paid to men not perfect, some of them very far from it. Would not these have been tenfold greater and more difficult to combat, had not the seen or confessed failings of the best admonished the Church to look to God and Christ alone?

These reasons are only conjectural, but they serve to show

that it is not from any necessity of time or means that the work of sanctification is not perfected before death. God could, if He saw fit, complete it at once; and perhaps He is pleased in some cases to do so. It is done by His power in all cases; and when He ordains that it take a long time, it is because He sees it to be best that it should be so. Even when the progress is most gradual, there is the infinite power of God's grace working along with the means. Let this thought encourage us to the use of all diligence both in the work of our own sanctification, knowing the mighty power that is working in us, and in seeking the salvation of others, for none is to be despaired of. The almighty grace that saves us can save and sanctify the most sinful of our brethren.

# THE SACRAMENTS

## 1. Introductory and Historical

THE Christian religion is distinguished above all others by its spirituality. It insists on the state of the heart towards God as the most essential thing: its duties are all summed up in love to God and man; its worship does not require solemn temples, mediating priests, or costly sacrifices; its ordinances are few and simple, and are chiefly the exercises of preaching and hearing God's word, prayer, and praise.

But there are two outward actions with material things that are recorded in the Gospels to have been instituted by Christ, and have been observed by all Christians (with few exceptions) all through the ages since Christ's time. These are Baptism and the Lord's Supper. They are not in the New Testament designated by any specific name, nor even mentioned together as institutions of the same kind. They were appointed by Christ at different times, and they are only referred to by the apostles separately as occasion arose to speak of each. Since, however, they are both ritual observances, and the only pieces of ritual distinctly appointed by Christ, it was natural that they should be classed together; and since an examination of what is said in the New Testament of them shows that they are similar in their nature and use, it is legitimate to regard them as forming a class, the conception of which may find place in the system of Christian doctrine. The name given to them is Sacrament; and since these ordinances are represented as connected with spiritual blessings, the Sacraments have been generally classed under the more general head of means of grace, as well as under that of Christian ordinances. In the former view their consideration belongs to doctrinal, in the latter to practical theology.

The Society of Friends (Quakers) do not think that these ordinances should be observed, because that seems to them inconsistent with the pure spirituality of the New Testament religion, and they consider that they were merely temporary appointments by way of accommodation to the circumstances of the time, as a transition from the elaborate ritual of the Old Testament to the perfect simplicity of the New.

But there is no indication given by Christ or His apostles of such a temporary character of these ordinances. On the contrary, He is recorded to have given His disciples the charge to baptize their converts, along with the assurance that He would be with them always, even to the end of the age (Matt. 28[20]); and Paul says that in the Lord's Supper we show the Lord's death till He come (1 Cor. 11[26]). He would hardly have given such careful instructions about the observance of it, or have referred so often both to it and to baptism, without a hint of their being shortly to be discontinued, if he had not believed them to be meant for continual observance in the Church.

Nor are such outward ordinances inconsistent with what Scripture teaches about the spirituality of the New Testament. The use of symbolic actions is due in general to the constitution of our nature as not merely spiritual but also corporeal, and God has graciously condescended to speak to us in such a way as to impress our senses. Since the symbolic rites of Christianity are simple, universally applicable, and easily intelligible, they are suitable to a rational and spiritual service. They have, indeed, in the course of the Church's history been so overlaid with cumbrous ceremonies and viewed as having magical powers, that the spirituality of Christian truth and worship has been impaired: but this is due to our conceptions of Christ's institutions, and we ought not to reject these on that account.

The name *sacramentum* seems to have been applied to baptism and the Lord's Supper first by Tertullian, to whom we owe a number of technical terms in theology. That word originally meant something consecrated, or the act of consecration, and was used in Roman law for the money deposited as a pledge by the parties in a suit, which was devoted to sacred or public uses. It was also applied to the oath of loyalty taken by Roman soldiers at their enlisting.

But in the Christian Church it was employed as the translation of the Greek μυστήριον in the old Latin version of the New Testament, and it seems to be in that sense that it is used by Tertullian. In his treatise *de Baptismo*, he calls it the sacrament of our water (*felix sacramentum aquœ nostrœ*), without any reference to the analogy of the military oath. He probably uses it in the sense of sacred sign. Μυστήριον sometimes means the hidden meaning of a symbol (Rev. $1^{20}$ $17^7$); and Tertullian, speaking of the Passover, says, "In this Moses had declared that there was a *sacramentum*," *i.e.* a secret meaning (*adv. Marc.* iv. 40). It is by a sort of transposition of the meaning that it came to be used for the symbol that contains the meaning, and it was used in a very loose and wide sense for anything figurative or symbolical.

In some places (*de Spect.* 24, *Scorpiace* 4) *sacramentum* is used by Tertullian in the sense of the military oath; and the reference seems to be to baptism, but that rite is not expressly mentioned.

Augustine formulates more distinctly the notion of sacraments when he says, "Dicuntur Sacramenta, quia in eis aliud videtur, aliud intelligitur. Quod videtur speciem habet corporalem, quod intelligitur fructum habet spiritalem," and again, "Accedit verbum ad elementum et fit sacramentum" (quotations and references in Hagenbach's *Dogmengeschichte*, p. 295). These statements lay down general principles about the sacraments that have been recognised by Protestants as scriptural and true—

(1) That there are in each sacrament two things, an outward sensible sign and a spiritual reality represented by it.

(2) That it is the spiritual reality that benefits our souls, and the outward sign can only be said to do so indirectly in so far as it represents it.

(3) That the word of God, which declares the spiritual thing signified by the material elements, must be associated with them to constitute a sacrament.

A more brief and general definition is also given by

Augustine when he calls a sacrament *signum rei sacræ*, and in this sense he applies the name to a great many different things, *e.g.* marriage, the ordination of priests, exorcism, the Sabbath, new moons, and the sacrifices of the Old Testament.

Accordingly, at and before this period there was no uniform understanding in the Church as to the number of the sacraments, some writers reckoning four and others six, while they varied as to which these were.

In the twelfth century a more precise definition was given by Hugo of St. Victor: "Sacramentum est corporale vel materiale elementum foris sensibiliter propositum, ex similitudine repræsentans, ex institutione significans, et ex sanctificatione continens aliquam invisibilem et spiritalem gratiam" (Hagenbach, *Dogmeng.* p. 452). This definition is noteworthy as containing the three points signalised in the Westminster definition, "represented, sealed, and applied." The representation is said to depend simply on the resemblance, the sealing (*significans*) on the institution of Christ, and the applying on sanctification, which is the work of the Spirit. Also, there is embodied in this definition the notion of divine institution, which our Catechism makes the foundation of its view.

Hugo also gave a briefer definition, which was adopted by Peter Lombard and became most common. "Sacramentum est visibilis forma invisibilis gratiæ in eo collatæ"; "ita signum est gratiæ Dei et invisibilis gratiæ forma, ut ejus imaginem gerat et causa existat" (Lomb. *apud Hagenbach*, *l.c.*).

This has formed the groundwork of many subsequent definitions in different branches of the Church. It omits the notion of sealing or being a pledge, which was contained in Hugo's first quoted definition; and it is noteworthy that the definition in the Church of England Catechism, which is founded upon it, adds this idea.

But in the scholastic age chief stress was laid on the notion that the sacraments contain or confer the grace which they represent; and not only was their function as seals or pledges overlooked, but even the primary notion of representing by resemblance was very much evacuated, and the name was given to ordinances which contain no such similitude to spiritual blessings as would naturally bring them to mind, e.g. the imposition of hands, or the pronouncing of absolution. Hence the Roman Catholic definitions are less distinct than the Protestant.

In those days, too, it came to be forgotten that if the sacraments are said to contain or confer grace, this is as Hugo expressed it, *ex sanctificatione*, and it was held instead to be *ex opere operato*.

The full definition of a sacrament as given in the Protestant Confessions cannot be justified till we have considered the purpose and efficacy of these ordinances; but if we take the general idea in which all the definitions coincide, we can show that there are certain ordinances to which it applies, and determine what these are. Such a general idea is expressed in the Shorter Catechism by the first part of the definition, "a holy ordinance instituted by Christ in which, by outward and sensible signs, Christ and the benefits of the New Covenant are represented." Roman Catholics agree with this so far as it goes; and it can be shown from Scripture that Baptism and the Lord's Supper have all these marks.

This being agreed on all hands, we undertake to show that no other standing ordinances of Christianity have all these marks, and in particular not those that the Church of Rome classes with them.

There is a propriety in limiting the description thus at this stage of the discussion, because it covers not only the Zwinglian view of sacraments in general, but the Roman Catholic view of the sacraments of the Old Testament. For while their definition of sacraments applies to those of the New Testament (*nova legis*), they do not refuse the name sacrament to those of the Old Testament.

It was in the twelfth century also that the number of the sacraments was decided to be the sacred number seven.

In regard to the five additional to Baptism and the Lord's Supper, we may observe—

1. The rite called Confirmation was in early times a part of baptism. After the washing with water, the person being baptized was anointed, and had the hands of the bishop laid

on him in token of his receiving the Holy Spirit. This custom probably was based upon the New Testament records of the apostles laying their hands on converts after their baptism, that they might receive the miraculous gifts of the Holy Spirit. As the office of baptizing was often delegated to others, while that of laying on of hands was performed only by apostles, when bishops came to be considered successors of the apostles, it was held to be their special privilege; and when bishops came to be not congregational but diocesan, as they could not always be present when baptism was administered, the imposition of their hands came to be a separate rite, and was explained as being a confirmation of the grace given in baptism. But in the New Testament it was extraordinary gifts, such as prophecy, tongues, powers of healing that were given by the apostles' hands, and as these have not been continued there is no evidence that this rite was meant by Christ to be perpetual in His Church.

2. The practice of auricular or private confession to a priest was a late corruption of religion; and the notion that this can be called a sacrament is so difficult to reconcile with any feasible definition of a sacrament, that even the schoolmen and Romanists are at a loss to say what is the outward sign in it, whether the works of penance or the words of absolution. So far from being at all analogous to baptism and the Lord's Supper, this rite is not even an institution of Christ at all, but one of the worst and most pernicious corruptions of Christianity.

3. The rite called Extreme Unction is based upon the passages in the New Testament (Jas. $5^{14}$, Mark $6^{13}$) that speak of the apostles or elders of the Church anointing the sick with oil in the name of the Lord. But that was plainly done with a view to their recovery, whether in a miraculous or medicinal or symbolic way. It came to be used in cases where recovery was not expected, as not merely a symbol but a means of communicating grace and help to the dying. For this there is no scriptural warrant whatever; it is a perversion of a practice used for quite a different purpose, and of which there is no evidence that it was meant to be perpetual.

4. Ordination is the setting apart of a person for office in the Church, and in several instances in the New Testament it appears to have been done by the laying on of hands. But it cannot be proved that this action was always used or held to be essential, or that it was meant to be the symbol of any spiritual thing. It is never explained or alluded to as baptism and the Supper are, and the action is one used on a great variety of occasions, in blessing, in presenting sacrifice, in healing, in bestowing charismata. There is no propriety, therefore, in regarding this as a sacrament.

5. That marriage should be regarded as a sacrament is one of the strangest of all the Roman Catholic doctrines, and is in contradiction to some of their other tenets. It is not a distinctively Christian institution, but was recognised by Christ as instituted at creation. He gave no precept as to the form of its celebration, and all His and the apostles' teaching about it is simply moral. Its elevation to sacramental rank is due to a misapprehension of Eph. $5^{32}$ "*sacramentum hoc magnum est*," where μυστήριον is used in the sense of secret or figure, but from which it is absurd to infer that it is a sacrament in the later and technical sense of the term.

## II. Nature and Relations of the Sacraments

It is an important characteristic of the sacraments that they represent Christ and His work of salvation not merely objectively in itself, but subjectively in its application to the believer. This appears even in their outward form. They are not merely symbolical spectacles to be gazed at; they are symbolical acts to be performed by or upon those whom they are designed to benefit; and their symbolical import lies not merely in the things used in them, but chiefly in the actions by which these things are administered to the receivers. In this they harmonise with the essential nature of Christianity, as being not a mere set of doctrines to be believed, but a personal dealing of the soul with God, not a theology but a religion. When the true idea of faith was lost sight of in the Church, and mere belief in doctrine took the place of trust in Christ, there were introduced beside the sacraments a multitude of symbols of a merely pictorial nature, such as crosses, pictures, candles, vestments, and the like, and even the sacraments were made to assume the aspect of mere representations of objective truths and realities, to the neglect of the actions in them that express our apprehension of these realities. But when Christianity is apprehended in its true character as a personal fellowship of trust and love between man and God through Jesus Christ, then it is seen how appropriately its outward symbols represent those divine and human actions by which that life of fellowship is begun and carried on. Hence in the Protestant Churches all merely scenic representations are or ought to be discarded, and the sacraments viewed as representing and confirming not merely the objective reality, but the application to us of the redemption that is in Christ.[1]

Now this application has, as we have seen in directly discussing it, two parts or sides, one in which man is passive or acted upon by God's Spirit, and the other in which being acted upon he acts also himself. These two aspects are presented to us in the two sacraments of the New Testament respectively, and serve to explain their leading differences. In baptism, as in circumcision, we have an outward action in which the subject is passive: he is washed with water; in the Lord's Supper, as in the Passover, we have one in which the subject is necessarily active: he eats and drinks. The former, therefore, approximately represents that moment or stage in spiritual life in which the soul is simply acted upon

[1] Hence Protestants, in opposition to Romanists, maintain as a general principle, "Nihil habet rationem sacramenti extra usum legitimum a Christo institutum seu extra actionem divinitus institutam" (*Form. Conc.* Part II. cap. vii. § 82).

There has been some controversy as to whether the sacraments are more properly defined as *actions* or as *signs*, Romanists and Lutherans holding the former, and most Reformed divines the latter. But it has been generally agreed that both views have an element of truth, and that the question is a minute and comparatively unimportant one. The Westminster divines in the Confession of Faith retain strictly the definition of them as signs, probably following the English and Irish Articles; but in the Catechisms describe them as ordinances, and declare in regard to each that the sign is an action. (Cf. *Helv. Post.*)

by the Spirit, which is distinctively called regeneration; the latter, that in which the soul is active, which is repentance, faith, the new life. These two are different in some important respects, and together they give a complete view of the way in which we are made partakers of Christ and His benefits. Thus while the objective reality represented is the same in both sacraments, the Saviour Himself with all His fulness of blessings, the two different forms in which these are symbolised represent the two parts or sides of the application of them to us. Thus there is a propriety in there being two, and only two such ordinances instituted by Christ; and some of their other points of difference are also seen from this point of view to be appropriate.

Regeneration, or that part of the Spirit's work in which man is passive, takes place once for all at the beginning of the spiritual life; hence baptism, the sacrament which especially represents this, is administered once only to the same individual. But the part of the Spirit's work in which man co-operates with Him is not a momentary act, but a long process continuing from the beginning of the spiritual life onwards to its perfection; therefore the sacrament that especially represents this is administered not once only, but frequently to believers in Christ.

Again, the former of these, in the order of nature, precedes the latter, as the implantation of the new life precedes its exercise; hence the sacrament of baptism is first administered, then that of the Supper.

Once more, regeneration, in which the soul is passive, is a work of which even infants are capable, and which is graciously done in many of them before they attain the use of reason; but repentance, faith, and new obedience by which the new life is carried on are not possible till the child comes to years of understanding. Hence there is a propriety in the administration of baptism to infants that does not exist in the case of the Lord's Supper. This is not, indeed, the only or principal ground of infant baptism. I do not enter on that subject at present, but simply refer to it as illustrating the characteristic differences of the two sacraments.

The mutual relation that we have observed between them

appears also if we view them in connection with the Jewish ceremonies and ordinances from which the outward forms were derived. Both have a very close relation to sacrifice. The Lord's Supper is not a sacrifice, as appears from its first observance; yet it presupposes a sacrifice, and is founded upon it. As the eating of the Passover required beforehand the sacrificing of it, so the eating of the broken bread and poured out wine points to the sacrifice of Christ our passover as an accomplished fact. Baptism is not so obviously connected with sacrifice; yet it also has a relation to it, for we are baptized into Christ's death (Rom. $6^3$). What the sacraments represent is chiefly the way in which we are made partakers of the sacrifice of Christ for us. Now we find from the Old Testament that there were two principal ways in which the efficacy of the sacrifices was conveyed to the people. The one was by the sprinkling of the blood, or washing with water, in which the ashes of a heifer slain for sin had been put; and the other was eating the flesh of the sacrifice in a sacred meal. These correspond to the outward symbols in the two Christian sacraments.

## BAPTISM

### ITS FORM, MEANING, AND EFFICACY

Taking up first the sacrament of Baptism, we may consider—

1. Its outward form. It seems obvious that the essential symbolical import of the ordinance is the cleansing of the soul from sin. Cleansing was the idea conveyed by the various washings of the Jews that formed the prototypes of Christian baptism, and this was recognised in the days of our Lord (Mark $7^{2-4}$). This is also alluded to in various passages in connection with the New Testament rite (Acts $22^{16}$, Eph. $5^{26}$, Tit. $3^5$, Heb. $10^{22}$, 1 Pet. $3^{21}$). There may not be in all these places an express reference to the sacrament, but it can hardly be doubted that they allude to it or to the spiritual reality it signifies, and they show that its idea is that of a cleansing by washing. This accordingly has been almost universally recognised as the primary meaning of the

rite, and from this the inference seems warrantable that in its administration any mode in which water is applied to the body of the person to be baptized, whether by sprinkling, pouring, or dipping, is legitimate as sufficiently indicating the cleansing use of the element. No doubt the entire immersion of the body exhibits this in a more complete and striking way, but other modes may express it sufficiently, and reasons of convenience and propriety may warrant their adoption in preference. This is the position that is maintained on this point by most Christians except those who are called Baptists, who contend for immersion as necessary—not that that is improper, or that sprinkling is absolutely required; but that the command is general, and does not prescribe any particular way of applying the water, while on grounds of expediency immersion is not suitable in this country and in the present state of society. The assertion that βαπτίζω always denotes a particular mode of washing, namely, by immersion, seems to be absolutely without foundation, and is given up by most competent scholars; nor can it be shown with any degree of probability that in all the cases of baptism recorded in the New Testament it was by dipping. On these points the Baptists seem to be entirely in the wrong. There is more plausibility in their contention on two other points: that the general custom of the ancient Church was to baptize by immersion, and that in one place at least (Rom. 6⁴, Col. 2¹²) Paul alludes to this form as having a spiritual significance.[1] In meeting these arguments some controversialists have taken an extreme and untenable position. They have held that the text in question does not contain any allusion to the plunging under the water and rising out of it, as figures of dying and rising with Christ; that it is a misunderstanding of the apostle's meaning to interpret it so, and that this misinterpretation gave rise to the practice of baptizing by immersion in the ancient Church. Now this

---

[1] In the *Teaching of the Twelve Apostles*, chap. vii., baptism is directed to be in (εἰς) living water, *i.e.* running, if possible; if not, in other water, either cold or warm; but if neither can be had, running nor standing, water is to be poured thrice on the head. Immersion seems to have been the ordinary rule, but when that cannot be done pouring is allowed.

would be a proper line to take if it were necessary to show that immersion is an improper mode of baptism, and pouring or sprinkling the only legitimate one. But that is not our position, and it is not advisable or safe to go so far. It seems impossible to deny that there is an allusion to the form of baptism in Rom. 6⁴, and consequently that the practice of baptizing by immersion was frequently used in the apostolic age as in subsequent times. All that is necessary for us to maintain is that this form is not essential to the validity of the ordinance. It is argued, indeed, that Paul's reference to it shows that the form has a spiritual significance, and therefore is an essential part of the sign; and some divines (*e.g.* Luther) in expounding the meaning and effect of baptism have made this its leading aspect.[1] But we have already seen that undoubtedly the idea of washing is the primary one in baptism. That is indicated in many passages of the New Testament, whereas that of dying and rising with Christ is only connected with baptism in one or two places in Paul's writings. Now these two ideas are so different that we cannot suppose that the same rite was designed directly and properly to represent them both; we must conclude, therefore, that the comparison to Christ's dying and rising again is merely an incidental allusion, and not the direct and principal significance of the rite. Had it been so the command must have been more express and precise to immerse than it can be proved to be.

We seem therefore led to the conclusion above indicated, that while immersion is a legitimate way of administering baptism, and one which in some respects brings out more vividly the idea of washing and cleansing, a mode also which has been frequently used in the apostolic and primitive times of the Church, and has given occasion to spiritual applications of its special actions; yet as the essential idea of the sacrament is that of cleansing, immersion is not absolutely necessary for its due administration, and being in certain circumstances inconvenient, may with advantage be dispensed

---

[1] In the present day Ebrard maintains in his *Dogmatik*, § 507, that the true idea of baptism is that of dying and rising to a new life in and with Christ, and not that of washing at all.

with.[1] This is the true position to take in regard to the outward form of baptism. It is hardly suitable to the freedom and spirituality of the New Testament to hold that we are strictly tied down to one particular method of applying water as a symbol of cleansing, or to imagine that the acceptability or efficacy of the ordinance depends upon the precise form of its administration. That would be to attach an importance to the external and ritual that our Lord and His apostles never do. We should not, on the other hand, maintain that sprinkling is *per se* more proper or consonant to apostolic usage than dipping, but should frankly say that the mode is indifferent, and that we adopt sprinkling simply because it is most convenient in our climate and our manners and customs. Taking this position, we can freely admit that in some respects immersion would be a more striking and expressive form, and can use all those expressions and allusions in Scripture that imply an entire washing, assuming that that is the ideal form of the ordinance, though it is not necessary or suitable to be actually practised among us. Some scope must be allowed to the imagination in the use of the sacred signs of the sacraments. They are meant not to be scenic displays and perfect resemblances, but suggestive emblems of divine truth.

[1] The Church of England in her baptismal service prescribes in the case of infants that they shall be dipped in the water as the proper mode, except when the parents declare that the child is too weak to bear it; though in the form for the baptism of those of riper years, dipping and pouring are put simply as alternatives. Wall in his *History of Infant Baptism* shows that dipping was first disused in France about the twelfth century, but continued in England till the reign of Elizabeth. The disuse of it he ascribes largely to the influence of divines who had been exiled in the Marian persecution, and become attached to the views and practices of Calvin and the continental Churches. He lays stress on the difference between pouring and sprinkling, holding the latter to be an unauthorised novelty introduced by the Westminster Directory, and he argues earnestly and quotes Jeremy Taylor and others of the same opinion for the restoration of the old practice of immersion in all but exceptional cases (chap. ix.). In this, however, they have not been successful; and I am not aware that even the modern Ritualists have revived this ancient practice, which would be certainly much more scriptural and proper than many they have adopted. The Church of Scotland seems to have followed the practice adopted by Calvin and Geneva of making pouring the ordinary method; but the Westminster Assembly has simply declared that dipping is not necessary, and that pouring or sprinkling is sufficient.

In the New Testament there is no evidence of any other ceremonies in baptism except the washing with water, nor is there any mention of them in the accounts of the ordinance in the *Didaché* or in Justin's *Apology*. But in course of time additions came to be made. Tertullian mentions as practised in his time threefold immersion, tasting a mixture of milk and honey (*de Cor.* 3), then anointing with oil, and laying on of hands by the bishop (*de Bapt.*); but he admits that for these things there is no direct Scripture authority, and that they rest on traditional custom. The introduction of them may have been due to the mysteries which formed an important and attractive part of the heathen religious worship, and which, after having lost their ancient power on popular faith, had a remarkable revival in the time of the Roman Empire. The influence of these remarkable rites probably affected the Gnostics first, and through them the Catholic Church. Baptism was looked on as the initiation into a new religious community, and it seemed proper that it should be accompanied with ceremonies similar to those by which men were admitted to the Eleusinian and other mysteries that were so famous. Language borrowed from these rites came to be applied to Christian ordinances, and a veil of secrecy, like that which enveloped the Gentile mysteries, was thrown around the special Christian services.

This tendency continued and increased along with other superstitions, and more ceremonies were added to the baptismal rite, such as exorcism, breathing on the baptized person, giving salt, and others.

Of the multifarious additions by which the simple institution of Christ had been overlaid in the Church of Rome, one, the marking the forehead with the sign of the cross, has been retained in the Church of England, though it may be remarked this was done only by a majority of one in the Convocation in 1562. The rite seems to have arisen from the practice mentioned by Tertullian (*de Cor.* 3) of making the sign of the cross on all sorts of occasions: it is mentioned by Augustine (*Conf.* i. 11) as used in baptism, but it has confessedly no Scripture authority, and on that account the Puritans and Presbyterians objected to it as tending to superstition. The Lutherans have retained not only the sign of the cross, but also the form of exorcism, though admitting them to have no divine authority.

In regard to the threefold immersion, there has been a curious variation in what was deemed the correct practice. Tertullian mentions the custom of trine immersion (or aspersion) in his argument against Praxeas (c. 25), for the distinction of the divine persons. But in the sixth century, when the Arians in Spain made use of the same rite to favour their doctrine that the Son and the Spirit are not one in substance with the Father, the orthodox adopted in opposition to them the practice of a single immersion.

2. As to the significance of baptism, all Christians are agreed that it is the cleansing of the soul from sin. This is the natural import of the sign, and it is referred to in various places of Scripture. The only question under this head is whether it symbolises only the cleansing of the pollution of sin by the work of the Spirit, or the removal of its guilt by the sacrifice of Christ, or both together. The former has been generally admitted, and on good grounds, since in several places baptism is connected with regeneration, and the baptism of water connected or contrasted with that of the Holy Ghost. Some divines contend that as the same symbol cannot have two different significations, the meaning of baptism should be confined to the reference that it confessedly has to regeneration, and that it introduces a confusion of ideas to see in it also an emblem of the sprinkling of the blood of Christ. Now this is so far valid that we ought not to consider the baptismal water as directly and specifically a type of the blood of Christ. For that there is no Scripture warrant. But neither should we regard it as directly and specifically an emblem of the Spirit: that would be a still more far-fetched comparison. We are not warranted to find any special meaning in the water, considered separately. The significance of the ordinance lies in the action of washing in which the water is employed. But when we look at this in its general nature and import we can hardly limit it to one part of the great blessing of deliverance from sin bestowed by Christ. We find that it is

connected with the remission of sins, not only by John the Baptist, but by Peter on the day of Pentecost (Acts 2³⁸). Thus sometimes the one side and sometimes the other of our salvation is brought out in connection with baptism or with the figure of washing embodied in it, and there is good ground for the comprehensive view taken in the Westminster Standards that baptism represents Christ and all the benefits of the New Covenant, justification and adoption, as well as regeneration and eternal life. Nor does this introduce any confusion or mixture of figures into the ordinance. For all these benefits are closely connected, and are all bestowed in Christ and by the Spirit. Forgiveness is more especially connected with the blood of Christ and renewal with the work of the Spirit; but, on the one hand, forgiveness is applied to us only by the Spirit working faith in us; and, on the other hand, sanctification is wrought in us by the Spirit using the person and work of Christ as the means of sanctifying us. Each is but a part or aspect of that one great salvation, meeting all our manifold needs, that is provided for us by God the Father, through the Son and by the Holy Ghost. Hence baptism, though it especially represents the work of the Spirit, is into the name of the Father, and of the Son, and of the Holy Ghost.[1] The fulness and comprehensiveness of the meaning conveyed by the rite is emphatically brought out in 1 Cor. 6¹¹, when the first clause, "but ye are washed," seems to be general, comprehending the two following as its parts, "but ye are sanctified; but ye are justified"; and then the final clauses apply to all together, and indicate the agency by which this great change is effected: "in the name of the Lord Jesus Christ and in the Spirit of our God."[2] It is

---

[1] So in other passages Paul connects the significance of baptism with the person of Christ (Gal. 3²⁷), and more particularly with His death (Rom. 6³·⁴, Col. 2¹¹). These passages afford the warrant for the expression in our Catechism that "baptism signifies and seals our engrafting into Christ," though I think that in these places Paul means not the outward rite, which he always called baptism into the name of Christ, but the spiritual reality which it represents. We partake of all His benefits when we are really united to Himself, and thus there is represented in baptism both our forgiveness and our renewal.

[2] That the sense of the comprehensive import of baptism was maintained in the early Church appears from the variety of names and titles by which they spoke of the ordinance, as φωτισμός, ἀνακαινισμός, ἀναγέννησις, υἱοποίησις, etc.

of considerable importance to bear in mind the fulness of meaning implied in the sacrament of baptism, not only for practical purposes, that we may exhibit to the people all that is signified in this divine ordinance, so that they may understand and appreciate it, but also on account of its doctrinal bearing on the efficacy of baptism. For, as we shall see presently, the theory that assigns a direct and causal efficacy to the outward rite has often led to a restriction of the meaning of it, so as to make this theory more consistent with experience. But we must undoubtedly preserve the unity of the object of baptism in all its aspects as representing, sealing, and applying. It cannot represent more or different things than it seals and applies, or there would be an unnatural combination of heterogeneous elements in the ordinance. No indication is given in Scripture of its having different objects in different respects. Though it is represented as both figuring and also in a sense accomplishing certain spiritual blessings, these are not separated from one another. It is by figuring and sealing that it communicates these blessings; whatever, therefore, it represents it also conveys when rightly used. If, therefore, there is reason to regard it as representing the entire change that God works in the soul of man through the application of Christ and His redemption by the Spirit, then its efficacy must be equally wide and comprehensive. This leads us to consider—

3. The efficacy of baptism. Since, as we have already seen, all Christians recognise in this ordinance a symbol of the cleansing of the soul by Christ, all must also agree that it has the effect that a most significant emblem directly appointed by Christ and solemnly administered in His name is naturally fitted to produce, that of keeping alive the memory of the spiritual washing, and impressing on men's minds its value and importance; an effect the same in kind as that produced, *e.g.*, by the Sabbath as an emblem of God's rest, or the stones set up at Gilgal in memory of the passage of the Jordan, or the frontlets and fringes on their garments that the Israelites were commanded to wear. Nor is this simplest and most universally admitted effect of the ordinance unworthy of consideration; for though most Christians

hold that this is but the lowest of its benefits, yet even this remembrance of divine truths and promises is of itself a help to the maintenance of true religion in the soul. This may not, indeed, appear as a distinct and separate effect of the sacrament in actual experience, for it is united with, and, as it were, absorbed in other and more precious influences; but it may be distinguished as an element in the complex whole, when we seek to analyse it into its component parts. Nearly all Christians, if we except the Socinians, some Arminians, and Zwingli in some of his statements, hold that this is not the whole design and effect of baptism; but that it does more than merely represent the cleansing of the soul from sin. And most would agree further, that one thing more that it does is to seal (*obsignare*) by a pledge (*pignus*) as well as a sign the gracious blessing that it represents. This idea of a seal ($\sigma\phi\rho\alpha\gamma\iota\varsigma$) is applied in the New Testament to circumcision (Rom. $4^{11}$), to which in another place (Col. $2^{11, 12}$) Paul makes baptism correspond; and therefore, though we do not find it anywhere expressly declared of the latter, the analogy of the Old Testament ordinance and the very nature of the case seems to warrant the connection of the same idea with baptism.[1] It is an outward symbolical ordinance appointed by Christ as Mediator, and accompanied with a promise of that which it represents (Acts $2^{39}$). Now, an outward thing given as a memorial by one who at the same time promises a benefit is just what is meant by a seal or token; and as these marks are all to be found in this ordinance, there can be no objection to giving it that name.

---

[1] The word "seal" seems to have been in common use among the Jews to describe circumcision, and to have had reference to its impressing a mark on the body; and it came afterwards to be used by Christian writers in reference to baptism, and may have led to the ceremony of signing with the cross. But when Paul calls circumcision a seal of the righteousness of faith, he seems to mean simply a token or pledge of it; and this is the sense in which the Reformed theologians have generally used the term. The sacraments are sometimes called sealing ordinances; but this is not exactly a scriptural expression: they are seals or tokens; but what we are sealed by is the Holy Spirit of God. The sacraments are not seals or pledges of our faith, as if they give any attestation or guarantee of it; but of the righteousness of faith, the objective work of Christ on which our faith rests. Dr. Halley's objections to the idea of their being seals are only valid against the notion of their attesting our faith or holiness.

But, further, since He who gives the pledge is the Amen, the faithful and true witness who cannot lie or deceive, it follows that He certainly performs what He promises in baptism whenever His promise is received in faith. When, therefore, the sign is used in faith, there is bestowed also that which is signified by it; and as the body is washed from the filth of the flesh, the soul seeking after God is purged from an evil conscience and born again to newness of life. This must be admitted in substance by all who believe that it is the work of God's Spirit and not of our own free will to apply to us the benefits purchased by Christ. Those, indeed, who think that salvation depends simply on a man's own choice to believe in Christ or not, can consistently hold that there is in baptism nothing more than a representation and confirmation of the doctrines and promises of the gospel, and a profession of faith in them on our part. Hence Socinians and some Arminians regard baptism as a mere sign or mark of our profession as Christians, or at most a pledge of God's promises to us, and of our obligation to faith and obedience, but not really a means of grace.

But we are constrained to take a higher view of the ordinance, not only by the general principle of our theology, that it is the Spirit that makes all outward means of grace effectual, so that if baptism does really confirm our faith as a sign and seal, it must also, by the agency of the Spirit, strengthen our spiritual life; but besides that, by the way in which baptism is often spoken of in the New Testament. It is said that by it we are saved (1 Pet. $3^{21}$). God is said to save us by the washing of regeneration (Tit. $3^5$), which most interpreters understand of baptism; and Christ is said to cleanse His Church by the washing of water in the word (Eph. $5^{26}$). These are strong expressions, and seem at first sight to give countenance to the doctrine of baptismal regeneration: and they are certainly inconsistent with any view that finds less in the ordinance than a means of grace as well as a sign and seal of it.

In regard to the subjects of baptism, it has been the doctrine and practice of Christians, that those from without the visible Church who profess their faith in Christ intelligently and credibly should be baptized.[1] Further, it has been the opinion of the great majority of Christians that the rite should be administered also to the infant children of such persons. But since the Reformation a section of the Protestant Church, to which many good and some great men have belonged, have denied this, and held that only those who being of full age make a profession of their own faith should be baptized. Those who have held this have generally maintained also that the ordinance can only be properly administered by entire immersion of the person in water, though there is no necessary connection between these two points. Those who held these views were called by their adversaries Anabaptists, *i.e.* rebaptizers, because they baptized by immersion, on their profession of faith, those who had been baptized by sprinkling in infancy. They call themselves Baptists, as if they alone gave true baptism. The former name is opprobrious and unfair, since they do not any more than other Christians repeat any baptism that they regard as real; the latter name, if strictly taken, conveys an injurious insinuation against those who differ from them, but it has been sanctioned by usage and disjoined from such an idea. The strictly proper term to designate their opinion as to the subject of baptism is anti-Pædobaptists, as the body of Christians who do not agree with them are Pædobaptists.

On this subject there are two distinct questions which it is well to consider apart and keep separate in our own minds, for much confusion sometimes arises from mixing them up together. The one is, what warrant have we for giving the sacrament of baptism to the infant children of believers? and

[1] Some, *e.g.* Dr. Halley, think that a profession of faith in Christ is not necessary for the baptism even of adults, but that it should be given by the ministers of the gospel to all who are willing to receive it. This is argued from Matt. 28$^{19}$, where the object of baptizing is held to be all the nations, and from the practice of the apostles, who, it is maintained, baptized men at once when sometimes no profession of faith is mentioned.

the other is, on what ground or principle is this done? These are manifestly quite different questions. The former inquires into the reason we have for our conduct, and that must be a direct or indirect command of Christ; the latter inquires into the reason of this command itself. For our warrant in baptizing infants it is sufficient to be able to show that Christ has appointed us to do so, and this would be a perfectly good reason even though we could not tell why or to what end infants are baptized.[1] But if we believe that there is reason and warrant for the practice, it is natural that we should seek to find out the ground and principle of it; and as in general the precepts of the New Testament are not mere arbitrary appointments, but laws appealing to the understanding, we may expect to be enabled to perceive on what grounds the command rests. Hence the two questions are naturally and closely connected. Still they are distinct in themselves and have distinct evidence bearing upon each, and it has sometimes happened that those who have adduced valid and satisfactory arguments for the right and duty of baptizing believers' infants have had very erroneous and untenable ideas of the ground or reason of that appointment. The two parts, therefore, should be considered separately; and the former as the simpler, and the necessary foundation of the latter, naturally comes first.

I. That the infants of believers are to be baptized appears from the following line of evidence, which is that generally employed by Reformed divines:—

1. The New Testament religion is organically connected with that of the Old Testament, and grew out of it. The Church is essentially the same in both dispensations. This has often been overlooked or denied by modern theologians, and the want of recognition of it has been one chief reason why some of them have failed to find sufficient evidence in

[1] The argument which in point of fact has been most frequently used for the baptism of infants is that taken from John 3⁵, which has been very often understood as asserting the absolute necessity of baptism for Christianity. In that form the argument is untenable, though I think a valid argument can be drawn from the significance of baptism as a sign of the truth declared in that passage, as I have endeavoured to show in my handbook on *The Christian Sacraments*, Part II. c. iv.

the New Testament or early Church for infant baptism. Schleiermacher maintained that Christianity stands only in the same relation to Judaism as to heathenism (*Der Christliche Glaube*, § 12). But the passages to which he appeals in support of this view do not really bear it out. They are those in which Paul speaks of faith in Christ as equally necessary for Jews and Gentiles (Rom. $2^{11,\ 12}$ $3^{21-24}$, 2 Cor. $5^{16,\ 17}$, Eph. $2^{13\ 18}$). In the passages where the first two of these texts occur Paul is simply proving that the Jews would not be saved merely because they had the law, and that they as well as Gentiles were guilty of sin; in the third it is manifestly individuals that are spoken of, and the relation of the two dispensations is not considered at all; and in the last quoted passage there is a distinct reference to the commonwealth of Israel as having the covenants of promise and the hope of salvation, so that when Christ is said to have reconciled both Jews and Gentiles to God, that must be understood of individuals, and not as if the Jewish Church needed reconciliation as much as Gentile bodies. And that Paul recognised a Church of God in the Old Testament essentially the same as that of the New Testament times, appears from his statements in Rom. $11^{17,\ 21}$ about the Gentiles being grafted into the Old Testament olive tree from which the Jews, the natural branches, were cut off. So also in Gal. $3^{14,\ 29}$ he speaks of Christians as inheriting the promise made to Abraham, and in Phil. $3^3$ he calls them the true circumcision (see also Eph. $2^{11\ 22}$). The same thing appears from the narrative in Acts, where we find that Paul maintained that he was truly a Jew faithful to the principles of the law and the prophets. Now, if Paul held this view, much less can it be doubted that the Twelve did so also, and we find it very distinctly implied in the Epistles of James and Peter. It seems, therefore, to be clearly made out as a matter of history, that though the coming of Christ and the establishment of the New Covenant did, indeed, make many important changes in the form and ordinances of the Church, yet in substance we are to recognise the old Church of God as continuing down into Christian times. The Jews who refused to believe in Jesus as the Messiah promised to the fathers became apostates from the religion of Israel, and separated themselves from the true Church of God which continued to exist among the disciples of Jesus.

2. In the Old Testament the children of God's people were admitted to circumcision, which was not merely a political but a religious ordinance, and corresponded to baptism in the New Testament. This statement is borne out in all its parts by undeniable facts. It is, of course, well known that when circumcision was appointed to Abraham as the token of God's covenant with him, it was commanded to be given to all the males of his household eight days old. This is a notorious matter of sacred history. But it is said by those who object to infant baptism, that circumcision was merely an external sign belonging to Israel as a nation, having respect to the temporal promises given to them; and not requiring any profession of religious faith on the part of those who had a right to it, but belonging to all Israelites as such. Hence it is said it affords no fair analogy to the ordinance of the new dispensation, which is not national, has no respect to any earthly inheritance, and implies a profession of faith in Christ in all who seek it for themselves. Now it is indeed to be admitted that there are differences between the two dispensations and their initiatory rites, and that in the ancient economy the Church of God was bound up with a particular nation, so that those who were members of the Church were also members of that body politic. But there is no doubt that circumcision was a religious ordinance, symbolising spiritual truths and giving a pledge of spiritual blessings. It was commanded to Abraham as the token of God's covenant with him long before there was any nation or any civil institutions at all connected with the covenant. Paul declares it to have been a sign and seal of the righteousness of faith (Rom. $4^{11}$), and everywhere speaks of it as a religious privilege. It is true that circumcision was not so expressly connected with a profession of faith in God as baptism in the New Testament is with faith in the Lord Jesus Christ, but there can be no other idea formed of its meaning than that it marked out those who received it as the people of God. And in the case of proselytes it clearly implied

faith in Jehovah as the God of Israel, while those who belonged to the nation by birth virtually kept up such a profession by continuing in a community that as such was dedicated to Jehovah, and looked forward to His promised salvation. Those who disregarded the laws of the theocracy were excluded from religious privileges, and those who openly rebelled against it were put to death. No doubt in practice these laws were not enforced, for very often the great body of the people were unfaithful and idolatrous. But such was the ideal of what Israel was to be, and it is by it that we must form our conception of its institutions. Circumcision, moreover, is closely analogous to baptism, not only in its initiatory character, but also in its symbolic nature and meaning. It was an emblem of the cleansing and renewing of the soul, and the giving of a new heart (Deut. $10^{16}$ $30^6$, Jer. $4^4$, Col. $2^{11}$), which is just what baptism signifies in the New Testament. The difference between them lies not in the spiritual things that they represent, nor yet in the efficacy that belongs to them, but only in the outward sign by which the renewing of the soul is figured.

Now we do not argue from this analogy directly that because circumcision was administered to infants, therefore baptism ought to be given them; that would be a very weak and precarious argument. But we say that the fact that the infant children of God's people were members of the Old Testament Church, proves that if it had been our Lord's will that they should not be members of the New Testament Church, that must have been expressly declared.

We freely concede (to the Baptists) that there might quite conceivably be a difference between the two dispensations in this respect, only we hold that the connection of the two, and the identity of the Church in both, makes it certain that the exclusion of children would have been a change, and their admission simply the continuance of the old rule. The burden of proof, therefore, lies with those who refuse infant baptism. If it could be shown that Christ and His apostles established a new rule in this matter, then we would at once admit that the analogy of circumcision was of no avail. But we contend that a new rule would have to be laid down to exclude infants from Church membership. The identity in substance of the ordinances in the two dispensations appears in this, that Paul in Col. 2:11, 12 calls baptism the circumcision of Christ. The disciples of Jesus were originally Jews, brought up in the Jewish Church, and familiar with its principles and laws. They did not conceive that they left that Church and entered a new one when they became followers of Jesus, though many of their old ordinances were abolished and some new ones appointed. So when Jesus commanded them to go and make disciples of all nations, baptizing them, etc., unless they were taught to the contrary they would certainly conclude that where the head of a family became a disciple his infant children as well as himself should be baptized. That had been the rule with regard to proselytes to Judaism. When any stranger desired to share in the religous privileges of Israel, especially in the Passover, the law was "let all his males be circumcised, and then let him come near and keep it; and he shall be as one born in the land" (Ex. 12:48). Unless, therefore, there was some indication to the contrary given by Jesus, the disciples must have presumed that the same course was to be followed with converts to Christianity. The burden of proof, therefore, lies with those who deny baptism to the infant children of professing Christians.

In Acts 15:1, 5 the Pharisaic party in the Church are represented as saying, "Except ye be circumcised ye cannot be saved." The circumcision contemplated was no doubt to have been performed not only on adult Gentile believers, but on their children. So Jews would naturally understand baptizing to include children, unless the opposite was specified.

3. But not only is there not the slightest indication that they are to be excluded, there are also various things that point in the other direction. Such are—(1) Our Lord's reception of infants when the disciples forbade their parents to bring them that He might lay His hands on them and bless them. It is true He did not baptize them or order them to be baptized, and a sufficient reason for that is that baptism as a Christian sacrament had not yet been instituted. But He gave them another token of His favour by laying

His hands on them, and He said, τῶν τοιούτων ἐστὶν ἡ βασιλεία τῶν οὐρανῶν (Matt. 19¹⁴). The word τοιούτων must refer not as some would have it, to believers as being like little children, but to infants themselves such as were then before Him; and the statement is that the kingdom of heaven includes them, and is given as the reason why they should be suffered to come to Jesus. Since infants are in the kingdom of God, and none can enter it but by the new birth, they must be capable of regeneration; and if so, it is proper that they should receive the sign and token of it. Can any man forbid water that these should not be baptized which receive the Holy Spirit as well as us?

(2) The words of Peter, Acts 2³⁹, "For to you is this promise, and to your children," more naturally refer to the households of Israel than to succeeding generations.

(3) The instances of the baptism of households by the apostles (Acts 16¹⁵, ³³, 1 Cor. 1¹⁶). It is important to observe the exact use to be made of these notices. It would be a very weak argument to assume the probability that there must have been infants in one or more of these cases, and that therefore they were baptized by Paul and ought to be baptized by the Church. For it is quite possible that all the members of these households were adults and all professed faith in Christ, and the instances are not so many as to make this a very violent improbability. If the burden of proof lay on our side, and we had to make out the right of the children of God's people to the seal of the covenant as a new thing, then I think these cases would be altogether worthless. But if our previous reasoning is good, we have not to make out this, but simply to show that there is no evidence for the withdrawal of a privilege already recognised and enjoyed. In that point of view the instances are significant, for they show us that the apostles acted just as they would have done if the old right of infants was to be maintained in the Church. They acted just as they would have done, on the principle that when anyone wished to enter the Christian Church he must bring his family with him: as the rule had been before, let all his males be circumcised: so it was now, let all his house be baptized.

We may therefore gather with considerable probability that this was the principle on which they acted.

(4) In 1 Cor. 7¹⁴ Paul states as a well-known fact that the children of believers are ἅγια, holy, *i.e.* in outward state, and in relation to God; and he bases this on the same general principle that the faith of the head of the house brought the whole family into this relation to God. Another view has been taken by some of this passage, who argue that if the children of believers were baptized Paul would have appealed to that and not merely to their being holy. But this is at best a mere probability, and Paul may have used the more general phrase, because in point of fact when the father was a heathen the children would not be baptized.

(5) Infant baptism is proved by sufficient evidence to have been the practice of the early Church. There is no doubt that the custom was universal in the time of Augustine, that it was common in the time of Tertullian, and that Origen found it established as an ancient custom, and there are probable references to it in the writings of Irenæus and Justin,[1] so that we may reasonably infer that it had been continued from apostolic times. Neander and other modern Church historians regard it as of later origin; but his opinion on this point seems to rest upon the circumstance that they cannot see evidence of it in the New Testament, and that again is to be traced to overlooking the organic connection and continuity of the Christian Church with that of the Old Testament.

It is apt to appear as a consideration favourable to Baptist views that there is no undoubted instance of infant baptism in the New Testament, whereas there are many cases recorded of adults baptized. But this is a mistaken view of the matter. There is really no case clearly decisive either way. The adults of whose baptism we read were not children of Christians, but converts from Judaism or heathenism; and on both views alike these should be baptized on their profession of faith. We have no record of a single

[1] Justin, *Apol.* i. 15.

case in which a child of believing parents was not baptized till he grew up. This would decide the case in favour of the Baptist view, but the other instances prove nothing for them.

The indications of the practice in regard to baptism given in the New Testament and early Christian writings seem to me sufficient to prove the continuance of an old practice, though they would hardly be satisfactory if we had to show the establishment of a new thing.

II. Let us inquire now what is the ground or principle on which the infant children of God's people receive the seal of the covenant.

Some have rested it on the ground that baptism is absolutely necessary to salvation, and that infants dying without it would be excluded from heaven. This view was largely prevalent in the ancient Church, and is held by those who have an extreme regard for antiquity, and interpret John $3^5$ as referring to baptism.[1] This, however, is manifestly a false and inadequate foundation for the observance. It is false, for the Bible does not lay it down that the sacrament of baptism is absolutely necessary to salvation. Further, even if this idea of the necessity of baptism were true, it would not afford a sufficient reason for baptizing all the infants of believers, but only those children, whether of believers or unbelievers, that seem to be in danger of death. The false interpretation of John $3^5$ as referring to baptism, and the use of it, thus understood, as the ground of infant baptism, prevailed early in the Church; but this just rendered possible the position taken up by Tertullian, that infants as a rule should not be baptized, and that the sacrament may more wisely be delayed to a maturer age.

The obvious inadequacy of this as a ground of infant baptism, has led to its being either supplemented or superseded by another theory, namely, that infants are to be baptized on the ground of the faith of others instead of their own. From an early period in the history of the Church sponsors or godfathers (*susceptores*, ἀνάδοχοι, *sponsores*, *compatres*) appeared on behalf of those who were to be baptized. They are

[1] So Wall, *History of Infant Baptism*; and even Goode, *Divine Rule of Faith and Practice*.

mentioned by Tertullian as a usual custom. Church historians are divided in opinion as to the origin of this custom. Neander, who denies the apostolic origin of infant baptism, thinks that they were introduced along with that. Mosheim, on the other hand, believes that they were originally admitted only in the case of adults, as witness and securities of the good faith of those who applied for baptism, and only afterwards allowed in the baptism of infants also. However this may be, it is certain that the institution ultimately took such a form as was adapted only to infant baptism. The sponsors were called to answer for the child, and profess faith and obedience on his behalf, and bound to care for his Christian education, that he might not nullify these professions when he grew up. In this system the infant was baptized on the ground of a vicarious profession of faith, and because, through the care of the sponsors, it was considered likely that he would himself in due time believe. Along with this there was combined (*e.g.* by Augustine and Aquinas) the idea that the faith not merely of the individual sponsors, but of the whole Church, was the ground of the baptism of infants (Aug. *Ep.* 98 ; Aquinas, quoted in Hagenbach, *Dogmengesch.* p. 459). In both of its parts, however, this notion of a vicarious profession of faith is entirely unfounded on Scripture ; and when infant baptism is rested on any such unscriptural and fictitious ground, great advantage is given to the views of those who deny it altogether.

Another untenable ground for infant baptism is that adopted by most of the older Lutheran theologians, and by Ebrard among the Reformed, that infants are capable of a certain kind of unconscious and germinal faith or repentance, so that when the sacrament of baptism is administered to them they may experience a certain germinal regeneration. This idea seems altogether fanciful, and to be rather the result of certain theological assumptions than of any observed facts or testimonies of Scripture.

The truth is, that all these theories are vitiated by the retention in one form or another of the idea of baptismal regeneration, whereas it is not till we entirely rid our minds of all notions of the outward act having as such any spiritual efficacy, and regard it simply as a sign and seal of the renewing wrought by the direct agency of the Spirit, that we can perceive the reason and propriety of its administration to the infant children of professing Christians. When we take this simple and scriptural view of the ordinance, then we perceive—

1. That there is nothing symbolised in it of which infants are not capable. It represents that part or side of the application of redemption in which man is passive, namely, regeneration, and not that in which he is active, namely, faith and repentance. Now, infants are capable of regeneration, though not of faith.

2. That God's covenant with His people has ever included their children as well as themselves; and He has given special promises that if parents, believing in Christ and walking with God in Him, faithfully and prayerfully bring up their children, they too will be regenerated by the Spirit (Prov. 22⁶, Is. 44³⁻⁵, Eph. 6⁴.

These promises must not, indeed, be so interpreted as to limit or fetter the sovereign and free grace of God, who has mercy on whom He will. But they afford a precious and blessed encouragement to believing parents in the discharge of their responsible duties in regard to their children. Indeed, without some such special assurance that God is willing to renew their children by His Spirit, it is hard to see how parents could contemplate with feelings of hope and joy the birth of children into the world. They know that their children inherit a corrupt nature, and will certainly commit sins if spared to grow up; and the prospect of their future life and destiny would be altogether a gloomy and sad one were it not for the assurance that God has a special regard to the children of His people, and has promised to make them His own children; so that if they plead these promises in believing prayer, and faithfully seek to discharge their duty, they may humbly but confidently trust that their children will indeed be born from above. Thus the right of the infants of professing Christians to be regarded as members of the Church depends not on their baptism, nor on any profession or promises made on their behalf, but on their birth of believers; and they receive baptism, not that they may be made holy, or dedicated to God, or admitted to the Church, but because they are already holy (1 Cor. 7$^{14}$), and members of the Church visible, in virtue of being the children of believers.

3. We see, further, as stated in the *Westminster Confession*, xxviii. 6, that "the efficacy of baptism is not tied to that moment of time wherein it is administered." This is a very important principle for the right understanding of the use of infant baptism, and it is one which depends upon a true conception of the efficacy of this sacrament. If the acting of the sacrament be direct and efficient, so as of itself, or by any power communicated to it, to produce regeneration or to co-operate to its production, then it is impossible to see how that power could be exercised at any other time than that of the action itself. The ordinance, from its very nature, is a transient act; and if it has any efficacy in itself at all, it must be exerted at the time when alone it has any existence. But if its efficacy be regarded as moral, depending on its being a sign and seal, the case is otherwise. A significant act, though it be transient and leave no permanent mark, yet since it can at any time be reported or remembered, may serve to recall what it signifies, even at a long distance of time. This is equally true of the influence such an action has on the mind as a seal or token of some promise. We can therefore easily understand how this mental and moral influence may be exerted by baptism when it is looked back upon long after its actual administration. Cases in which this must be its mode of working occur even apart from infant baptism. A young man may have been baptized after a profession of faith apparently sincere, and afterwards come to see that he had not then been truly converted, and may be led at a later period to a really saving change and a true profession of faith. In such a case it is universally agreed that he should not be rebaptized, as that sacrament is not to be repeated. But as it never can be right to deprive anyone entitled to it of the spiritual benefit of the ordinance, it follows that it must be possible for him to derive as much good from the memory of his former baptism as he could from a fresh administration of the ordinance. It is as truly to him a sign and seal of his new birth when he remembers having

received it before he was truly converted, as it would be could he receive it. Just so it is in the case of those who are baptized in infancy. When they come to believe in the Lord Jesus Christ, whether in earlier or later years, then looking back to their baptism in that faith they find in it a confirmation of God's promises on which they rely, and that strengthens and increases their faith. They suffer no loss, therefore, in being baptized in infancy, while as yet incapable of that faith by which alone the sacrament becomes an effectual means of grace. Nay, they gain greatly by it. For the sacrament is a far more significant symbol and a far more affecting seal of God's grace, just because it is given to infants.

Some evangelical divines maintain, and among them Dr. Cunningham very strongly, that the normal type of baptism is to be found in the ordinance as administered to adults, and that the baptism of infants is to be regarded as an abnormal and exceptional case,—an administration of it which is warranted by the word of God, but one in which we cannot so clearly see the meaning and design of the sacrament. They have been led to this position by dwelling on the principle that the sacraments in general are not means of obtaining the spiritual things signified in them, but seals or confirmations of the fact that these blessings have been already received. On that principle it is argued they ought to be given only to those who have received Christ by faith; and this is only fully apparent when a profession of faith precedes their administration. When that is so, we can say that in all cases the sacrament, if it is not a false profession, seals and confirms to the receiver the promises of the covenant. This alternative, however, cannot be put in the case of infant baptism. In it there is no possibility of a false profession on the part of the receiver, being an infant; and yet it cannot be said, on the other hand, that the sacrament is always a seal of grace actually bestowed. Hence this administration is regarded as a somewhat exceptional case, in which the full meaning and effect of the rite does not clearly appear.

It may be doubted, however, whether it is necessary to take up this position, and it certainly seems an improbable thing that our Lord would have made such institutions in

His Church as led to the result that the way in which the ordinance is most commonly administered in a body of professing Christians should be an abnormal form of it that to some extent disguises or veils its full meaning.

But may not the baptism of infants be regarded as a type of what is or ought to be the normal state of things in the Christian Church? It represents the regeneration of the soul in infancy: the propriety of the symbol is only justified by the possibility of that, and the common use of the administration may be held to indicate that in Christian households that should be the usual case. God's appointment of it may be taken to convey an assurance of His willingness to take the children of His people to be His, and to renew and save them even in their infancy; and may it not be that when Christian parents are faithful to their duty in training up their children for Him, and do this in humble, believing, and prayerful dependence on His gracious aid, He will not fail in His part of the covenant, and that they will assuredly be born again? Does not the fact that God has appointed as the ordinary lot of the children of believing parents that they shall receive the sign of the new birth, seem to indicate that it is His will that the reality should correspond to the symbol, and that, as a rule, the children of believers should be born again in infancy? May it not be due to the unbelief and unfaithfulness and want of due care in training their children that this is not more frequently the case? And should not Christian parents pray more earnestly and believingly than they do that their children may be regenerated from their birth; and are they not warranted in humble faith to bring them up on the presumption that they have been so born again when dedicated to God, humbly presuming this when nothing appears to the contrary, not because they have been baptized or because that rite has any regenerating power, but because the appointment of it for the children of His people solemnly declares as a general truth that God is willing and anxious to have these children as His own?

What has been said about the grounds and reasons of infant baptism may indicate how to answer another question on which there have been differences of opinion and practice. Whose children ought to be baptized? It is clear that if the principles on which we maintain infant baptism be correct, it is only the children of those who profess their faith in Christ that have a right to the ordinance. It is because they are members of Christian families that they are recognised as members of the Church visible. Clearly, therefore, their parents must be such as make a profession of Christianity, or at least one of them must be such. Paul in 1 Cor. 7$^{14}$ represents a household as sanctified even when the husband or the wife may be an unbeliever. Hence it has been generally held by the Reformed Churches that a profession of faith by one of the parents entitles the children to baptism. It has sometimes been held that persons might be regarded as members of the visible Church even though they do not make a personal profession of faith, and that all who have been themselves baptized and not excluded from the Church are such, and, therefore, their children may be baptized. Some who are of this opinion hold that for the Lord's Supper a distinct profession of faith is needed. Others, again, have maintained that it, too, does not require a profession of faith, although this latter view is nearly obsolete.

But in either form the theory seems untenable. It proceeds upon the assumption that a profession of faith in those who are capable of it is not necessary for membership of the Church visible. Of course, all who maintain infant baptism admit that the children of believers are in a sense members of the Church though they do not and cannot profess faith in Christ; but that is because they are incapable of doing so, and because there is from God's covenant promise reason to believe that they are born again; but with this necessary exception it is held that membership in the visible Church implies a profession of faith in all who are capable of it. If this be not so we make the invisible and visible two different Churches, an idea of which there is no hint in Scripture, and which leads to great confusion. The true conception seems rather to be that there is but one Church which in different aspects is invisible and visible, as known only to God and as imperfectly recognised by men. If this be so, then the condition of membership of the Church visible in the case of adults is just a profession of what constitutes membership of the Church invisible, *i.e.* faith in Christ, and none can be regarded as members of the Church visible except those who make such a profession. In accordance with this view the terms believers, those who profess faith, members of the Church visible, are used as convertible terms in our standards. (See *Conf.* xxviii. 4; Larger Cat. 166; Shorter Cat. 95.)

I do not here inquire what sort of a profession is to be made, or what evidence the Church should require of its sincerity: that is a different point which will come before us at a later stage. Dr. Hodge, I think, has somewhat confused his treatment of the subject by mixing up these two questions. There are differences of opinion as to what amount of particularity is required in a profession of faith, and what rule the Church is to follow in judging of professions made; but these are matters of detail and practical application, and whatever may be said about them it is important to settle the principle that only those who profess their faith in Christ are entitled to have their children baptized. Indeed, it is hard to see how any who do not do so can undertake the obligations which must necessarily accompany the ordinance, since it is a sign and seal of the covenant of grace.

This question is also sometimes confused by being put in this form: whether only the children of communicants should be baptized. Most Protestants have held that the qualifications for the two sacraments are the same, and that those whose children are to be baptized should also be admitted to the Lord's Supper, and should observe that ordinance. Some, however, have thought that higher qualifications are required for the latter sacrament than for the former; and many without formally maintaining this in theory act upon it practically. In such cases, when men profess intelligently faith in Christ as their Saviour, and yet for some conscientious reason abstain from coming to His table, it may not be necessary to deal with them strictly in the way of censure. Their neglect of the Communion may be a sin, yet if it proceed from mistaken ideas or scruples it can hardly be regarded as a very scandalous one; and in a person whose profession and conduct are in other respects unexceptionable, it may be best to deal with it by instruction and persuasion rather than by exclusion from other privileges. The Communion is not the only mark of the people of Christ, indeed it is rather a privilege than a mark. The one essential mark is a profession of faith in Christ, and that may be made in various ways. A man may be admitted to Church membership on such a profession by being himself baptized, or by having his children baptized, or by receiving a token of admittance to the Lord's table, and any of these acts gives him a right to all the rest. If he is himself baptized he acquires the right of coming to the Communion and having his children baptized; if he has a child baptized he acquires a right to the Communion, and *vice versâ*. That which really gives him the right is the profession of his faith, and which of the ordinances he receives in the first instance depends simply on which of them he is in circumstances to need. What is important, therefore, is not that those who receive baptism for their children be actually communicants, but that they be such as would be admitted to communion if they desired it, and, of course, also ought to be exhorted to come forward.

## BAPTISMAL REGENERATION

Before passing from the subject of the efficacy of baptism, we must consider more particularly the doctrine of Baptismal Regeneration, which has been maintained by many divines and Churches, though in very different senses by some and by others respectively.

From a very early period in the history of the Church the term regeneration (ἀναγέννησις) was applied to baptism, as by Justin Martyr describing the Christian worship in his *Apology*. The words of Christ in John 3⁵ were understood of baptism, and it was held to be absolutely necessary for salvation. There was in the post-apostolic times a strong tendency to attach undue importance to outward rites, and to exaggerate the value and powers of the sacraments. Much of the language used of them by the Fathers is rhetorical and somewhat inflated and bombastic; so that we can hardly gather from their statements any clear and precise doctrine. It came, however, to be generally maintained that the regeneration spoken of in Scripture is effected in baptism (hence the phrase baptismal regeneration has much Patristic authority); but there seem to have been very different views as to what was meant by it. The difference of the views held generally in the East about grace and free will, from those of Augustine that prevailed in the West, would necessarily imply a different idea of regeneration. There are also statements in the writings of Origen, Chrysostom, and Basil [1] that baptism is a symbol or type of the purification and new life of the soul, and indications that some at least of the statements of the Fathers about regeneration by baptism are to be understood as instances of the figure of putting the sign for the thing signified. While it must be admitted that the Fathers generally had an excessive and superstitious idea of the efficacy of the sacrament, it has been sufficiently proved that they are not really unanimous in holding baptismal regeneration, and certainly not in the sense of the later Church of Rome.

But as the Augustinian doctrine of regeneration was established as orthodox, while at the same time the ritualistic tendency steadily increased, there was formed a more definite doctrine of sacramental efficacy, which was reduced to a metaphysical system by the scholastic philosophy, and became the symbolical doctrine of the Roman Catholic Church. That doctrine is a thoroughly materialistic one, making the effects of the sacraments exactly analogous to those supposed to be wrought by magic, in which certain outward things were believed to be endowed, by certain charms or spells, with the power of producing wonderful effects. Baptism is declared to be the instrumental cause of justification and regeneration, and to produce these results *ex opere operato* in the case of all who receive it and do not put an obstacle in the way (*non ponentibus obicem*). The scriptural evidence alleged for it is

---

[1] Origen, *adv. Cels.* iii., ed. Spencer, p. 142, Eng. trans. c. li.; Chrysostom, *in Joh.* iii.; Basil, *de Spir. S.* c. xv.

John 3[5], Eph. 5[26], Tit. 3[5], Acts 22[16], 1 Pet. 3[21], and it rests upon a particular interpretation of these texts, especially of the first.

It is assumed that when our Lord said, "Except a man be born of water," etc., He referred to the sacrament of baptism. Even this is not certain; and if any baptism be directly meant, it can only be that which John and the disciples of Jesus were then administering. That there may have been an allusion to this is not improbable; but what Jesus directly spoke of was the idea of baptism, or the reality which it represents. Some think that He declared two things to be necessary to enter the kingdom of heaven—birth of water, i.e. baptism, and birth of the Spirit, i.e. regeneration. But against this is the fact that the preposition is not repeated: it is simply ἐξ ὕδατος καὶ πνεύματος; and in all the other forms of the statement in this discourse, only one thing is mentioned—begotten again, or from above, of Spirit. Jesus seems therefore to speak of one thing only, that baptism with the Holy Spirit which John had declared He would bestow (Matt. 3[11], John 1[33]). This does not refer to the Christian ordinance of baptism, as Roman Catholic and Lutheran expositors groundlessly assume, but to the spiritual renewal of which baptism was the symbol. Jesus expected Nicodemus as a teacher of Israel to know the things of which He was speaking: now he could not have known about a sacrament not then instituted; but he might have known of the needed and promised renewal by the Spirit, from such passages as Isa. 44[3], Ezek. 36[25, 26], where the Spirit is metaphorically designated by water. The interpretation which takes water and Spirit to be one idea = the Spirit working like water, seems the most natural and suitable to the context.

In Tit. 3[5] God is said to have saved us διὰ λουτροῦ παλιγγενεσίας, κ.τ.λ., which contains, I think, a reference to baptism, though that is not quite certain. But the washing (or laver) of regeneration does not necessarily mean that which causes regeneration; it is analogous to "the baptism of repentance," and may naturally mean accompanying or symbolising regeneration.

Similar is Eph. $5^{26}$, a highly figurative passage, where baptism is probably, though not certainly, referred to, and Christ is said to have cleansed His Church by it in the word. It is declared here that baptism is a means by which, along with the word, Christ sanctifies His people; and this we cordially believe without holding that the outward ordinance has any regenerating power.

In 1 Pet. $3^{21}$ baptism is said to save us; but it is called a figure, and the reality is not the putting away of the filth of the flesh, but the inquiry of a good conscience after God.

In Acts $22^{16}$ it is generally assumed that the words, wash away thy sins, refer to forgiveness. But it seems more in accordance with the meaning of like exhortations elsewhere in Scripture to understand them of repentance and forsaking sin (see Isa. $1^{16}$, Jas. $4^8$, 2 Cor. $7^1$).

These passages therefore can all be understood in a proper and natural sense without implying the Romish doctrine of baptismal regeneration, and therefore cannot be regarded as proof of it. If it were proved by other evidence they could be interpreted as declaring it, but they do not necessarily or naturally touch it. Now, so far from being proved by any other evidence, the doctrine in question is conclusively disproved by several considerations.

The great principle that runs through the New Testament, and is expressly and plainly stated in many places, that sinners are saved by simple faith in the Lord Jesus Christ, is diametrically opposed to this Romish doctrine. In the Epistle to the Romans, Paul emphatically states, and proves from the Old Testament, that we are justified by faith without the works of the law, and makes no mention of baptism or any other rite as necessary until he comes to speak afterwards incidentally of baptism as pledging the believer to a life of holiness. Exactly similar is the tenor of his Epistle to the Galatians, which contains, amid declarations as strong of salvation by faith, only one solitary allusion ($3^{27}$) to baptism. So also it is in his other Epistles. John gives as his own, or reports as his Master's, many precious sayings about salvation and eternal life by faith in Jesus, and about the new birth of

God; but there is not a single reference to baptism in his writings, save the doubtful one in John 3⁵. The same great truth of salvation by faith is taught or assumed by the other New Testament writers. Now this is entirely overthrown by the Romish doctrine of baptismal regeneration. If it be only by baptism that the new life is imparted, then it is not true that whosoever believeth in Jesus shall not perish, but have eternal life; and if baptism always regenerates the soul, then it is not true that he that believeth not the Son shall not see life. Even the exceptions that Romanists are forced to make on either side, as that martyrdom or the desire of receiving baptism suffice without it, and that the purpose of mortal sin places an obstacle in the way that prevents its efficacy, do not suffice to bring their doctrine into consistency with the teaching of Scripture. For there may be true and great faith without the desire of baptism, e.g. in Quakers who reject the ordinance entirely, and one baptized in infancy may never come to believe in the Saviour. Unless, therefore, we are to give up the doctrine of salvation by grace through faith, we must reject that of the Church of Rome on baptismal regeneration.

Experience also witnesses decisively against it. Although regeneration itself is a secret and mysterious thing, yet wherever it is real it will and must show itself in its effects of godliness, purity, and uprightness of life. It is a mere empty name or imagination if it does not do so. Now the Romish theory is, that all who are baptized and have not interposed the obstacle of sin are renewed in heart and life. We should expect, therefore, to find this manifested in their character and conduct, and we must bring the doctrine to this test of experience and fact. No doubt, in the case of those who have been baptized when of full age, there is always the possibility of an incalculable element coming in, for we cannot tell whether or not there was an obstacle put in the way of the efficacy of the sacrament. But in the vast multitudes who have been baptized in infancy there is no such uncertainty; for as infants cannot interpose any obstacle, it is certain, according to the Church of Rome, that they are all regenerated in baptism. But what says history and experience to this? Have there not been multitudes baptized in infancy who have given no evidence whatever of godliness or practical Christianity, nay, who have been notorious for vices and crimes of the grossest kind? One instance, at least, we have in the New Testament of a man who was certainly baptized and yet not regenerated, Simon Magus. Of course it is possible to form a theory to explain such cases—as that the baptismal grace was very early stifled and destroyed in these men; but we appeal to the plain facts of the case, and ask if it is reasonable to expect us to believe in a change so momentous as that which is alleged to have taken place when there are absolutely no traces in the actual facts. We have no evidence of the reality of regeneration in the history of the world or the Church, except from what we see of the fruits of the Spirit as contrasted with the works of the flesh: we do observe that these are very generally found in connection with the sincere profession of faith in Christ, but we also find that they are not at all invariably, or even nearly so, connected with the rite of baptism. We conclude, therefore, that baptismal regeneration, in the sense of the Church of Rome, is as much a superstitious fiction as cures by magical spells or charms.

The practical consequences of this tenet are most mischievous, for by means of it all that is good and sound in the doctrine of original sin and efficacious grace, as held even by the most Augustinian Romish divines, is virtually neutralised. Though it be held in theory that all men are born in sin, and need a great change before they can be saved or made fit for heaven; yet, since it is also taught that that change is effected in baptism, and in the case of infants without any possible doubt, then, as all within the external pale of the Church are baptized in infancy, they are led to regard themselves as free from all indwelling sin, needing no saving change, and able to merit God's favour by works of obedience. Thus all the humbling and alarming power of the doctrine of original sin is taken away and a basis laid for carelessness, low morality, and presumptuous self-confidence.

This doctrine also tends to make those of original sin and regeneration appear mere unreal technicalities. For if there is no greater difference between men dead in sin and those born again by the Spirit than there is to be seen between the baptized and the unbaptized, most people will think that this is in reality, in many cases, no moral difference at all, and that these doctrines are mere fictions of theologians, and not realities of human life and experience. The only way in which these cardinal doctrines of Christianity can be upheld is making them correspond to the moral character of men, and not to their mere ecclesiastical position or reception of outward rites. If it be held that only those who manifest Christian virtues can be known to be really born again, and that all who display an utterly worldly character are unregenerate whether baptized or not, then we can fully maintain and prove the doctrines of depravity and regeneration as great and palpable realities, but not otherwise.

A doctrine of baptismal regeneration is also maintained in the Lutheran Church, but in a very different sense from the Romish one, and far less anti-scriptural and dangerous. There is, however, some difficulty in stating precisely what the Lutheran view is, for different divines of that Church have given very diverse statements on the subject, and the forms of expression used by some are not very clear or intelligible. Neither Luther's own statements nor those of the symbolical books of his Church seem to differ essentially from the Reformed doctrine, though they emphasise different points in it. Attaching so much importance to justification by faith, they naturally deny the magical power that Romanists ascribe to the rite as a mere outward act *ex opere operato*, and make its efficacy to depend entirely on the word of God and the faith of the receiver. But at the same time they are anxious to represent it as not a merely subjective and uncertain thing, but a real objective certainty; hence they attach great importance to the word that is associated with the sign in the sacrament.[1] There is the divine word of promise, assuring us of forgiveness and regeneration, the outward sign exhibiting and confirming this, and faith receiving it; and when the sign is received in faith upon the word of promise, the thing signified by it is also certainly received. Thus

[1] See Luther's *Shorter Catechism*, part iv.

where there is faith the sacraments are always connected with the spiritual blessings that they represent, and we may be truly said to be washed from our sins and receive new life in baptism. This is exactly the doctrine of Calvin and his disciples, with only this difference, that the Lutherans hold that in such cases the spiritual blessing is bestowed or conveyed through the sacramental action, while Calvinists hold that it is given directly by the Holy Spirit, the sacrament being only the sign and seal of His work. But this only applies to the baptism of adults; while both the Lutheran and Reformed Churches agreed that infants also are to be baptized, and a difference of view emerged in regard to them. Luther attempted to carry out his view of faith being the condition of the efficacy of baptism by maintaining that infants may and do have faith, receiving it in answer to the prayer of the Church; but this was a position so obviously inconsistent with fact that it could not be held, except in the modified form, that they may have the germ or principle of faith, though incapable of its actual exercise, and in this form it was not applicable for the purpose designed.[1] Hence it came to be held by later Lutherans that in the case of infants, baptism is certainly accompanied by regeneration; while it was still held that in the case of adults it is so only when they exercise faith in the promises made and sealed in it. Such is the doctrine, *e.g.*, of Buddeus. But it was evidently illogical to make so great a distinction between the effect of baptism in the case of infants and of adults, and the tendency was to assimilate the latter case to the former, and to hold that baptism in all cases conveys to the soul a certain spiritual influence, imparting a new life, unless that is hindered by positive unbelief. Some modern Lutherans, such as Martensen, hold that baptism effects a regeneration, not, indeed, of the personal or conscious life of those who receive it, but of the nature or substance which is beyond the range of conscious-

[1] Spanheim says that the questions between Lutherans and Reformed on baptism are, whether all infants are regenerated by it? whether it is not merely a sign and seal and moral instrument of regeneration, but also has a causal efficacy, and so is ordinarily necessary, not merely as a commanded duty, but as an indispensable means?

ness, laying the foundation for the spiritual or glorified corporeity that believers look for at the last day. But this idea has no foundation in Scripture, for there is nothing to indicate that regeneration or being begotten of God is employed in two distinct senses there, and the future resurrection and glorification of the body is connected, not with baptism or any change effected by that ordinance, but with the indwelling of the Spirit of Christ in believers (Rom. $8^{11}$). It is also, as Martensen admits, a theory incapable of being verified by experience. It appears, then, that we must regard this view, as Oosterzee expresses it, "as extra-scriptural theosophy, not apostolic theology, and equally not the theology of the Reformation" (*Dogmatics*, § cxxxviii. 4. 10).

It seems to be sufficiently made out that the early divines of the English Church held substantially the same views on baptism as those of the Reformed Churches on the Continent. Their general doctrine was Calvinistic, and on this point they agreed with Calvin in ascribing as much as possible to baptism in the way of representing, sealing, and applying the highest blessings of salvation to believers, while denying to it any inherent physical or magical efficacy apart from faith. Burnet's exposition of the article (27) on baptism is substantially sound and good, and the article itself does not materially differ from the other Reformed Confessions, nor does the Westminster Confession depart from it in substance. In the Catechism it is distinctly said that it is not by the outward sign, but by the inward spiritual grace, that we are made children of grace, though at the outset the catechumen is made to say, "In my baptism I was made a member of Christ, the child of God, and an inheritor of the kingdom of heaven." But in the offices for the baptism both of infants and of adults, prayers are offered for their regeneration before the administration, and thanks given for it after. These in their most obvious sense seem to imply regeneration in baptism, and are perplexing to those who do not hold that doctrine. The earlier Anglican divines understood them as proceeding on the charitable assumption that the baptized either did, or in due time would believe; and in regard to infants, some of them seem to have held that when any are regenerated in infancy this is usually done at baptism. But in the course of time various tendencies came into play, leading men away from this position. Archbishop Laud and his followers introduced many Romanising doctrines and practices, and among these the doctrine of baptismal regeneration. But it has been held by Anglican divines in very different and sometimes fluctuating senses. Some of them, e.g. Jeremy Taylor, seem at times to coincide exactly with the Church of Rome, ascribing all the spiritual blessings of Christianity to the outward rite of baptism, though at other times they speak of faith, repentance, and other graces being required as dispositions for it, at least in the case of adults. The idea seems to be held by some that though baptism may not always produce the new life, yet that is not to be had without it; but Taylor admits that the blessings of baptism may sometimes be given before the ordinance, as in the case of Cornelius, and that in other instances they may not appear till long after. This seems, after all, to come back very nearly to Calvin's doctrine, that baptism does really convey the graces that it signifies when there is faith, but that its efficacy is not limited to the time of its administration.

Another class of Anglican divines, of whom Waterland may be mentioned as an example, make baptismal regeneration consist in a relative change, not a real and inward one.[1] It is being adopted into the family of God, put into the relation of His children; but it does not produce any real change in the disposition or character of the soul. In this way many of the difficulties that beset the idea of a spiritual change being effected by an outward rite are got rid of, and it is

---

[1] There may be said to be three views among Anglicans as to how men are said to be regenerate in baptism—

1. That they receive a germ of eternal life, which is a faculty only, not character. Goulbourn, Browne, and High Church writers.

2. That they receive an outward status, ecclesiastical regeneration. Waterland.

3. That they receive the sign and seal of spiritual regeneration, and are said by a figure to receive the thing itself. Usher, Hooker, Moule.

made more easy to maintain that all who are baptized are in this sense born again. But it gives a very peculiar and unnatural sense to the term regeneration, and tends greatly to obscure and throw into the shade the real doctrine of Scripture as to that great change. Those who take this view usually attempt to compare it with the more scriptural idea of regeneration, and are found passing from one sense of the word to another, according to the exigencies of their position.

Thus the doctrine of baptismal regeneration in all its various forms leads either to inextricable confusion or to anti-scriptural dogmas. But it has really no support in Scripture. Baptism is the divinely-appointed sign of regeneration; and sometimes our regeneration is called a baptism into Christ. The sacrament gives us the assurance that God grants forgiveness and renewal to all who believe in Christ, and is willing to bestow these blessings on their children also; and so it is a blessed help to our faith and progress in holiness. But it has no magical or mystical efficacy, nor is it indispensable, so that there can be no regeneration without it.

## The Lord's Supper

### ITS FORM, MEANING, AND EFFICACY

In treating of the second of the Christian sacraments, the Lord's Supper, we may follow the same plan as in the former, and consider—

I. The external sign in this ordinance. The institution of it is recorded by the first three evangelists, and by Paul in 1 Cor. 11$^{23}$. All these narratives agree in telling us that on the night in which He was betrayed, Jesus took bread, etc.; and the statement of Paul plainly shows that this was meant to be a permanent observance from time to time among Christians, and was actually kept as such by the early Churches. Hence it appears that the outward part of the sacrament consists of the giving and receiving and eating bread, and the giving and receiving and drinking of a cup of wine, with thanksgiving to God. There is really little more to be said positively than this, and this seems perfectly plain and sufficient. Yet there have been many questions as to the outward rite.

1. As to the matter of the elements, the Romish Church holds that the bread must be unleavened, on the ground that Christ instituted the sacrament after the Passover, when only unleavened bread was eaten. The Greek Church, on the contrary, requires the use of leavened bread, holding that the Supper at which the sacrament was instituted was not the paschal feast, but one held by anticipation on the day before it. The historical question is one of those difficult points, in regard to the details of our Lord's life on earth, about which the opinions of competent judges are still very much divided; but whatever may be the truth, it is obvious that Jesus did not specially select either the one kind of bread or the other, but took whichever He used simply because it was the one then at hand. And as there is no indication of any spiritual significance being attached to the kind of bread used, the conclusion seems to be that it is a matter of indifference whether it be leavened or unleavened, and that the bread commonly in use where the sacrament is kept ought to be taken. In like manner, questions were raised in ancient times, and have been renewed in the present day, in regard to the cup. There can be no doubt that what Jesus used was wine, as that was what was drunk in the cup of blessing at the Passover, and He calls it the fruit of the vine.[1] There were some in the first or second century who from extreme asceticism thought it their duty to abstain from all intoxicating drinks, and therefore would not use wine in the Lord's Supper, but put water in its place. Hence they were called Hydroparastatæ; and cases are referred to in various ages of individuals who could not bear the taste or smell of wine. The possibility of such cases is one of the arguments used by Romanists for refusing the cup to the laity. The difficulties, therefore, that are raised by some in the present day as to the use of wine in the

[1] It is pretty certain that as used by Jesus it was mixed with water, and I do not think there can be any objection to that practice if no symbolical meaning is attached to it, as is done by some in the Church of England.

Lord's Supper are not altogether new in the history of the Church. As to the settlement of such questions, it is plain that no precise limitation is given as to the nature of the cup. Our Saviour took that which was in common use at the time, and we best conform to His example when we use the wine that is generally drunk as a beverage among us. To attempt to define the particular kind of wine used by Him, whether fermented or unfermented, and to insist on the use of that alone, is just the same unwarranted particularity as the rules of the Greek and Romish Churches about the bread. I do not think it necessary to the ordinance that the wine used should be intoxicating, nor do I inquire whether the unfermented wine used by some is really wine at all; the simple fact that it is not an ordinary drink for nourishment and refreshment makes it unsuitable for the ordinance. If those who advocate it could bring it into common use, then it would be not inappropriate to the sacrament; but to use a peculiar drink that no one would think of taking in ordinary life, is to depart from the simplicity and significance of the ordinance. As for those who cannot safely take any wine that has intoxicating qualities, the number of such can only be very small; and it has been held by the best divines that such may use water or some ordinary beverage, rather than either abstain from the Supper entirely, or receive the bread only and not the cup (see De Moor, *in Marck. Comp.* chap. xxxi. § 6). Such is the remedy provided for extreme cases; but surely the danger of the taste of wine to reclaimed drunkards may be practically reduced to a nullity by the use of light wine mixed, if need be, with water, and by the very small sips that each communicant takes. Those who hold that the use of any intoxicating drink is absolutely and in itself wrong, are, it is to be feared, adopting the principles of those ancient heretics who held similar views; and these lead to much more serious errors. To such Manichean principles no concession can be made; but to those who abstain on grounds of expediency and Christian charity every encouragement should be given. If it should come to be the general practice of professing

Christians to abstain from wine in common life, then it might be natural and proper enough to use some other beverage in the Communion, for the spirit of the institution is that that be used which is ordinarily drunk for refreshment. But on this matter the general arrangements of the Church must be made in accordance with the views and practices of the greater part of its members, while special provision should be made for any exceptional cases that may occur. We ought, however, carefully to avoid laying any stress on the precise nature or qualities of the beverage used, for that is of no consequence to the religious use of the ordinance, and would only tend to involve men's consciences in perplexity. It may be better in itself to use purer and lighter wines than those commonly drunk among us, but the only safe rule to adopt for the Lord's Supper is to use the kind that is customary in ordinary life. The appropriateness of the symbol depends not on its being of any special nature or colour, but on its being a customary, pleasant, and refreshing drink.

2. As to the action in the sacrament, there has been some controversy about the breaking of the bread. Romanists and Lutherans do not break the bread in the actual administration of the Supper, but have it previously divided into round cakes or wafers, which they give to the communicants. The Reformed Churches, however, consider that it is more in accordance with Christ's example, and the simplicity and significance of the ordinance, to use just the ordinary bread, and to break it at the table as part of the sacramental rite.[1]

There is also a question which has a historical interest in the annals of the Scottish Church as to the posture of

[1] It has generally been held by Reformed divines that breaking the bread is a part of the symbolism of the sacrament; and if our Lord used the expression, Broken for you, in the institution, this would be clearly established. The word κλώμενον, however, in 1 Cor. 11$^{24}$ is of doubtful authenticity, so that we cannot be absolutely certain on this point; but it is at least highly probable that the breaking the bread is a significant action, and ought never to be omitted. Lutherans hold that the function of the minister is only *Consecrare et distribuere.* Buddeus, lib. v. chap. i. § 13. See also Spanheim, *Elenchus Controversiarum.*

the communicants. At the last Supper of our Lord and His disciples they reclined on couches, for that was the usual attitude at meals and feasts.[1] It seems evident also that in the apostolic age the ordinary posture at table was retained in the Supper, for that ordinance was observed in connection with the *agapæ* or love-feasts, which must have been conducted after the manner of ordinary entertainments. Paul's references to the abuses connected with the observance of the sacrament at Corinth in 1 Cor. 11 all presuppose that it was kept in this way. A relic or survival of this ancient usage is to be seen in the fact that even to this day the Pope communicates sitting. In the third century we have an indication in an incidental expression of Dionysius of Alexandria that standing was a customary posture at the Lord's table (Eus. *H. E.* vii. 9).[2] Afterwards, along with more superstitious ideas about the sacrament, the custom of kneeling came in, earlier in the East, where forms of servile adoration were more common, than in the West; and this was finally established in the Church as the proper and necessary adjunct to the doctrine of Transubstantiation.[3] If the body of our Lord be really present in or under the appearance of bread and wine, then clearly it may and should be worshipped with such adoration as is expressed by kneeling. It is not easy to say whether the doctrine produced the attitude, or the posture of worship led to the belief in the bread being the object of worship; probably the two corruptions went on by degrees hand in hand, and mutually promoted each other.

At the Reformation the doctrine of Transubstantiation was exploded by the Reformers, and in most of the Protestant Churches the attitude connected with it was more or less modified. The Lutherans adopted the practice of standing or walking by the table, which was still allowed to have the

---

[1] ἀνέκειτο (Matt. 26²⁰), ἀνέπεσε (Luke 22¹⁴).   [2] τραπέζῃ παραστάντα.

[3] It was only made a fixed rule for the whole Church by Pope Honorius III. in 1217, two years after the Lateran Council had established the doctrine of Transubstantiation. Previously it had been the custom in Italy, but not in Germany. (See Neander, *K. G.* ii. 515.)

position and form of an altar; most of the Reformed Churches, however, went back to the more primitive form of sitting at a real table, the minister being at the head of it, like the host at a common meal. In the Church of England the practice of kneeling was retained, though in the earlier times of the Reformation it was not insisted on. John Knox, for example, was allowed at Berwick and Newcastle to dispense the Communion to the people sitting; but he endeavoured in vain to get the prescription of kneeling excluded from the Liturgy, and only succeeded in obtaining the insertion of a rubric, distinctly guarding against that being supposed to imply any adoration of the elements. This rubric was omitted in the revision of the Prayer-Book in the beginning of Elizabeth's reign, but reinserted after the Restoration in 1660.

In the Church of Scotland the sitting posture was adopted from the beginning of the Reformation. Kneeling at the Communion was one of the five Articles of Perth sought to be imposed by the Royal and Prelatical party, but ever resisted by the Presbyterian; and this continues to be the usage in Presbyterian and Congregational Churches to the present day.

In favour of it are the following considerations:—

(1) It is most conformed to the example of Christ, and the earliest practice of the Church.

(2) It is most appropriate to the nature of the ordinance as a feast, and indicates most significantly the freedom and nearness of access to God that believers enjoy.

(3) The kneeling posture has been closely connected with false doctrine and idolatry, and the danger of these is best avoided by the adoption of the older attitude.

In regard to the mode of administering the sacraments in general, our Church has held strongly the essential principle that they are not to be dissociated from the preaching of the word, to which they are to be regarded as appendages. Hence the normal practice is that they be administered after sermon; and when in special circumstances this cannot be, there should at least be some exposition of the great truths of the gospel. This is a great safeguard against superstition.

II. In regard to the significance of the Lord's Supper, there is little room for discussion, for it is expressly stated by our Saviour in the words of institution that the bread signifies His body and the wine His blood. That this is so in some sense, whatever more may be true of the sacrament, is admitted by all. It is to be observed, however, that these elements do not represent Christ's body and blood abstractly and in themselves, but His body as broken and His blood as shed for us. Some writers, in explaining the symbolism of the ordinance, are led in what I think is a wrong direction by failing to observe this. They take the bread as representing Christ's body in itself, and often more particularly His body as it now is glorified in heaven; and they fancy that some resemblance or connection is indicated between it and the material element of bread. Thus Alford, commenting on the words of institution in Matt. 26, explains the bread by reference to the truth that in Christ all things consist, so that literally His glorified body is the staff of life to the universe. But this is surely a far too general explanation of this, the most specifically Christian, ordinance of the New Testament. It must represent not what Christ's body is to the world at large, but what it is to His own believing people. A further objection is, that it destroys the parallelism of the two parts of the sacrament, for Alford is obliged to give a quite different explanation of the cup from that which he gives of the bread.[1]

The true view of the meaning of the symbols is indicated by the fact that the body of Christ is represented as broken, and His blood as poured out, and that Paul declares that in this ordinance we show the Lord's death. The simple meaning of both parts of the sign is to represent the death of Christ; His body and blood in this connection stand simply

[1] Similarly, Dorner thinks that the symbolising of Christ's death is not the chief thing, and that the breaking of the bread is rather to be understood of its distribution (*Glaubenslehre*, ii. 850, 851). This is the view of the Lutheran dogmatists. (See Buddeus, lib. v. c. 1, § 13.)

for His death, as is plain from 1 Cor. 11$^{27}$, where guilty of the body and blood of the Lord can only mean guilty of His death. This is the view taken by our standards (see Confession, xxix. 1, 7 ; Larger Catechism, 168, 170, 174), and is practically important.

This simple and scriptural view of the meaning of the elements enables us to see a natural and consistent meaning in the various other parts of the ordinance. Thus the giving of the bread and wine represents the presentation of Christ crucified in the gospel, and shows the freeness of God's offer of Him to sinners ; the circumstance that it is by the hands of men that the elements are given, shows the outward means by which the gospel is made known ; and the custom, which we believe to be most scriptural, of all the communicants handing them one to another, and not all receiving them from the minister, teaches that all believers have a work to do in testifying of Christ to their brethren, and seeking to lead them to receive Him. Then the receiving of the elements represents the faith by which we receive and rest on Christ as offered to us in the gospel ; and the nourishment and refreshment that bread and wine give to the body symbolise the spiritual life and blessedness that come through faith in Christ. Thus the whole ordinance, though as simple as possible, is yet very rich in spiritual meaning.

III. As to the efficacy of the Lord's Supper, the question resolves itself into an inquiry about the connection between the sign and the thing signified ; and the great division of opinion may be said to be on the point whether that connection is bodily or spiritual. Nearly all Christians admit that there is a real connection, so that the body and blood of Christ may be said to be really present to believers in the Supper ; but there is a great difference as to the nature of the presence asserted by different Churches. Pretty early in the history of the Church exaggerated language came to be used about this as well as the other sacrament, and effects and blessings were ascribed to it that properly belong only to the spiritual realities represented by it. With the increasing tendency to superstitious and material ideas, these views gained the upper hand, and at the Fourth Lateran Council in 1215 Transubstantiation was decreed as the faith of the Church.

#### 1. ROMAN CATHOLIC DOCTRINE

This doctrine, which was confirmed by the Council of Trent, may be analysed into the following positions:—

1. That Christ's body and blood are really present, contained under the appearance of bread and wine, the substance of the bread being changed into the body, and that of the wine into the blood of Christ, the accidents of the bread and wine alone remaining (see *Conc. Lat.* iv. c. i., *apud* Hagenbach, *D. G.* p. 469). The peculiar form of this doctrine is due to the fact, that while it was held that the elements are changed into the body and blood of Christ, it is obvious that there is no change whatever in the appearance which they present to the senses. In order to reconcile these two things, recourse was had to the metaphysical distinction of substance and accidents. This distinction was understood by the realistic philosophers of that scholastic age as one of different parts of things that had each an objective reality, and might exist apart from one another. The substance or essence of a thing, the "form" of Aristotle, the "idea" of Plato, was regarded as a real entity, and hence it was possible to conceive that it might be removed or changed, though the accidents, *i.e.* the non-essential qualities, remained the same. This is what was held to take place in the consecrated elements. The accidents or qualities of whiteness, roundness, taste, nutritiousness remain, but the substance in which they inhered is entirely changed, and instead of it there is present the body and blood of Christ. These accidents, however, do not properly belong to the body of Christ, and so it has generally been held that they exist without any subject in which they properly inhere.[1] This doctrine is obviously based entirely

---

[1] This metaphysical subtlety is supposed to be a literal interpretation of Christ's words: "This is My body"!

High Anglicans also profess to give a literal interpretation. Wilberforce, *Doctrine of the Eucharist*, says the words assert an identity of subject and predicate (p. 98) which consists in this, that the subject and predicate make

on the realistic theory of the real existence of the forms or essences of things, and its ground is entirely removed if that theory be not true. But it must appear in the light of modern philosophy that the theory of Realism has no evidence to support it. There is, indeed, an intelligible distinction between substance and accident, and in the logical study of any object of thought or knowledge we must analyse it into these two. We find in it certain qualities which we can by abstraction contemplate separately, and we call them accidents; but we also find that we cannot conceive of any of them existing by itself, but must imagine it as inherent in something, and therefore we say that there is besides the qualities a something in which they inhere, which we call substance. But while we can conceive all the qualities of an object separately, we have no reason to believe that they can exist separately from the substance. The distinction is entirely due to our power of abstraction, and consists simply in different aspects of things; but the only things that we really know to exist are not substances and qualities separately, but substances possessing qualities. A round white piece of bread we know to exist, and we can think of its roundness, whiteness, and other qualities separately, and we know also that there is something that is round, white, etc.; but we only know the substance by its qualities, and apart from these we have no means of distinguishing one substance from another.

2. Transubstantiation is held to be effected by the act of the priest pronouncing in Latin the words of institution, *Hoc est corpus meum.* It only needs that he be duly ordained by a bishop having unbroken apostolic succession, and that he have the intention of doing what the Church does in the sacrament. This assumed power is, indeed, the chief dis-

up together a real but heterogeneous whole (p. 99), so that he who receives the one receives the other also. So long as we remain in the region of the senses, and take account only of that which is visible to the outward world, the *sacramentum* is all which we know of; but judge of the matter by faith and revelation, and we are sure that the *res sacramenti* is present also (p. 102). Thus, as he says, he differs only verbally from Thomas Aquinas, for by substance he meant, according to the Aristotelian conception, not the material, but that which is an object only to the intellect, the *res sacramenti* (p. 108).

tinction and prerogative of the priestly office, and marks it out on the Romish theory as an order superior to that of ordinary Christians. The priest possesses this tremendous power of making bread into the body of the Lord for the spiritual life of the people (*conficere corpus domini*), and the bishop possesses the still higher prerogative of giving that power to whom he will. Thus the hierarchy in the Roman Catholic Church is not a mere titular gradation or distinction of rank and authority, but a distinction of orders resting on the possession of mysterious supernatural power. So far all is consistent.

The doctrine of the necessity of the priest's intention, however, introduces an element of embarrassment. For no one can possibly be certain of the secret intention of another's heart; and yet if the priest go through the outward actions never so regularly without it, the mysterious change does not take place, and the bread and wine remain what they were. Yet on the reality of the change depends the worship that is given to them. If they are not really transubstantiated, then, even on the Romish theory, the worship of them would be idolatry. Hence no Romanist can be absolutely sure that he is not guilty of that sin, for he can have no certainty as to the intention of the priest in any particular case. This inconsistency, however, seems to be inseparable from the system; for if once such power is ascribed to the priest, it would be monstrous to say that he could exercise it against or without his own will.

3. Another point in the Romish doctrine of the Lord's Supper is that in it a sacrifice is offered by the priest to God for the remission of sins. The priest, having changed the elements into the body and blood of Christ, proceeds to offer them to God; and this is held to be a repetition of the sacrifice of Christ on the Cross, and to procure pardon not only for those present and joining in the service, but for any for whom it may be offered, and for the dead as well as the living. This sacrificial idea harmonises well with that of Transubstantiation; and though it is of independent origin and growth, its development seems to have nearly kept pace

with the other. That, as we have seen, arose from the gradual materialising of the symbolical meaning of the sacrament and the words of institution. The doctrine of the sacrifice in the Eucharist sprang from a perversion of another Christian idea. The New Testament teaching is that all believers are priests to God, and as such are called to offer, not propitiatory, but eucharistic sacrifices. They do this by dedicating themselves to God (Rom. 12¹), and also by offering praise and thanks, and by deeds of benevolence and charity (Heb. 13¹⁵, ¹⁶). The gifts that they contributed for pious purposes might, in this sense, be called offerings or sacrifices; and in early times, before the language had been perverted to an unscriptural effect, it was freely used. Now it was anciently the custom that the bread and wine used in the Lord's Supper were contributed by the freewill offerings of the people, as the provisions of the *agapæ* also were; and the presentation of them came to form a part of the worship, like the offertory in the Church of England, and to be accompanied with prayers for the acceptance of the gifts as thank-offerings and expressions of the self-dedication of the worshippers. This stage in the progress of the worship is illustrated copiously by Bunsen in his work on Hippolytus and his age. Gradually, however, the true idea of the universal priesthood of believers was forgotten, and that of the priesthood of Christian ministers came in its stead; and then the original meaning of the prayers offering the elements was no longer understood, and they began to be regarded as sacrifices offered by the clergy as priests; and as the prayers of oblation were accompanied with those for forgiveness and other spiritual blessings, the sacrifice came to be regarded as expiatory. This perversion of scriptural ideas, harmonising with the idea of the real presence of the body and blood of Christ, led on to the full-blown Romish doctrine of the sacrifice of the Mass—a doctrine glaringly inconsistent with the emphatic statements of Scripture, that there is no other propitiation for our sins but the one perfect and all-sufficient sacrifice of Christ. This doctrine of sacrifice may be said to be the most radical and fatal error in the Romish view of the sacrament. It altogether alters and perverts its meaning, for it ascribes to it an efficacy quite different from that which it has as received by communicants. On the sacrificial theory it has a power not at all of applying Christ's benefits to us, but of procuring from God these benefits by an additional offering of Christ, and thus it may benefit those who do not partake of it at all, but are merely spectators; nay, even those who are absent or dead. Anything more entirely opposed to the nature and character of the ordinance as represented in Scripture, it is impossible to conceive.

Still further, it is maintained that the true body and blood of Christ are received by the mouths of the communicants; and, finally, that they are received by all alike, whether good or bad, believing or unbelieving, though they are salutary only to the former and deadly to the latter. But as these points are of comparatively less importance in the Romish system, while they are maintained also by Lutherans and play a more leading part in their doctrine, we may defer any remarks on them till we have examined the principle of the Lutheran view.

### B. LUTHERAN DOCTRINE

Luther, who did such noble service to the cause of pure Christianity by restoring the great truths of the gospel after they had been buried for ages in the Roman Catholic Church, rejected the most fundamental and dangerous principles of the Romish doctrine of the Supper, namely, the notion of its being a sacrifice, the change of the substance of the elements, and the dependence of the presence of Christ on the act of the priest. Thus he and all his followers deny the first three of the positions implied in the Romish doctrine, and by doing so entirely alter its nature and spirit. The Supper is no longer regarded as a propitiatory offering or a repetition of the sacrifice of Christ, it is rather looked on as an act of communion with Christ. So far we can perfectly sympathise and agree with the Lutheran doctrine. It was an immense improvement on the Romish view, and swept away its most unscriptural parts. But Luther still clung to a real presence of the body and blood of Christ in the sacrament. He held that the substance of the bread and wine was not indeed changed, but still remained along with the accidents; but that the substance of the body and blood of Christ was also present in, with, or under the bread and wine. This position is what is generally described as consubstantiation; but that term does not occur in the authorised Lutheran standards, and is repudiated by some of their theologians (*e.g.* Buddeus). Something like the same idea had been maintained by John of Damascus in the Greek Church before the scholastic doctrine of Transubstantiation was wrought out. The illustration used by him and also by Luther is that of the existence of fire in a live coal where the coal remains what it was, but is not merely coal but coal with fire in it. There is, however, this obvious difficulty, that in the consecrated elements there is no sensible appearance of anything more than bread and wine, and that if Christ's body be really present it is strange that it should not be perceptible by any of our senses. What do we mean when we say that a body is present to us, except that it presents itself as an object to one or more of our senses? The notion of a real but entirely insensible presence of the body of Christ along with the real bread seems even more difficult to grasp than that of a presence as the substance of the accidents of bread. Another difficulty of the Lutheran notion of the real presence, is how the body of Christ can be present in so many places when the sacrament is administered at once. In order to evade this, Luther and his disciples have adopted the theory that the divine attribute of ubiquity is communicated to the human nature of Christ in virtue of the hypostatic union. This, however, rests upon a wrong view of the union of deity and humanity in Christ's person, and tends to destroy the reality of His human nature. Besides, even if this view of the hypostatic union were true, it would be inappropriate for the purpose in hand; for it would manifestly prove too much, since on that theory Christ's body might be said to be present everywhere in every piece of bread as well as in the Supper. The consideration of this might lead us to suppose that the Lutherans really meant by the assertion of the presence of Christ's body in the Supper, that we really are made partakers of Christ in this ordinance; and in this even Zwinglians and Calvinists would agree with them. But that Luther and his followers meant more than this appears from their other positions. They maintain—

2. That the body and blood of Christ are received by the mouths of the communicants (*manducatio oralis*), and not simply by faith in their hearts. It is explained, indeed, that this is not done in an ordinary natural way, but in a supernatural and heavenly manner; not so that the Saviour's body is torn by the teeth, but yet so that it is really received by the mouth in, with, or under the bread and wine. On this point the Lutherans insist strongly; also—

3. That not only believers who worthily partake of the ordinance in the exercise of faith, but all who receive it even though they have no faith, receive and eat and drink the real body and blood of Christ, though it is only when there is faith in the soul that such reception is profitable and life-giving. This position they support by the saying of Paul, that he that eats and drinks unworthily is guilty of the body and blood of the Lord,—inferring from that that such a one must really receive the Lord's body and blood, for unless he did so he could not be guilty of a sin against them. Then they use this as a proof of the oral reception; for they argue, if the Lord's body be received even by unbelievers it cannot be by faith that it is received, since they have no faith; it must therefore be by the bodily mouth in the act of eating, which is common to all communicants alike, whether believing or not.

It seems probable that Luther's great aim in retaining so firmly as he did these points in the previously current doctrine of the Supper, was to preserve the objective character of the blessing bestowed in it, which seemed to him to be endangered by the way in which Zwingli and his friends spoke of it. When they described the sacrament as a commemoration of the death of Christ, and said that His body and blood are only present to our faith, they seemed to Luther to make the communion with Christ in the sacrament to depend on our own subjective thoughts, and so to be merely imaginary. Perhaps in reality some of their expressions were inadequate, and gave some occasion to such an idea. But Luther in his anxiety to maintain a real communion with Christ not dependent on our thoughts or feelings, but certain and independent, thought it necessary to assert a real presence of Christ in the elements, even to those who have no faith, and from this flowed the three positions just indicated. The biblical evidence for them he thought he found in the words of Christ, "This is My body," which he insisted must be literally understood; and all the difficulties and contradictions that his doctrine was shown to involve he regarded as mere objections of rationalists, to be met by a simple appeal to the omnipotence of God, and the fact that there are in His word mysteries transcending human reason. This, indeed, would be a sufficient answer to the objections, if the doctrine against which they are made were certainly taught in Scripture. But the very question is whether it is so taught, and Luther's argument constantly turns round in a circle, or assumes what needs to be proved.

### C. ZWINGLIAN DOCTRINE

The element that was overlooked by Luther was clearly and emphatically brought out by Zwingli, that the Lord's Supper refers to the death of Christ for us. The fundamental idea in his teaching is, that the broken bread and outpoured wine represents the death of Christ; and in some of his statements he did not go beyond this, and asserted, or was understood to assert, that the bread and wine are nothing more than signs of Christ's broken body and shed blood, recalling to our memory what He has done for us and the blessings He has obtained. The use of them is simply that they lead us to think of Christ as our Saviour, and that in them we profess our faith in Him. This was all the length the Swiss Protestants would go at an earlier stage of the discussion, when the only alternatives present to their minds were the Romish and Lutheran doctrines, both of which they recognised as superstitious, and not founded on Scripture. But afterwards, when some of the Lutherans, particularly Brentz, Bucer, and Melancthon, departing from Luther's idea of a local bodily presence and oral reception of Christ, maintained a spiritual communion with Him in the Supper; and when Calvin, whose views otherwise were akin to theirs, also adopted that intermediate idea, the followers of Zwingli came to see that they could and should recognise the sacraments as not merely signs, but also seals and means of grace which the Holy Spirit uses to maintain and promote our real though spiritual communion with Christ. This view was expressed in the *Consensus Tigurinus*, 1549, and in most of the Reformed Confessions, though some of them incline towards ascribing much, and others to ascribing little, to the sacrament. The old Zwinglian doctrine of their being mere signs or badges and nothing more, was afterwards held only by the Socinians and some Arminians, because their general system of doctrine did not recognise any supernatural work of the Spirit in the conversion and sanctification of men.

## *b*. REFORMED DOCTRINE

The doctrine in which the great body of the evangelical Churches have ultimately acquiesced may be best explained by a brief exposition of the statements of the Westminster Standards. We may take the Shorter Catechism as the briefest and most comprehensive. "The Lord's Supper is a sacrament, wherein by giving and receiving bread and wine, according to Christ's appointment (the outward action), His death is showed forth." This is the first object and effect of it, and it is this commemorative character of the ordinance that was lost sight of by Luther, and especially brought out by Zwingli. It is expressly asserted in the very words of the Catechism by Paul (1 Cor. 11[26]), and it is this aspect of the sacrament as a commemoration of the one sacrifice of Christ that most directly excludes the Romish doctrine of its being itself a sacrifice.

But, further, "the worthy receivers are . . . made partakers of His body and blood, with all His benefits, to their spiritual nourishment and growth in grace." This is the aspect of the Supper that was overlooked by Zwingli and brought into due recognition especially by Calvin : that in the ordinance we do not merely commemorate the death of Christ for us, but also have communion with Him as the food of our souls. That this also is a true and scriptural idea appears from what our Lord says in John 6 about our abiding in Him by eating His flesh and drinking His blood, and also by the words of Paul (1 Cor. 10$^{16}$). The Lord's Supper is a means of grace as well as a sign and seal of the covenant; because in the right observance of it we do feed upon Christ, and our souls are nourished by Him as the bread of life.

This is done, the Catechism explains, "not after a corporal or carnal manner, but by faith." The negative statement here excludes the Romish and Lutheran doctrines of a bodily reception of Christ's body and blood with the mouth, either as underlying the accidents of the bread and wine, or as locally present in, with, or under them. In opposition to these views it is said they are received by faith. Here, however, it is to be observed, faith is spoken of as the mode of receiving, in opposition to any corporal or carnal manner, and not as the power by which the reception is effected. The statement must be understood in harmony with what the Catechism had just before said, that the sacraments became effectual by the blessing of Christ, and the working of His Spirit in them that by faith receive them. The faith itself by which we feed upon Christ is the gift of God and the work of His Spirit, who in the right use of the sacrament applies to us the redemption purchased by Christ. It is clear also that on this view only those who have faith, *i.e.* the worthy receivers, are made partakers of Christ ; those who have no faith cannot receive Him in this spiritual way, and as there is no other reception of Christ in the sacrament, unbelievers can only receive the external elements of bread and wine.

So far all the Reformed Churches are agreed, and these are the most essential points of the doctrine. But there is among them some difference of view and statement as to what precisely is meant by the body and blood of Christ which believers are said to receive. There were some who understood by this the exalted and glorified humanity of Christ, and held that in a mysterious way we are made partakers of this; not, indeed, as the Lutherans thought, by its being present in, with, or under the bread and wine, but by a certain virtue or power flowing from it. This was the opinion of Calvin, and it was associated by him with a speculation about the essence of Christ's glorified body consisting of power, so that it could be said that we are really united to the substance of His flesh and blood, although He is in heaven and we on earth. Of the Reformed Confessions, the one which most strongly expresses this view is the Gallican, Art. xxxvi., and it is worthy of note that the French National Synod at Rochelle in 1571 refused to comply with a request to alter the wording of that article so as to exclude the word substance, though the next Synod in the following year added an explanation, that they did not condemn those Churches that could not agree to the statement that Christ feeds us with the substance of His flesh and blood. The Belgic Confession seems also to incline in the same direction, Art. xxxv.; but it does not seem to have been regarded as teaching so explicitly the doctrine of Calvin as the Gallican, since it was unanimously approved, without exception or alteration, at the Synod of Dort, not only by all the members of the Synod, but by all the representatives of foreign Churches. The old Scottish Confession of 1560 also speaks very strongly against the Zwinglian view of the sacraments as "nothing else but naked and bare signs," and says that "as the eternal Godhead has given to the flesh of Christ Jesus (which of its own condition and nature was mortal and corruptible) life and immortality, so does Christ's flesh and blood, eaten and drunken by us, give us the same prerogatives." But the later Helvetic Confession, the Heidelberg Catechism, the XXXIX. Articles, and the Westminster Standards, contain another and simpler view of the subject. Instead of understanding the body and blood of Christ, which, they declare, believers really receive, to be His glorified humanity in heaven, they explain it as meaning His body as broken and His blood as shed for us, i.e. His death. *Conf.* xxix. 7, " receive and feed upon Christ crucified, and all the benefits of His death." This seems a simpler and more scriptural view of the matter. The body and blood of Christ means His death; the communion of His body and blood is exactly parallel to the fellowship of His sufferings, being crucified with Him, planted together in the likeness of His death, etc. This is the union with Christ, dwelling in Him and He in us, which we have by faith through the operation of the Holy Spirit, and which is represented and sealed to us by the outward elements and actions of the Supper.

The various attempts that were made in the sixteenth and seventeenth centuries to effect a union of the Lutheran and Reformed Churches on the ground of the common principle above indicated all failed, and all interest in such efforts was lost in the decay of spiritual life and sound doctrine during the rationalistic age, when the views of many on the sacraments fell back to the Socinian, or to yet lower forms of opinion. The union of the Churches in Prussia and other parts of Germany in 1817 was largely a work of statecraft, and was brought about by simply allowing each body to retain its own belief and worship. It was not based on any common principles, even to a limited extent, in regard to the doctrine of the Supper, and therefore had not directly any doctrinal significance or importance. But the movement towards union led many theologians to attempt a reconciliation of the sacramental views of the different Churches, and to endeavour not only to mark out a foundation of principles held in common, but to develop a more mature form of the doctrine than any single one previously held, which might unite harmoniously the elements of truth contained in each. Schleiermacher states very clearly and correctly the positions of the different Churches, and points out the common ground which they occupy as protesting against Romanism on the one hand and Socinianism on the other; and he also indicates the three different forms of opinion within this common ground, the Zwinglian and Lutheran being the two more extreme, and the Calvinistic occupying a central position. He does not himself attempt the development of a system that could embrace the true points of them all in a higher unity, but he declares that to be the desideratum and problem for theology in this department.

Ebrard, in his work on *The Doctrine of the Lord's Supper*, has grappled with this problem, and endeavoured to solve it mainly by a further working out and more distinct articulation of Calvin's view; but his theory has not found acceptance either with the adherents of the Lutheran doctrine, such as Kahnis, or with a Presbyterian divine like Dr. Hodge, who stands substantially and almost literally in the same position as the *Consensus Tigurinus*.

Kahnis is not quite a thorough-going adherent of the Lutheran doctrine on this point, but has been severely blamed by Hengstenberg for deviating from orthodoxy in regard to the Lord's Supper as well as other points, and he admits that the doctrine of Luther has its weak and untenable side. He holds that the words of institution cannot be interpreted literally, and that they do not refer to Christ's glorified body in heaven, but to that which was crucified on Calvary. He sums up his view thus: "The progress from the symbolical apprehension (Zwingli) proceeds from the point of view, that divinely-ordained symbols, which are appropriated to us for enjoyment, are a visible word of God, *i.e.* a sacrament. What is appropriated to us is the death of Christ in its power, especially forgiveness of sins. While everyone, even the unworthy, objectively receives this divine pledge of the sacrificial death of Christ, yet it is only to the believer for the forgiveness of sins. Only so can the Lutheran determination of the purpose of the Supper be maintained. But he who receives the death of Christ in its efficacy, the forgiveness of sins, enters into mysterious connection with the body of Christ itself, since the forgiveness of sins is the power inhering in the body of Christ. Only so, I believe, can the substance of the Lutheran doctrine of the Supper be maintained; and if I am not mistaken there lies herein the possibility of a higher union of the Lutheran and Reformed doctrine" (*Zeugniss von den Grundwahrheiten des Protestantismus*, p. 29).

This seems a better mode of reconciliation than that of

Ebrard, and, in fact, we could accept almost every word of the above statement.

That the difference even between the Lutheran and Reformed Churches is at bottom not so great as it has often appeared in controversy, may be seen from the interesting fact observed by Ebrard (*Abendmahl*, ii. p. 778), that in the classical hymn of the Lutheran Church ("*Schmücke dich O liebe Seele*") the Reformed modes of expressions are used. The thing that the best Lutheran divines had mainly at heart was to maintain that the believer's communion with Christ in the sacrament is a reality, and not a mere imagination or subjective exercise of faith and feeling; but the form they adopted to express this was a very unfortunate one, and gave too much countenance to superstitious notions.

We, too, are anxious to maintain that our communion with Christ in the Supper is not a merely imaginary one, due merely to the strength and liveliness of our faith, but real and true, depending on what is sure and certain, apart from our changing moods. But we think this can be maintained perfectly well without making the partaking of Christ depend on the outward elements or actions in the sacrament, by recognising that it is due to the blessing of Christ at the first institution of the sacrament and the working of His Spirit in our hearts.

Considerable confusion is caused by the various uses of the phrases presence, real, objective, subjective, spiritual.

This may be cleared up by asking in each case what is present? and when?

If that which is present be the literal body of Christ, as now glorified in heaven, then since that body is still material, if it be really present at all, it must be present in a bodily way; it may be said to be a heavenly, mysterious, supernatural presence, to denote that a special agency of divine power is at work in it; but to speak of the spiritual presence of a body seems utterly meaningless. If the question then is as to the glorified body of Christ, we should deny its real presence.

But if the question is as to Christ Himself, we maintain

that He is really present, according to His promise: "Lo, I am with you always," etc.; and this presence, though spiritual, is also objective, and not merely subjective.

We also say that His body and blood are present. If these words be understood to mean the death of Christ, it is present to our faith, the evidence of things not seen: this may be called a subjective presence.

Again, where is the presence? If it be held to be in the elements, we deny that it is real; but if it be in the soul of the believer when he receives the elements, then we say it is real, though spiritual; and this is what is sometimes meant by a subjective as distinguished from an objective presence. In this sense, too, we recognise a presence, not only of Christ, but of His body and blood, *i.e.* of His death.

In regard to the subjects of the Lord's Supper, or the persons to whom it should be administered, it follows necessarily and obviously from what we have seen to be the scriptural doctrine of its nature and efficacy, that they are believers professing their faith in Christ. It is only those who have faith in the Lord Jesus who really feed upon Him in the sacrament; to others it is merely an external rite without meaning or use, and their merely formal observance of it cannot profit them, but tends rather to burden their hearts, and involves the guilt of despising and abusing a most significant and solemn ordinance of Christ. It is clear also from what is recorded of the sacrament in the New Testament that it is meant for true Christians only.

When it was instituted our Lord was alone with His disciples, and addressed them as His friends who trusted in Him as the Messiah and Saviour.

It was observed by the early believers after the day of Pentecost as a mark and token of their discipleship (Acts $2^{46}$); it is the disciples that come together to break bread (Acts $20^7$); and Paul represents the ordinance as binding those who partake of it in a common and holy brotherhood, just as the sacrifices in Jewish and heathen worship implied that the offerers were of these religious fellowships (1 Cor. $10^{16-21}$).

There are doubtless two aspects in which the qualifications necessary for the Lord's Supper may be viewed, and two different modes of stating them according as we look to the duty of the individual applicant or at that of the Church. It is one question, Who ought to come to the Lord's table, or Ought I, for one, to do so? and another question, Who ought to be admitted by the Church? But the answers to both questions are closely connected, and both flow from the same general principle as to the nature and efficacy of the sacrament. The answer to the former must be that it is only true believers that ought to come, and consequently that the point for everyone to consider for himself is whether he is truly a believer in Christ or not. This is a matter on which we believe a man may, by the teaching of the Spirit, attain a certain knowledge for himself. But it is not possible for others to know certainly whether he is sincere and right in his profession or not. Hence, while it is only true believers in Christ that ought to come to the Lord's table, yet when the question is, who should be admitted by the Church, the answer must be, those who make a credible profession of faith. The difference between the common principle and practice of the Reformed Churches and those of the Anabaptists and Plymouthists in the present day consists in this, that the former recognise, while the latter do not recognise, the above distinction. On this question Jonathan Edwards and the Independents are on the side of the common Reformed doctrine, and do not deny or ignore the distinction. On this point, therefore, they do not really differ from Presbyterians.

Independents do not say that none should be admitted but those who are really converted, or that the Church can certainly tell who are so.

Presbyterians do not say that any should be admitted of whom the Church does not form a judgment that they are converted.

The difference between them is solely as to what is the ground of this judgment.

Dr. Hodge says (*Syst. Theol.* iii. 569) that Edwards in

his Essay on the Qualifications for Communion lays down one proposition and proves another; that what he proposes to prove is, that only those who in the judgment of the Church are godly or gracious persons are to be admitted, but that all his arguments are directed to prove that those who come to the Christian sacraments profess to be Christians. This is not the case in point of fact with all his arguments, for several of them are manifestly directed to prove the former proposition, and, if they are valid, do prove it. It is to be observed also that Edwards always joins together profession and visibility, and considers the profession of the applicant one main ground of the Church's judgment. Such are his arguments from the representations of the Church in the parables, and the way the Churches are addressed in the Epistles. Dr. Hodge does not hold that a man's own profession is the only ground of his admission, it must be a credible profession, and the only point of difference would seem to be what kind or amount of corroboration from life and character does the profession require. But this is merely a question of detail, not of principle, as Dr. Hodge seems to represent it. In fact, Dr. Hodge may much more plausibly be charged with logical inconsistency here than Edwards. For once and again in his discussion of the subject he dwells on the evils and dangers of limiting the Church to the communicants (pp. 572, 577–579), and advocates the right of giving baptism to the children of those themselves baptized though they are not admitted as communicants. But this can only be done on the assumption either that Church membership does not imply a profession of faith, or that the Lord's Supper requires something more. Yet he does not admit either of these, and, moreover, he expressly holds that the qualifications for both sacraments are the same (p. 574). How these positions are to be reconciled I cannot see.

The general principle held alike by Presbyterians and Independents seems to be simply this, that those who make a credible profession of faith are to be treated as true believers and members of the visible Church, entitled and bound to receive the sacraments, and that their children are to be baptized.

It is the duty of the Church to judge of the profession of applicants, and there is a slight difference of opinion as to the evidence required to make a profession credible in the eyes of the Church.

# ESCHATOLOGY

## I. MEANING OF LIFE AND DEATH IN THE NEW TESTAMENT

### 1. IN THE TEACHING OF JESUS

IN several of His sayings recorded in the synoptic Gospels Jesus associates the idea of life or eternal life with that of the kingdom of God as parallel and synonymous terms. This statement in my Cunningham Lectures on *The Kingdom of God* (pp. 134, 135) is objected to by Mr. V. H. Stanton in his work, *The Jewish and the Christian Messiah* (p. 222 n.), in which he has expressed very generous appreciation and agreement with much in my exposition of the biblical notion of the kingdom of God. He thinks that Matt. $25^{31\text{ff.}}$ is the only passage which would seem to support so strong a statement. There the Judge says to those on His right hand, "Inherit the kingdom prepared for you" (v.$^{34}$), while in v.$^{46}$ it is explained, "The righteous shall go into life eternal." But is there not the same parallel use of these expressions in the Sermon on the Mount, since in Matt. $7^{14}$ Jesus says, "Strait is the gate, and narrow is the way, that leadeth unto life"; and in v.$^{21}$, "Not every one that saith to Me, Lord, Lord, shall enter the kingdom of heaven"; and again all the synoptic evangelists tell of the rich young ruler inquiring, "What shall I do that I may inherit eternal life?" and Jesus' saying in connection with that incident, "How hardly shall they that have riches enter the kingdom of God"? It might perhaps be thought that these sayings only refer to eternal life as a future blessing, and connect it with the kingdom of God in its ultimate manifestation in glory, but not with that kingdom as already present in Jesus' coming and work, and therefore that life is not absolutely identified with the kingdom. This seems to be Mr. Stanton's view. But there are other passages where life is not so plainly connected with the kingdom of God, but where it is opposed to death in such a way as to show that Jesus spoke of life as a blessing now enjoyed by those who believed in Him, in contrast to worldlings.

One of the most striking characteristics of our Lord's mode of speaking was, that He described bodily death in the case of His disciples as a sleep (Matt. $9^{24}$, Mark $5^{39}$, Luke $8^{52}$, John $11^{11}$); while, on the other hand, He spoke of some who were living in this world as dead, or having no life in them. This latter form of speech occurs repeatedly in the Fourth Gospel; in the others the most distinct instance is Jesus' striking saying to the disciple who asked leave to go and bury his father before obeying the call to follow Him, "Let the dead bury their dead" (Matt. $8^{22}$, Luke $9^{60}$). The Master saw the danger of this disciple being drawn back into a worldly life by what in itself was a proper and dutiful office, and so He said, Those who are dead to Me and My message may be left to do such services, there is more urgent and blessed work which only the living can do; thou, who hast received life, art called to follow Me and proclaim the kingdom of God. Here, especially in the form in which Luke gives the saying, it is implied that the kingdom of God involves the possession of a life of which the world is destitute, and the preaching of the kingdom is the spreading of that life.[1] This is in accordance with the sayings recorded in John $5^{24, 25}$, "He that heareth My word, and believeth on Him that sent Me, hath eternal life . . . hath passed out of death into life . . . the hour cometh, and now is, when the dead shall hear the voice of the Son of God; and they that hear shall live"; and that life or eternal life is only to be had by faith in Christ is also declared in John $5^{41}$ $6^{40, 47, 51, 53, 54}$ $10^{10, 27}$. These passages clearly speak of a life to be received even now, and no otherwise is it meant when

---

[1] There is a temptation to adduce in support of this Luke $5^{10}$, ἀνθρώπους ἔσῃ ζωγρῶν, "thou shalt take alive (or possibly revive) men"; cf. 2 Tim. $2^{26}$ R.V. But this would be very precarious, and the meaning of 2 Tim. $2^{26}$ is doubtful.

Jesus, impressing on those who would be His disciples the necessity of giving up whatever would cause them to offend, said solemnly, " It is good for thee to enter into life halt or maimed," etc. (Matt. 18$^{8,\ 9}$, Mark 9$^{43,\ 45,\ 47}$). For it cannot be supposed that on entering the final glory of the kingdom any of the saved could be described as halt or maimed; that must refer to their now obtaining the true life at the cost of what would have made their natures full and complete in this world.

But what exactly did Jesus mean by that eternal life, the absence of which in worldly men He called death ? His sayings about it show that He regarded it as having relation to God : " He is not the God of the dead, but of the living: for all live to Him " (Luke 20$^{38}$). God is the source of all life ; and that life only is worthy of the name in which man is united to God. But this union must be a moral one. According to the teaching of the law and the prophets, Jesus declared that to have eternal life we must keep the commandments, the first and greatest of which is to love God with all the heart, and the second to love our neighbour as ourself (Luke 10$^{29}$, Matt. 19$^{17}$, and parallels). A soul possessed with supreme love to God, and with that love to men that is in agreement with God's regard for them, is united to God by ties of love and sympathy ; and this fellowship with God is what Jesus calls life. Where this is absent there is death. So in the parable of the Prodigal, the younger son while forgetful of his father, and spending his substance in a way abhorrent to him, is described as dead, lost, being to his father as if he were not ; but when he returned with a penitent affection to his father he is alive again, once more a sharer in the feelings and emotions that form the life of the family. Thus we see how it was that Jesus connected life with the kingdom of God. For that kingdom was in His view a family, its members are children of the King ; nay, the connection is an even closer one, for His Spirit is in them, and so they are partakers of a life which others have not.

This conclusion, drawn from the synoptic Gospels, is in beautiful accordance with the statement in Jesus' prayer in John 17$^3$, " This is eternal life, that they know Thee the only true God, and Him whom Thou hast sent, Jesus Christ." To know must here mean not merely intellectual knowledge, but personal acquaintance, such knowledge of the true character of God as can only be obtained through sympathy and love; and it is because Jesus is the perfect revelation of God's character, and could say, " He that hath seen Me hath seen the Father," that He could also declare that eternal life included the knowledge of Himself as well as of His Father.

Here may be considered that memorable saying so often repeated by Jesus in slightly varying forms, " He that findeth his life shall lose it; and he that loseth his life for My sake shall find it " (Matt. 10$^{39}$); " Whosoever would save his life shall lose it; and whosoever shall lose his life for My sake shall find it " (Matt. 16$^{25}$, Mark 8$^{35}$, Luke 9$^{25}$); " He that loveth his life loseth it; and he that hateth his life in this world shall keep it unto life eternal " (John 12$^{25}$). The last of these forms of this saying indicates most clearly the key to its meaning, though that may be gathered from the others also. For in all alike the word for life is not ζωή, that living which is opposed to being dead, and which is associated with the kingdom of God, but ψυχή, the soul, the personal animal life in which one is conscious of pleasure and pain, joy or sorrow. But in the saying as given by John it is distinctly life of the soul in this world that is spoken of in contrast to keeping the soul unto eternal life (ζωή). He that loveth or would save his life is he who lives for his personal enjoyment of earthly things, whether pleasure, or honour, or power, or love from this earth and his fellow-men, and is opposed to him who hateth and loseth his own enjoyment of such things for Christ's sake and the gospel's; that is, whose great and all-absorbing aim is to have Jesus as his Lord and King, and the glad tidings of God's kingdom as his chief joy. Of the former Jesus said he shall lose, or even now is losing his life: and so regarding what is certain and already begun as present, He describes the former as actually dead and the latter as living.

Life, then, in general, we may say, is, according to Christ's teaching, the conscious exercise of personal activities; life in this world is their exercise upon things sensible and intelligible; but since all finite things are mutable and pass away, the activity that is exercised only on them cannot be eternal, but tends to exhaust and destroy itself. Life to God is the conscious exercise of the soul's activities towards God in trust, love, gratitude, praise, prayer, obedience; and since God is eternal and infinite, His being, attributes, word and works afford an everlasting and inexhaustible object for such activities; hence the life that consists in them is everlasting. Addison sings—

> "Through all eternity to Thee
> A joyful song I'll raise,
> For, oh, eternity's too short
> To utter all Thy praise."

And what he says of praise may be said equally of every other devout exercise of the soul to God.

But a soul to which sense and the world are the highest objects of regard is destitute of such exercises towards God; and if it has voluntarily forsaken God and turned away from Him to the world, it is in a state of alienation under His displeasure, and in this state cannot exercise towards Him those religious activities in which life to God consists. For such this life is only possible through a revelation of God, which will show that sinners who have disobeyed and displeased Him may yet come to Him in humility, contrition of heart, and trust in His mercy. Now, this is the revelation that was made dimly and gradually at the beginning, and perfectly in Jesus Christ.

This conception of life may be applied to the highest life of all, that of God Himself. "The Father," said Jesus, "hath life in Himself" (John $5^{26}$). He hath life, He is the living Father (John $6^{57}$), the living and true God; and as such He is contrasted in the Old Testament with the dead idols of the heathen, in that they have no activity, neither see, nor hear, nor speak, nor do anything (Isa. $41^{23,\ 24}$, Ps. 115, Dan. $5^{23}$), whereas the true God knows, and wills, and loves, and speaks, and acts. But, further, He has this life, this fulness of activity, in Himself; He is not dependent as we are on objects outside of Himself to draw out His activity. "Before the mountains were brought forth, or ever Thou hadst made the earth and the world, from everlasting Thou art God," as truly the living God then as ever after. For, says Jesus, "Thou lovedst Me before the foundation of the world." "I had glory with Thee before the world was." The living Father had an eternal object of His love in the Son, who is one with Him; and thus He has life in Himself, the most intense activity of the highest spiritual emotions in the contemplation and love of Him who is the brightness of His glory and the express image of His person. He is the fountain of life, for He hath given to the Son to have life in Himself; and He said, "As the living Father hath sent Me, and I live by the Father; so he that eateth Me, even he shall live by Me."

### 2. IN THE EPISTLE OF JAMES

In the Epistle of James life and death are spoken of incidentally and without any full explanations, but substantially in the same way as in the sayings of Jesus recorded in the synoptic Gospels. In Jas. $1^{12}$ we read of "the crown of life which the Lord promised to them that love Him," the genitive being that of apposition, the crown which consists of life; and in chap. $2^5$ we read, "the kingdom which He promised to them that love Him." This confirms the identification of life with the kingdom of God. Again in chap. $1^{15}$ we find, "sin when it is full grown bringeth forth death." Thus life and death seem to be regarded as ultimate results rather than as present states. Death is the product of the full development of sin; life, the crown of tried and tested love. But the germ of life at least is present in believers, for ($1^{18}$) God has "brought us forth by the word of truth," and ($1^{21}$) "the implanted word is able to save our souls." The life that we have in this world is but a vapour that appears for a little and then vanishes away ($4^{14}$), and the corruption and rust of earthly riches shall at last eat into those who have made them their portion, and the end shall be a day of slaughter ($5^{1-5}$). On the other hand, he who turns a sinner from the error of his way shall save his soul out of death ($5^{20}$). Thus it would appear that even in this world the sinful, ungodly life is really death, while that which is animated by an active faith in God's word of truth is alone really worthy of the name of life. But it should be observed that while James emphasises the natural connection of death with sin and life, with faith and love as each the fruit and development of these opposite moral states (cf. $3^{11-18}$), he yet intimates very plainly that these issues come about not merely by a natural sequence, but by the supreme authority and will of the just and gracious God. "There is one lawgiver and judge, who is able to save and to destroy" ($4^{12}$). We look for the issue of our life here as the husbandman does for the harvest, but also as the coming of the Lord in person: the Judge standeth before the door ($5^{7-9}$). So in order to be saved from death it is needful not only that a sinner be turned from the error of his ways, but that his sins be forgiven him ($5^{15}$); and a Christian brother is not only to endeavour to convert a sinner, but also to pray for him ($5^{16-18}$).

Altogether the views of life and death implied in the Epistle of James seem to be as nearly as possible the same as those in our Lord's discourses in the synoptic Gospels.

### 3. IN THE TEACHING OF PAUL

In the writings of Paul the use of the terms life and death is very frequent and somewhat various. To ascertain, if possible, what precise ideas he attached to them, it will be best to examine the various passages in which they occur, in what is most probably the chronological order in which they were written.

Taking, then, first the earliest of his Epistles, the First to the Thessalonians, we find in chap. $5^{10}$ a weighty expression of the fundamental Christian faith about Christ, "who died for us, that whether we wake or sleep, we should live together with Him." Here we may observe that Paul does not give the name of death to the believer's end of bodily life, but calls it sleep, as he does also in chap. $4^{13, 15}$ and 1 Cor. $15^{20}$, using in this reference the language of Jesus about Lazarus and Jairus' daughter; while in other places he speaks of it as "departing," or "being absent from the body." He does not entirely avoid the common word death, and he uses it of men in general and of the ungodly; but of Christians he employs by preference phrases which indicate that in their case death has been robbed of its sting, and is no longer properly to be called by that name. It is significant, however, that in the case of our Saviour here and always where death is mentioned, it is never said of Him, as of Stephen, He fell asleep; what He bore was death in its truest sense. Further, it is to be noted that Christ gives us a life with Himself that is independent of the life or death of the body; a life that we have here and now while we are awake as to earthly existence, and that we have equally when the death of the body brings us into a state of sleep. This is exactly in accordance with Jesus' words in John 11[25, 26]; and it is difficult to avoid the conclusion that Paul knew of these or similar words, whether by tradition or otherwise. It may also be observed that in the preceding verse this life with Christ is identified with salvation and opposed to wrath, *i.e.* the wrath of God.

In 2 Thessalonians there is no use of the terms life and death, but in Gal. 2[19, 20] an important statement is made: "I through the law died to the law, that I might live unto God. I have been crucified with Christ; yet I live; no longer I, but Christ liveth in me." From this text, compared with the one previously considered, it appears that the life which was there described simply as living with Christ consists in having Christ living in us. This is that idea of mystical or spiritual union with Christ which is so familiar and essential in the theology of Paul as well as in that of John, and which is so vividly illustrated in our Lord's images of the Bread of Life and the True Vine in John 6 and 15. Another point that this passage adds to the former is, that the believer's life with Christ is preceded by a death which is also with him, and is called here a dying to the law. It is not a continuous state, but an event happening once for all: "I died" ($\dot{a}\pi\acute{e}\theta a\nu o\nu$); and it is effected by being crucified with Christ. This dying is to the law, *i.e.* in relation to law, not the Jewish law in particular, but God's law in general; it is a final removal from the dominion of law, for that is the scope of the apostle's argument. There may be a reference indicated by the clause "through the law" to the penal character of death; but plainly it is not the idea of the suffering involved in death that is prominent, but that of its being a cessation of the activities of life: it delivers me from the law, because it makes me virtually cease to be, so far as the law is concerned.

In Gal. $3^{21}$ "to give life" means to give to men spiritually dead the power of serving and pleasing God, so that they should be able to attain righteousness; and in Gal. $6^8$ eternal life is opposed to φθορά, corruption, the result of sowing to the flesh. This latter seems to convey the idea of wasting away, perishing along with the perishing flesh, in opposition to enduring everlasting activity in and with the Spirit, which is eternal.

In the Epistles to the Corinthians, as the contents are of very varied character, so also is the use of the terms life and death. In 1 Cor. $3^{22}$ and 2 Cor. $7^3$ they are used in the ordinary physical sense, and in 1 Cor. $7^{39}$ and $15^{18-20}$ "live" occurs in this sense, but its opposite is "fall asleep." In the latter passage (v.$^{18}$) it is said as one of the consequences of the denial of Christ's resurrection, "Then they also which have fallen asleep in Christ have perished," a broad distinction being thus made between the physical death of believers and that perishing which is elsewhere used as a synonym for death (2 Cor. $2^{16}$). As to the important text 1 Cor. $15^{22}$, "As in Adam all die, so in Christ shall all be made alive," interpreters are divided, some taking all in its fullest sense, and understanding "die" and "be made alive" of physical death and resurrection; while others would explain the statement to be, "as in Adam all who are in him die, so in Christ shall all who are in Him be made alive," and understand by "made alive" the communication of spiritual life. But the former view seems to be the more natural, and seems to be required by v.$^{24}$, where they that are Christ's are mentioned as one order of those who are to be raised. Further on in this chapter (v.$^{31}$) a familiar and easily intelligible use of "die" occurs, "I die daily," *i.e.* I am in continual danger of death; and the same idiom is found in 2 Cor. $1^{8,\ 9}$ $4^{10-14}$. In this last passage, however, the life that is contrasted with the continual imminence of bodily death is spiritual, consisting of the renewal of the inward man in faith and hope.

The statement in 2 Cor. 5$^{15}$, " one died for all, therefore all died," is of great importance, as it is one of those in which death is represented as the blessing that Christ has obtained for us, *i.e.* dying in and with Him, as Gal. 2$^{19, 20}$. Here it is not called specifically dying to the law or to any particular thing, but simply dying in virtue of Christ's death on our behalf. As united to Him and represented by Him, we share His death with all its consequences. The meaning of this is more fully explained in the Epistle to the Romans, to which we next come.

Here there is at chap. 1$^{32}$ a statement about the heathen who sin, that they know the judgment of God, that they who do such things are worthy of death. On the meaning of "death" here there is considerable difference of opinion; but the probability is that it is used in a general sense for punishment inflicted by God in the future state. Paul is asserting the moral and religious knowledge that the heathen had or might have had; but as this assumed various forms in the mythology of different peoples, he expresses it altogether from his own point of view. In Rom. 2$^{7, 13}$ he describes more fully the righteous judgment of God, and sets " eternal life " (v.$^7$) as the reward of the righteous over against anger and wrath, tribulation and anguish (v.$^8$), which is the punishment of the wicked; and in the following verses identifies the former with glory, honour, and peace (v.$^{10}$), and the latter with perishing (v.$^{12}$). Here, more distinctly than anywhere else, Paul associates eternal life with true happiness, and perishing with misery, probably on account of the nature of the subject and the fulness with which he desires to describe the divine judgment so as to show its impartiality. The term death in the important passage, Rom. 5$^{12-21}$, has been variously understood, and some, as Hodge, take it to denote the penal consequence of sin in general; but it is more natural, and seems, indeed, to be necessary in v.$^{14}$, to understand it of the decease of the body, as Meyer and Godet take it. So it is parallel to 1 Cor. 15$^{22}$.

But in the 6th and 7th chapters of this Epistle we find

the fullest exposition of the idea already indicated in those to the Galatians and Corinthians, that death with Christ is the great blessing that believers receive. The conception of death that explains this bold paradox is that of cessation of all correspondence with the previous environment, or of all relation to the world in which the life was formerly lived. So Paul says, "we died to sin" (Rom. $6^2$), and goes on to explain that this was by becoming one plant with Christ (v.$^5$), of whom he also says, "He died to sin" (v.$^{10}$). This shows that by dying to sin the apostle does not here mean a moral change, ceasing to love and serve sin, for that never could be said of Christ; but a legal change, ceasing to be under its condemnation, according to the principle stated in v.$^7$, "he that died has been justified from sin"; since he has suffered the last penalty of the law, he is altogether separated from the sin that condemned him. Paul's argument is, that since it is in this way that grace abounds, it cannot legitimately be made a motive for continuing in sin; since, if we are justified only by being separated from sin by the death of Christ, we cannot willingly keep up any connection with it; and since we die with Christ only to live with Him, and His life is a life to God, our life must henceforth be that also. In the practical enforcement of this appeal he again speaks of death as the end and wages of sin (vv.$^{21, 23}$) in the same sense as in the 1st and 2nd chapters: and then in chap. $7^{1-6}$ he gives a further illustration of the believer's death with Christ, describing it as a death to the law, so as to show how it is that, as he said before, "we are not under law" ($6^{14}$). In the illustration, death is used in the ordinary physical sense; and in the application, the point of comparison is that it removes a person from all the relations and obligations of this world, and makes him as it were non-existent.

The notions of dying and living are applied in a somewhat different sense in the subsequent paragraph ($7^{8-13}$), in which he explains from his own experience how the law though not itself sin, is yet to fallen man the occasion of sin, so that we can be freed from sin only by being freed from the law. "Apart from the law," he says, "sin is dead: and I was alive apart from the law once; but when the commandment came sin revived, and I died." To whatever period of his life Paul refers, it is plain from the previous verse that he speaks of sin and law as in his own knowledge. He was not really apart from the law, but he did not know it in its real meaning and breadth; and as long as this was so the sin that was really in him was dead, not putting forth any activity or energy; and he was alive with no sense of sin and confident of God's favour, feeling no hindrance to his activity in works of obedience. But when the commandment came home to him sin sprang into life and activity within him, and he lost his former confidence and became utterly paralysed in his efforts after holiness. Here as elsewhere the general idea of life is functional activity, and of death the absence of it, while there is included also that of happiness in the former and misery in the latter.

In the paragraph that describes the believer's deliverance from sin ($8^{1-13}$), life and death are employed as in Gal. $6^8$ to express the ultimate consequences of walking after the flesh and after the Spirit, by reason of the perishable nature of the one and the divine nature of the other.

The same idea of death and rising again with Christ as the way of our deliverance, both from the guilt and from the power of sin, is found in Col. $2^{11}-3^4$ in a more condensed form, in which a wealth of ideas is so packed into a brief compass that it is not easy to unfold them all. Christians have been buried with Christ in baptism ($2^{11}$), they have died with Him from the rudiments of the world ($2^{20}$), i.e. they have been delivered from these by being removed out of their sphere. This has been effected by the death of Christ, into which they enter by believing acceptance of Him in baptism, and in which God forgives all their transgressions and cancels the bond of a condemning law that hindered their efforts after holiness. But along with this legal deliverance from guilt there is a spiritual quickening to new life ($2^{13}$) from a death in sin, which is a state of inability and impotence to true goodness. This new life is with Christ, nay, it is Christ Himself living in them ($3^{1-4}$), and shall be fully manifested when Christ shall be revealed at His coming. This spiritual quickening, as well as the death in sin out of which it brings us, is more fully described in the parallel passage in Eph. $2^{1-10}$, where it is not complicated with the deliverance from law which Paul's special purpose in writing to the Colossians led him to interweave with it. In a later passage ($4^{17-19}$) the state of spiritual death is described as involving darkness of understanding, hardness of heart, loss of feeling, vanity of mind, *i.e.* cessation of all the functions of moral and religious life.

In the Epistle to the Philippians and the Pastoral Epistles, Paul makes many touching references to his own approaching departure, and uses the words life and death generally in their common physical sense, while he makes repeated reference to that eternal life which is the hope and promise of the gospel. In 1 Tim. $4^8$ godliness is said to have the promise of this life and of that which is to come, not in the sense in which we generally use that phrase of the present and the future time of existence, for the word is not βίος but ζωή, but rather of life, the exercise of the soul's highest functions, both now and in a future state. Opposed to this is the description in chap. $5^6$ of one living in pleasure as dead while she liveth, which is explained by Eph. $2^{1\text{ff}}$. The life that is in Christ is described in 1 Tim. $6^{19}$ as the life that is life indeed (ὄντως). Paul's latest Epistle contains a weighty statement that repeats as it were the keynote struck on this subject in his earliest (1 Thess. $5^{10}$), when he says (2 Tim. $1^{10}$) that Christ Jesus has abolished death (*i.e.* disabled it, made it powerless), and brought life and immortality to light by the gospel.

From this survey of the Pauline Epistles we may gather what was the essential idea of life and death in the apostle's mind. He employs these terms, as we have seen, in a rich variety of applications, but this gives us all the more certainty in our inference as to the idea he had of them; for if we find that one conception is suitable to all these different applications, there can be little doubt that it is the true one. Now it is plain (1) that the notion of life being mere existence, and death non-existence, will not satisfy the conditions; for though in a few places this notion might be put on the terms, consistently with the apostle's meaning, in many more it would be quite inapplicable. Those who maintain what is called the ontological sense of these terms are obliged either to interpret some passages in a very unnatural way, especially those in which men living in the world are described as dead in sins, or else to make the definition of death the cessation of an activity[1] which we believe is the true conception, but is very different from mere existence. If the ontological sense merely means that existence or non-existence is always included in the idea, that is true, of course, of life; but it is not the fact that death in Paul's writings, always includes the idea of non-existence. But it appears also (2) that the notion of life being simply holiness or happiness, and death the absence or opposite of these, is equally unfounded. There are some passages where such an explanation might be possible, but it is not suggested by any, and it would be quite inconsistent with many. Life, no doubt, is conceived as a blessing and death as an evil, but we cannot explain away the radical meaning of the words into these notions.

In distinction from both of these explanations, it appears that the notion of life in general, with Paul, is the same as that which we gather from the sayings of Jesus in the Gospels—the exercise of personal functions and activities, the nature of these determining the different kinds of life of which he speaks. The exercise of bodily or animal functions, such as respiration, sensibility, movement, constitutes physical life: when, in addition to these, there is intelligence, volition, desires, and passions, but no regard for God and moral goodness, then men though living in the world are spiritually dead, they are what Paul calls natural ($\psi\upsilon\chi\iota\kappa o\iota$) or animal men; where there is a personal knowledge of God who is spirit, and a regard for the things of spirit, there is life in the highest and truest sense; and since it unites us to God and Christ, this life is eternal. But Paul also makes very prominent the penal aspect of death as not only the consequence, but the judgment and wages of sin; and in some

---

[1] This definition is given by M. Petavel in his able and thoughtful book, *The Problem of Immortality*, p. 215, although he calls the sense for which he contends ontological, as if life were synonymous with existence.

passages this is the main idea associated with it. This is
so especially where he speaks of the death of Christ for our
sins. There the emphasis lies not on the mere cessation of
physical life-functions, nor on the sufferings He endured in
dying, but on His being made sin, made a curse for us, and
by bearing that death which is the wages of sin, reconciling
us to God.

#### 4. IN THE EPISTLE TO THE HEBREWS

In the Epistle to the Hebrews the most remarkable expression bearing on the usage of the terms life and death is the phrase "dead works" (νεκρῶν ἔργων), which occurs twice in that Epistle ($6^1$ $9^{14}$), and nowhere else in New Testament. In the former of these places they are mentioned as needing to be repented of, and in the latter as what we need to be cleansed from by the blood of Christ. The first mention is so incidental that the context affords no light as to the precise idea conveyed by the epithet "dead"; but in the other it may be noticed that it is an argument à fortiori from the efficacy of the Levitical sacrifices within their limited sphere to the greater power of the blood of Christ, and that one of the two things named in the former clause, "the ashes of a heifer sprinkling the unclean," had special reference (see Num. 19) to the cleansing from pollution caused by contact with a dead body; also that the contrast to dead works is emphatically put as to serve the living God, the absence of the article—θεῷ ζῶντι—bringing out the force of the epithet "living." From these considerations it would appear that in the mind of the writer dead works are such as belong to the sphere of death, i.e. the world which is separated from the living God, and are polluted by the touch of sin—the soul's death. The view of Trench and others, that the phrase denotes works of external obedience in which there is no heart, and so describes an intermediate class between positively evil and truly good works, though expressing what is in itself a great truth, and applicable to Heb. $6^1$, is not suitable to the context in $9^{14}$, for surely it is meant to teach that the blood of Christ cleanses from all sin, and not merely from that of heartless service. Besides, if this were the meaning of the term "dead works," we should expect to find it used much more frequently, since the evil of mere mechanical heartless obedience is frequently exposed in Scripture.

Generally in this Epistle death is used in its simplest literal sense, and there is not connected with it that wealth of ideas that appears in Paul's writings; but in $2^{14}$ the devil is said to have the power of death, and to have been destroyed, or rather rendered powerless, by Christ through His death. Here it does not seem necessary or natural to understand by "death" anything more than physical death; and as the sacred writer unquestionably connected death with sin (see $9^{27,\ 28}$), his meaning is that the devil as the tempter and accuser of men invests death with the power and terror that it has for the guilty.

### 5. IN THE FIRST EPISTLE OF PETER

The First Epistle of Peter has for its keynote that Christians are the true Israel of God, the people of His own possession in the new dispensation, though scattered abroad, strangers and persecuted in the world. This appears in the salutation ($1^{1,\ 2}$) where the mention of obedience and sprinkling of the blood of Christ alludes to the making of the covenant with Israel (Ex. $24^{7,\ 8}$); also very plainly in chap. $2^{9-11}$, and less obviously but really in other places. It is also taught that believers have this position and privilege in virtue of a new birth ($1^{3,\ 23}\ 2^2$), and this is connected also with the death and rising again of Christ. While this Epistle contains so much that resembles Paul's to the Ephesians, there is not in it any description of the unregenerate state as one of death, like that in Eph. 2,[1] though its moral character is described in a very similar way (1 Pet. $4^{3,\ 4}$). The state of the ungodly is conceived as a life of sin from which we are delivered by a death to sin connected with the death of Christ. He "bore our sins in His own body upon

---

[1] It is arbitrary and unnatural to interpret νεκροῖς in $4^6$ in that sense, especially as it would be a solitary example of it in the Epistle.

(or perhaps 'up to,' as R.V. marg.[1]) the tree, that we, having died to sin, might live to righteousness" ($2^{24}$); and since Christ has "suffered in the flesh, we are to arm ourselves with the same mind: for He that hath suffered in the flesh hath ceased from sin, in order to live no longer by the lusts of men, but by the will of God" ($4^{1.2}$). These statements are very like Paul's, but it has been questioned whether they express the same idea of deliverance by death from the guilt of sin as is conveyed in Rom. $6^7$. But Peter clearly represents Christ's death not merely as our example, but as our redemption, both from the guilt and power of sin, and His resurrection as the power that effects our regeneration ($1^3$) and salvation ($3^{21}$); and it seems probable that He as well as Paul had the idea of the mystical union of believers with Christ, in virtue of which they are freed from the death which is the wages of sin, through dying in and with Him, and raised to a new life of forgiveness and holiness through His rising from the dead.

### 6. IN THE SECOND EPISTLE OF PETER

The Second Epistle bearing Peter's name, though it differs very greatly in many respects from the First, so that its authenticity on literary grounds cannot be held to be certain, yet has the same conception of life as given to Christians by divine power, making them partakers of divine nature as opposed to the corruption that is in the world through lust ($1^{3.4}$). The physical death of a believer is spoken of as a departure or a putting off the tabernacle in which he is here ($1^{14.15}$). On the other hand, false teachers who bring in impious and immoral tenets are described as bringing upon themselves as a judgment swift destruction ($2^{1.3}$). They are compared to irrational brutes that have no end before them but wasting away ($\phi\theta o \rho \dot{a}$), and the moral corruption of ungodly men has for its consequence a similar

---

[1] I prefer this rendering on account of the accusative ξύλον, and consider it to indicate that Christ was bearing our sins all through His earthly life up to the Cross, on which He exhausted and made an end of them, dying to sin that we might do so also.

complete wasting away ($2^{12}$). The whole world is to pass away on the day of the Lord's coming and judgment, while true Christians look for new heavens and a new earth wherein dwelleth righteousness ($3^{10-13}$). The word death does not occur in the Epistle, but the opposite of the life which believers receive from God is the destruction which is so often and solemnly mentioned as both the natural and the judicial consequence of an impenitent course of life, according to the impulses of lusts and pleasures.

### 7. IN THE TEACHING OF JOHN

Of all the New Testament writers, John makes the notions of life and death the most prominent in his presentation of the Gospel, for by him Christianity is conceived as being essentially eternal life. He has intimated very definitely the purpose of his Gospel and his First Epistle, and in both cases it has reference to this. Of the Gospel he says (John $20^{31}$), "These are written, that ye may believe that Jesus is the Christ, the Son of God; and that believing ye may have life in His name"; *i.e.* his record of the signs by which Jesus manifested His glory was designed to lead to faith in His divine nature and mission those who as yet had it not, and through that faith they would have life in Him. In the opening of his First Epistle he says, with reference to his apostolic teaching (1 John $1^3$), "That which we have seen and heard declare we unto you also, that ye also may have fellowship with us: yea, and our fellowship is with the Father, and with His Son Jesus Christ"; and then he goes on to tell the purpose of his present letter (v.$^4$): "And these things write we unto you, that our joy may be fulfilled," *i.e.* your joy and mine together made full.[1] How this is to be done

---

[1] Some expositors (*e.g.* Westcott) take v.$^3$ as well as v.$^4$ to denote the purpose of the Epistle; but there seem to be good reasons for understanding the former as a reference to the apostle's testimony in general: the aim in $1^3$ is not equivalent to that in $5^{13}$; the Epistle does not consist of testimony to the life of Christ but of inferences from it, and a needless tautology is avoided by distinguishing the general purpose of the apostle's ministry in v.$^3$, and the special aim of the Epistle, v.$^4$. This does not necessarily imply that the Gospel was written before the Epistle, as the reference may be to oral testimony.

he declares more particularly towards the close (5¹³), "These things have I written unto you, that ye may know that ye have eternal life; even unto you that believe on the name of the Son of God." The Epistle, then, is intended for those who have already received the testimony of the Gospel, and is designed to show them what is involved in their faith in Christ; hence it gives the subjective as the Gospel gives the objective side of Christianity. Eternal life is obtained by faith in Christ; but that faith may not at first be self-conscious or fully assured, hence believers need to be shown that they have indeed eternal life in Christ, and the assurance of this is what completes their joy. Since these three passages that state the purpose of the Gospel and of the Epistle correspond so exactly, it may be safely inferred that the "eternal life" of John 21³¹ is the same as "the fellowship with the Father, and with His Son Jesus Christ," of 1 John 1³; and this is confirmed by the fact that Christ has just been described as "the eternal life which was with the Father, and was manifested unto us" (v.²). This is otherwise expressed by saying that "God gave unto us eternal life, and this life is in His Son" (chap. 5¹¹); "in Him was life" (John 1⁴). These statements show that when Jesus is called, and calls Himself, the life, the meaning is not merely the giver of life, but one who is essentially living, and whose very presence and reception constitutes the true life of every soul that has it.

## II. THE INTERMEDIATE STATE

In regard to the intermediate state or condition of souls after death, there are just two important theological questions; the one is, whether there is any possibility of conversion for the ungodly; and the other is, whether there are any penal or purgatorial sufferings for the godly in the unseen world. These I propose now to consider.

1. The whole representations that Scripture gives of the state of the dead prove that there is in it a wide difference between the godly and the ungodly. At death the spirit returns to God who gave it; when we make our bed in Sheol, God is there. Now, to be ushered into the immediate

presence of God with consciousness, memory, and conscience in full and active operation, must needs of itself produce the most opposite feelings, according as men have been reconciled to Him here or not. If we are at peace with God, having our sins forgiven and our hearts turned to Him, to be in His presence will be the source of comfort and joy; while for those who are still His enemies, lying under His holy wrath, and full of dislike and hatred of His character, the very presence of God will be a continual torment. Moreover, for the Christian to depart is to be with Christ, the Saviour whom he trusts, and whom having not seen he loves; to be absent from the body is to be present with the Lord, and that to him is far better. But for him who has despised and rejected the Saviour offered in the Gospel, the presence of Christ will add to the pangs of an evil conscience and enhance the misery of his state. Thus it is plain, even from the most general and least figurative descriptions of the unseen world, that there are in it two opposite states of happiness or misery appointed for souls, according as they are reconciled to God or not. So, too, it is said, "The wicked is driven away in his wickedness: but the righteous hath hope in his death" (Prov. 14$^{32}$). Judas is said on his death to have gone to his own place; while Jesus said to the penitent robber, "To-day shalt thou be with Me in Paradise." This uniform strain of scriptural representation is confirmed by our Lord's parable of the Rich Man and Lazarus, when both are described as being in the place of souls between death and the resurrection, but the one comforted and the other tormented.

Now, the question is, whether there is any possibility of a change or transition in the other world from the miserable state of the ungodly to the blessedness of the godly. It has been the general opinion of the Church that there is not, but that the condition of each man is finally fixed at death.[1] But in modern times some have thought that there are indications in Scripture that such a change may be possible

---

[1] Even the Roman Catholic doctrine of Purgatory admits this; for while it asserts a purifying process for those who, though saved, are not perfectly freed from sin, it allows no possibility of salvation to those who are not reconciled to God in this life.

at least in some cases, and that this affords some relief from the difficulties of God's providence, since heathens who have not had the gospel preached to them in this life may have an opportunity of hearing and believing it in the other world. It cannot be doubted, however, that the general impression produced by the scriptural statements on the subject favours what has been the common opinion. In the parable of Lazarus, Abraham is represented as saying to the rich man, when he prayed that Lazarus might be sent to him, first, that he has simply received what he had chosen; and, second, that between them is a great gulf fixed, which cannot be crossed on either side: and though this is a parable, and its imagery cannot be pressed in detail, this point seems to have a meaning, and to describe an unchangeable state. There is, indeed, another view of this parable which makes it teach quite a different doctrine, which is put briefly and clearly in a letter of Charles Kingsley's (*Life*, i. p. 394). "Our Lord represents Dives as still Abraham's child, under no despair, not cut off from Abraham's sympathy, and under a direct moral training of which you see the fruit. He is gradually weaned from the selfish desire of indulgence for himself to live and care for his brethren, a divine step forward in his life which of itself proves him not to be lost.[1] The impossibility of Lazarus getting to him, or *vice versâ*, expresses plainly the great truth, that each being where he ought to be at that time, interchange of place, *i.e.* of spiritual state, is impossible. But it says nothing against Dives rising out of his torment when he has learnt the lesson of it, and going where he ought to go." On this I would observe, that the great lesson of the parable is a warning against that worldliness or unbelief which looks only to the things that are seen, and is blind to unseen things: and that the rich man's request for his brethren gives no sign of any change in that respect, but betrays the same exclusive regard to outward things, so that it can hardly be considered an indication of a better state of mind; while the statement about the great gulf fixed, seems to imply an absolute and final separation. If we inquire, not what meaning may be put on the parable, but what it naturally teaches, I think we must

[1] See also Plumptre, *The Spirits in Prison*, p. 60.

take the common view of it. But this passage does not stand alone. We are told (Eccles. 9¹⁰), "there is no work, nor device, nor knowledge, nor wisdom, in Sheol, whither thou goest." "The night cometh, wherein no man can work" (John 9⁴, cf. 11⁹, ¹⁰), which seems to imply that there is no activity in the soul's separate state such as could effect a change of condition. Further, in all the descriptions of the last judgment it is for the things done in the body that men are said to be judged, hence it would appear that nothing that affects men's eternal destinies takes place in the disembodied state. Again, our Lord's parable of the barren fig-tree (Luke 13⁶⁻⁹), taken in connection with the incidents that gave rise to it, the slaying of the Galileans by Herod, and the eighteen men being killed by the fall of the tower, shows that death is the cutting down of the tree, the end of its respite and probation. There are, however, some texts commonly quoted in support of this, and used even by Hodge (*Syst. Theol.* iii. p. 725), that are not applicable: Eccles. 11³, "where the tree falleth, there it shall be": Matt. 25¹⁰, when the bridegroom comes the door is shut; Rev. 22¹¹, "he that is unjust, let him be unjust still." The last two passages refer not to death, but to the coming of Christ. Perhaps also Heb. 9²⁷ is not conclusive.

On the other hand, the possibility of conversion in Hades has been thought to be implied in two passages of 1 Pet., 3¹⁸⁻²⁰ and 4⁶.

Now, these texts are exceedingly obscure, and beset with difficulties on every side. All attempted renderings are open to some objection or other, and take some of the words or phrases in an unusual or improper sense. The two great classes of interpretation are those that understand the passage of a personal preaching of Christ in the other world, and those that refer it to His preaching by His Spirit to men in this world. Now, it is obvious that if any of the latter class be correct, the passage has no bearing whatever on the state of the dead. I am inclined, however, to think that it is more natural to understand the first of the passages in Peter of a personal preaching by Christ in Hades; and if so, I think it must be to those who disobeyed Noah's call to repentance, and were destroyed in the Flood.

But this interpretation is not free from very considerable grammatical difficulties, so that one cannot feel quite certain of its truth ; and to base on the passage, which, so understood, refers to a single and unique event, a general doctrine of the possibility of conversion in Hades, is doubly precarious.

In 1 Pet. 4⁶ I think grammatical and contextual reasons require us to understand νεκροῖς as those who are now dead, and that the preaching of the gospel spoken of was not after but before their death, which is referred to in the clause that declares the purpose of the preaching ἵνα κριθῶσι, κ.τ.λ.

Our Lord's words in Matt. 12³² have been held by Augustine and many since to imply that some sins are forgiven in the future life; but this is a very precarious inference indeed. The phrase αἰὼν μέλλων, as Meyer points out, would not include the state of the dead before the judgment and second coming of Messiah, and it is doubtful whether it refers to the future life of individuals at all.

In the parallel passage in Mark 3²⁹ the phrase is simply εἰς τὸν αἰῶνα. A limited negative does not always imply that the affirmative is true beyond the limits mentioned.

It ought, however, to be considered that the teaching of the sacred writers is designed for those who hear it, and not necessarily to be applied to those who do not and cannot do so. They declare that those who reject Christ in this life cannot hope to be saved by Him in the life to come. But that does not necessarily imply that the same is true of those who never heard of Him at all. In the case of those of the kingdom of God who die in infancy, we must suppose that they come to the knowledge of Christ in the future life, when or how we know not ; and possibly the same may be the case with others. The argument from analogy has some force, that as we do not believe that death interrupts the consciousness of the soul, there is reason to believe that it is still capable of thinking, feeling, willing, and so of repentance and turning to God. It is clear that Christ and His salvation are known in the spirit world ; and those who in the darkness of heathenism have been feeling after God, if haply they might find Him, and loving and longing for goodness, will assuredly be drawn to God and Christ, and find peace there. But for those who have heard the gospel here and neglected or refused it, what will there be there to change their hearts? Jesus gives solemn warning that in the case of everyone there is a limit to the day of grace, after which it will be too late. Men may be so hardened in sin that it is impossible to renew them again unto repentance: and for such there can be no possibility of salvation in the life to come.

When the Bible speaks of those who have refused God's call, calling on Him and not being answered (Prov. 1$^{28}$), of many seeking to enter the kingdom of God and not being able because the door is shut (Luke 13$^{24-27}$), the meaning is not that true spiritual repentance ever can be in vain, but that the mere selfish desire of salvation that may arise in the most wicked soul, when the evil consequences of sin are felt, will not be accepted by God. In the place of souls it may well be that the consequences of sin are so keenly felt that none can but desire deliverance; but in those who have heard the gospel message and not obeyed it, this will not produce real repentance. In the case of all such the parable of Lazarus and the teaching of Scripture in general seems to show that a final separation is made at death. In regard to those whose moral life is not at all developed in this world we ought not to be so positive, but to acknowledge that we do not know how God brings them to a personal decision and faith in Christ, whether immediately at death or by the revelations of the unseen world.

The question ultimately comes to this, Can there be genuine repentance in the future life? for if any soul truly turns to God anywhere and at any time, we may be sure that God will grant forgiveness, and the state of misery will be changed into one of blessedness; and in the case of those who have died in ignorance of God and Christ, and come to know the Saviour first in the future state, repentance may be possible; but if men have neglected and refused in this life to obey God's gracious call, what likelihood is there that they will comply with it after death, or that God will work more powerfully on their souls than He has done here?

II. The other question as to the state of the dead is whether there are any penal or purgatorial sufferings for the godly in that state. That there are such has been held in various ways, the most extreme and materialistic one being the Roman Catholic doctrine of Purgatory. That doctrine rests upon the distinction between the eternal and the temporal punishment due to sin. All who die in communion and peace with the Church are held to have the eternal punishment of their sins remitted, through the merit of Christ. But there is also held to be a temporal punishment to be borne by sinners themselves; and if that is not fully endured in this life, by sufferings or penances, it must be expiated by sufferings in the future state. Hence all Christians who are not perfectly sanctified, and have not made satisfaction for all their venial sins, go to a place or state called Purgatory, where they suffer, with more or less severity, for a longer or shorter period, according to their desert. The Church has power, however, to apply her treasury of merit, from the good works of the saints, as well as the efficacy of prayers and sacraments, to mitigate, shorten, or remit their purgatorial pains.

This is the formal and official doctrine of the Church of Rome on the subject, which is of faith for her members. The more particular statements as to the place of Purgatory, the nature of the sufferings there as by fire, are representations commonly used and tolerated, if not sanctioned, by the Church. It is hardly fair to make much of them in controverting the doctrine, except in so far as they show with what terrible effect the dogma can be wielded as a weapon to keep men in subjection to priestly rule.

In regard to this doctrine, even in its more general form, it may be noted—

1. It is entirely without Scripture support. Even its advocates do not profess to bring a full and explicit proof from the Bible, but rest it mainly on tradition and the authority of the Church, which we cannot admit as sources of doctrine. The only passages adduced in its support are our Lord's saying that the sin against the Holy Spirit shall not be forgiven either in this world or in that which is to come, —a passage from which, as we have seen, the inference is precarious to forgiveness at all after death, and doubly so to

Purgatory; and Paul's words in 1 Cor. $3^{12-15}$, where, however, he is speaking of the work of building up the Church, and says that if one who is himself a believer is careless how he does this and brings in those who in the end cannot stand the test, he shall suffer loss and be saved as through fire, *i.e.*, with pain and difficulty. But the day is that of Christ's coming, and the passage says nothing of the intermediate state.

2. It is contradicted by the express teaching of Scripture, that the souls of believers pass into a state of happiness immediately on their death. When Paul wrote to the Philippians, he says that he was not yet perfect ($3^{13}$); yet that for him to die would be to be with Christ, which would be gain to him ($1^{21, 23}$). The thief on the Cross, converted at the last hour of a life of sin, was as far from perfect as could well be conceived; yet Jesus said to him, "To-day shalt thou be with Me in paradise" (Luke $23^{43}$). Jesus also describes Lazarus as carried by angels to Abraham's bosom, where he is comforted (Luke $16^{22}$); and John in apocalyptic vision heard a voice from heaven: "Blessed are the dead," etc. (Rev. $14^{13}$).

3. The doctrine on which Purgatory rests, of the punishment of venial sins having to be borne after the eternal condemnation is removed, is unscriptural and false. It implies that the sufferings of Christians in this life are penal inflictions, whereas they are constantly represented in the Bible as fatherly chastisements; it assumes that their repentance, good deeds, and self-denial are truly expiatory, making atonement for their sins; while Scripture teaches that the only sacrifice for sin is that of Christ, and that His blood cleanses from all sin. Still more unscriptural are the doctrines of works of supererogation and of the Church's treasury of merit and power to apply it, which are implied in the practical use made by Romanists of the doctrine of Purgatory.

The most plausible defence of it is that made by Möhler and others, that those who are but imperfectly sanctified in this life must be purified after death, and that this is the nature and design of the pains of Purgatory. But this entirely alters the character of the doctrine, and overthrows its principle. For it is necessary to the Roman Catholic system that the sufferings be expiatory. If they are not so, or even if, besides this, they are disciplinary and purifying, then the whole doctrine of the power of the Church to mitigate or shorten them falls to the ground. For if they are necessary in order to remove the remaining stains of sin, then the merits or sufferings of others can have no fitness to supply their place, nor would it be any real blessing to the departed soul to be saved from a process of purification which, however painful, would be the means, and the only means, of bringing him to perfection in holiness. The Roman Catholic doctrine of Purgatory is a corruption of earlier ideas about the purifying of the soul and the terror of the last judgment. Clemens Alex. (*Strom.* vii. 6) speaks of the soul being purified by spiritual fire, but not in reference to the future life. Origen connected the purgatorial fire with the burning up of the world at the last day. Augustine is generally said to have placed the fire in Hades; but his views were doubtful and vacillating. Pope Gregory I. (590) first distinctly asserted it; and the pains were at first conceived as purifying, as they are represented with such moral insight by Dante. The nature of the doctrine was, however, entirely changed by the notions of human satisfactions and merits which arose in the scholastic age; and the granting of indulgences from the time of the Crusades onwards led to gross practical abuses.

Apart from the Roman Catholic doctrine of Purgatory, it has been thought by some that there must be a process of purification in the state of the dead for those who, though truly believers in Christ, are not perfect in holiness at their death; and that the statement of the Westminster Confession, that "the souls of the righteous being then made perfect in holiness, are received into the highest heavens, where they behold the face of God in light and glory" (xxxii. 1), is exaggerated, and not borne out by Scripture. Dr. Luckock[1] says that this, which he admits to be the common belief, "invests a mere physical process with that sanctifying influence which

---

[1] *The Intermediate State*, p. 64.

can only be exercised through the operation of the will." He thinks that if we could remove the subordinate evils that have made the Roman doctrine of Purgatory a byword; and leave only the dominant idea of a progressive cleansing, commencing immediately after death and lasting on till the work is complete, a great end would be gained. In this cleansing the soul must suffer acutely; but only in a spiritual way, as in penitential sorrow.

Both this view and that of moral perfection at death seem to be inferences from Scripture rather than its direct teaching. The phrase in Heb. 12$^{23}$, "the spirits of just men made perfect," does not refer to perfection in holiness, but to the completion of blessedness which the Old Testament saints received (Heb. 11$^{40}$); and the other passages simply say they are at rest, with Christ, in paradise. It is inferred from the statements that they are blessed, and in a state far better than here, that they must be entirely free from sin; and, on the other hand, from the fact that believers are not free from sin up to death, that they must be purified from it by a gradual process hereafter, and that this must imply suffering. Neither inference is certain, and the latter, I think, the more precarious.

### III. THE FINAL STATES

It has been the prevalent belief of the Christian Church in all ages that after the last judgment the state of men is inevitably fixed, and that the blessedness of the saved and the punishment of the lost shall be everlasting or final; and this seems to have been due to the general impression made by the teaching of Scripture on this solemn subject. There has been no doubt that the happiness of the saints in heaven shall be eternal; and it might be a pleasing task to attempt to gather from Scripture, and to depict, as far as our faculties will allow, the nature of their blessedness. But, unhappily, it is more necessary for the theologian to consider the darker side of the future state, which is a painful and terrible subject of contemplation. It is more necessary, not from the greater importance of the subject, or because it has been more fully revealed, but merely because it has been called in question, and because it is needful to consider and estimate the reasons that have been urged against it. The belief that some of God's creatures and our fellowmen are to suffer for ever, that sin and punishment are to be eternal in the universe of the God of love, is so awful and distressing to our souls, that if it were possible to avoid it we should be right glad to adopt an opposite opinion. It is a baseless calumny on those who maintain it as a Bible doctrine, to say or insinuate, as is sometimes done, that they have a malignant or cruel delight in the thought of the endless suffering of their fellows. The men who have taught it most earnestly have been in many cases distinguished by the most self-denying philanthropic zeal for the salvation of lost sinners. Their very apprehension of the awful doom awaiting the impenitent has quickened their zeal and anxiety to present the Saviour to them and to lead them to Him. They feel the awfulness of the doom which they are constrained to declare, and they are often sorely tempted to soften down or explain away the teaching of Scripture on the subject. The various theories that have been adopted to remove or relieve the burden on the mind and heart that the ordinary doctrine does certainly impose, present themselves to our mind in an attractive guise, and we cannot help feeling a hope that some of them might be found to be true. The doctrine of eternal punishment presents difficulties both to our reason and to our feelings. If we were asked to judge for ourselves what we should think the most fitting issue of the world's history, we should probably say that it would be most worthy of a God of infinite power, wisdom, and love to bring all His creatures ultimately to a state of holiness and happiness in fellowship with Himself, however far they might wander from Him at one period of their existence. It seems more suitable to the unity that we look for in all works of wisdom, that all things should tend to this single issue of good in which God would be most highly glorified, than that there should be a perpetual duality of good and evil in the world. Thus even our reason left to itself would revolt from the idea of eternal punishment. Still more do our feelings sink oppressed under the weight of the thought of final and hopeless misery. We can hardly imagine how we could contemplate such a thing with any composure, or that any sin could be so great as to make us feel that eternal punishment is a just and necessary doom. These difficulties of the head and of the heart do not need to be urged on us by the opponents of the doctrine, they are ready enough to present themselves, and hard enough to get rid of even without that. If it were possible to yield to them without giving up the essential principles of the gospel, as well as going against the plain and solemn statements of Scripture, we should be ready enough to do so. But we must appeal to the word of God, and be guided by its teaching. Let us first consider the teaching of Scripture, and then the various ways in which it has been attempted to get rid of the difficulties of thought and feeling by denying eternal punishment.

There are several passages where the adjective αἰώνιος is applied to the future punishment of the impenitent as well as to the blessedness of the saved, and these have generally been taken to imply that both are everlasting. But it is maintained by Dr. Cox, Dean Farrar, and others, that in the New Testament αἰώνιος never means everlasting, but always "of or belonging to an age," "age-long," "aeonian." Now αἰών does indeed generally, and often in the New Testament, mean age, lifetime, period. But it seems quite clear that the phrases, εἰς τὸν αἰῶνα, εἰς τοὺς αἰῶνας τῶν αἰ., are used for Heb. לְעוֹלָם וָעֶד, which mean "for ever," and that αἰώνιος is used for the adjectival form of עֹלָם, e.g. Ps. 24$^7$, so that there does not seem to be any reason to doubt that it often means everlasting. This is held by most Greek scholars, and given in the lexicons as a meaning of αἰών and αἰώνιος; and apparently with right. Plato in a passage expressly treating of the subject (Timaeus, pp. 37, 38), uses αἰών for eternity in the strict sense as opposed to time, and αἰώνιος as synonymous with ἀΐδιος. Dean Farrar quotes a similar passage from Philo (*Eternal Hope*, p. 199). αἰώνιος is freely rendered in Latin by "aeternus," which was often used in the strict sense. In some places of the New Testament the meaning everlasting seems to be necessary (*e.g.* 2 Cor. 4$^{17, 18}$, 1 John 1$^2$, John 17$^3$), where Dr. Cox's explanation is very forced and unnatural. The view that it always means of an age, age-long, requires the assumption of a doctrine of æons that does not seem to be borne out by Scripture. The fact that these phrases are sometimes used of things or relations that are not endless, does not prove that the words themselves do not properly mean everlasting, because it is a very common thing in all languages that words denoting infinitude should be employed of things that are not infinite. So ἄπειρος undoubtedly means "boundless," although Homer applies it to the Hellespont. So in Ex. 21$^5$ and Philem.$^{15}$ "for ever" correctly translates לְעֹלָם, εἰς τὸν αἰῶνα, αἰώνιον, and it would be absurd to say that the English word "*ever*" means an age or a lifetime. I think it clear, therefore, that αἰώνιος may and sometimes does mean eternal, *i.e.* either everlasting or independent of time entirely; and the statement of Kingsley, endorsed by Cox (*Salvator Mundi*, pp. 121, 122), that it never has either of these meanings, seems entirely untenable. This, however, does not prove that it always has either of these senses; for, as I have just said, it is sometimes, like all similar terms, modified by the nature of what it is applied to, and its real meaning in each place where it occurs must be determined by the text and context.

Now let us look at the passages in the New Testament where the future punishment of the ungodly is spoken of. I shall not refer to two in Matt. 5$^{22}$ and $^{29, 30}$, because it seems very probable that these contain only a figurative allusion to the valley of Hinnom, where the bodies of malefactors were cast out to be burned. But Matt. 10$^{28}$ and Luke 12$^5$ undoubtedly speak of Gehenna as a place of suffering after death. Again, Matt. 18$^{8, 9}$ speaks of being cast εἰς τὸ πῦρ τὸ αἰώνιον, εἰς τὴν γέενναν τοῦ πυρός, and the parallel passage (Mark 9$^{43}$) speaks of τὸ πῦρ τὸ ἄσβεστον = γέεννα. Here it is quite clear αἰώνιος = ἄσβεστος, and cannot mean age-long. Nor do I think that we can possibly avoid understanding these words of suffering after death. Though there may be an allusion to the valley of Hinnom based on Isa. 66$^{24}$, yet the thing shadowed forth by the figure is the opposite of the life, which is spoken of as future. The expression πῦρ αἰώνιον occurs again in Matt.

$25^{41}$, in the parable of the Sheep and the Goats, where it is said to have been prepared for the devil and his angels; and is explained in v.$^{46}$ as κόλασις αἰώνιος, where the same epithet is applied to the life of the saved. There is nothing whatever to indicate that αἰώνιος here means age-long; and the whole parable suggests the idea of a final judgment. Much stress is laid by Farrar and Cox on the use of the word κόλασις here, since, according to the usage of classical Greek and the definitions of Plato and Aristotle, that word is distinguished from τιμωρία, retributive punishment, as meaning chastisement or suffering inflicted for the correction and reformation of the offender. But this distinction seems not to be observed in biblical Greek, and in the only other place where κόλασις occurs (1 John $4^{18}$) it cannot have that meaning, nor can the verb κολάζω in Acts $4^{21}$ and 2 Pet. $2^9$. The words παιδεύω and παιδεία seem to have come in New Testament use in place of κολάζω and κόλασις.

We have also our Lord's words on the unpardonable sin (Matt. $12^{31, 32}$, Mark $3^{28, 29}$, cf. 1 John $5^{16}$).

1 Pet. $4^{17, 18}$ points to a twofold issue of the history of mankind, and a terrible doom for the ungodly and unbelieving.

See also 2 Pet. $2^{3, 17, 21}$ $3^7$, Jude $^{13-15}$.

Paul's representations on this subject are chiefly two— (1) That of the day of judgment, when all shall appear before the tribunal of Christ to receive each according to his deeds, and where there shall be a separation of men into two great classes (Rom. $2^{6-9}$ $14^{10}$, 2 Cor. $5^{10}$); (2) that the end of the rejectors and enemies of Christ is destruction, ὄλεθρος, 1 Thess. $5^3$; ὄλεθρος αἰώνιος, 2 Thess. $1^9$; ἀπώλεια, Phil. $1^{28}$ $3^{19}$. He speaks repeatedly of those who are being saved (οἱ σωζόμενοι), and of those who are perishing (οἱ ἀπολλύμενοι), 2 Cor. $2^{16}$ $4^3$, and says that to the latter the gospel is a savour of death unto death; and that the end and wages of sin is death (Rom. $6^{21, 23}$).

The Epistle to the Hebrews speaks of some whom it is impossible to renew again to repentance ($6^{4, 6}$), and describes in terrible terms the doom of apostates ($10^{26, 31, 39}$).

In the Book of Revelation we have presented in vision

the great judgment and the lake of fire; and there are express statements of the endless nature of the punishment of the wicked ($14^{11}$ $20^{10, 15}$ $21^8$), and of the final and unchangeable state of men ($22^{11}$).

The attempt to explain these many and varied testimonies as describing only suffering that is temporary, though it may be many ages long, and that is ultimately to lead to conversion and restoration, seems to me on the most careful consideration to be altogether unsuccessful. They appear plainly and emphatically to assert a doom that is final and hopeless, and also one that involves terrible suffering, though whether that suffering is to be everlasting or to issue in final extinction of conscious being is not so clear. Some of the passages taken literally would lead to the former and others to the latter alternative. Probably none of them ought to be pressed in their literal sense.

### I. UNIVERSALISM

Of the alternative views on this subject the most complete and thoroughgoing is that of the ultimate restitution of all intelligent creatures to fellowship with God, or universalism. The advocates of this view hold that though some shall be condemned at the judgment as transgressors of the law, and as not having believed in Christ the Saviour, and though in consequence of this they shall be consigned to suffering as the punishment of their sin; yet sooner or later, it may be after long ages of misery, they shall be brought to repentance, and ultimately delivered and saved. It is essential to this theory, with whatever modifications it may be held, that the wicked shall be brought to repentance and moral reformation before their sufferings cease. This is involved in the nature of restitution, and is indeed seen and felt to be necessary by all thoughtful and earnest men. However painful the idea of eternal suffering may be, and undoubtedly is, the notion of ungodly and wicked creatures being for ever happy is absolutely intolerable. Indeed, the difficulty connected with the common doctrine lies as much in the idea of eternal sin as in that of eternal misery, and the more spiritually-minded of its opponents put in the foreground of their attacks the everlasting duration of moral evil as implying a failure of God's goodness and victory over His love. The theory of restitution, then, requires us to believe that all creatures shall ultimately be converted from sin to God. But now the question arises—By what means is this to be effected? Some would answer by saying that the sufferings inflicted in the future life are themselves the means of purification, that they are designed and inflicted for this end, and will lead to it sooner or later in the case of all. This was the view of Origen, and is the consistent carrying out of the doctrine of the universal Fatherhood of God in its absolute and unrestricted application. All punishment is regarded as merely disciplinary and corrective, inflicted for the offender's good, and all properly retributive punishment is denied. Hence it follows that the final issue of all punishment inflicted by God must be the reformation of the criminal, and that the infliction can in no case be eternal, since God's punishment must attain its end. But this view is not consistent with the facts of human nature and divine government. It is not the case that suffering invariably tends to moral improvement. In many cases within the range of our experience it has no such effect, and it is a very shallow view of man's character to suppose that it can be changed by mere suffering from the love of sin to the love of goodness and of God. That may inspire terror and shrinking from the consequences of sin, but it cannot of itself produce any real hatred of sin, or reconciliation to God. Suffering may be used by God as a means of perfecting the holiness of His people and overcoming their remaining habits of sin where there has been first wrought in the soul a real love of holiness and turning from sin, but it is impossible that by itself it can effect a change of heart. The idea of suffering being of itself a converting agency is ably exposed by Julius Müller in his work on *Sin*, who shows how inconsistent that is with the idea of redemption. For if men could be restored by punishments, what need was there of redemption? Is it to be supposed that punishment is the means of salvation for those who refuse to receive the redemption of Christ? Then punishment would be a more powerful means of good than the cross of Christ. But perhaps it may be said that the restitution of all is to be effected, not by the mere infliction of punishment, but by moral means,—by the same means as conversion is effected in this life, the offer of the grace of God in Christ, and the working of the Spirit of God in the sinner's heart. But if these have been refused and resisted here, what certainty is there that they shall prove effectual hereafter? Whatever view we take of the reason why many are not converted here, whether we ascribe it to their own free will or to the absence of the effectual grace of God, the same reason may prevent their conversion hereafter. Or can it be said that a state in which the wicked are finally separated from the godly, and made to feel the awful effects of separation from God, is more favourable to their conversion than the position in which many are in this life under all the influences of God's grace? If there is to be any certainty of the final restitution of all, we seem to be always driven back to the assumption that suffering itself must have this effect, and that, accordingly, seems to be what is tacitly presumed even when not asserted by its advocates.

The theory of universal restitution has been attempted to be supported by Scripture, and especially by a series of passages in Paul's writings which it is necessary to examine. In Rom. $5^{18}$ the restoration in Christ seems to be made coextensive with the condemnation in Adam, and both are said to be εἰς πάντας ἀνθρώπους. Most interpreters, however, explain this passage so that it does not affirm universal salvation; some, as Meyer, holding that it refers only to the objective side of redemption, the gracious will of God by which it is designed for all men, without regard to the conditions on which the subjective enjoyment of it depends; and others, like Hodge, that by all men here we are to understand all who are in Adam on the one hand, and all who are in Christ on the other. Either of these interpretations seems admissible, while the latter is the more satisfactory. 1 Cor. $15^{22}$ is a parallel statement, and in vv.$^{24-28}$ Paul declares that Christ must reign till He has put down all authority and power. This of itself might denote only a triumph over enemies, destroying for ever their power to rebel, and not necessarily a restoration; but when he says (v.²⁸) that the end is that God may be all in all, that seems to imply a spiritual union of all souls to God. So it is understood by Neander, Pfleiderer, and others. But Meyer, Weiss, and others hold that the connection of the passage, as well as Paul's teaching elsewhere, excludes that idea; since the reign which God exercises over all can be no other than that which Christ had, and which consists not in the conversion or annihilation of all hostile powers, but in their being made powerless and subjected to His will.

In Rom. 11²⁵⁻³² Paul certainly teaches that during the time of Israel's unbelief and rejection, the fulness of the Gentiles is to be brought in, and then all Israel is to be saved. But that seems clearly to refer to those living at the time of the fulfilment of the prophecy, and not to those who are dead before that; and though v.³² seems to have a more universal reference, it only declares the gracious design of God in His providential dealings, without asserting that it shall be actually accomplished in all men.

The statements in Eph. 1¹⁰ and Col. 1²⁰ speak of God gathering together all things under Christ as head, which is simply parallel to 1 Cor. 15²⁴⁻²⁷; and reconciling all things to Himself through Christ, which it is very difficult to explain, since the proper meaning of reconciliation can apply neither to innocent nor to inanimate beings. But we cannot let an obscure and doubtful statement neutralise the express and solemn testimony of so many other places as to the final condemnation of the wicked. On any view, we must either limit τὰ πάντα in some way, or take ἀποκαταλλάξαι in an improper or modified sense; and if we do not take the latter alternative, we must regard τὰ πάντα as limited by the mention of the Church, v.¹⁸, which is not an impossible view. If τὰ πάντα be absolutely universal, reconcile must be used in a very wide sense, including different meanings in reference to holy angels, redeemed men, and inanimate things. This is hardly consistent with the continued existence of devils and men unconverted and suffering punishment, but it is consistent with their ultimate annihilation. So it is understood by Sabatier with much probability.

## 2. CONDITIONAL IMMORTALITY

A less extreme and thoroughgoing attempt to remove the difficulties of the common doctrine is the theory of Annihilation or Conditional Immortality; *i.e.*, that the human soul is not essentially immortal, but only receives eternal life as a gift of God, and that those who reject Christ shall sooner or later cease to exist as conscious and sentient beings. This view was held in the ancient Church by Arnobius,[1] and has been revived by some modern writers: Samuel Minton, in a work entitled *The Glory of Christ*; Edw. White, *Life in Christ*; Petavel, *The Problem of Immortality*, and others mentioned there by him. It has been put in different forms. By some it has been maintained that there is no future life at all for the wicked; but this seems so clearly opposed to the scriptural doctrines of the General Resurrection and Last Judgment, that it has obtained little favour; and the more usual form of this theory has been that, after a period of suffering as the punishment of their sins, the wicked shall cease to exist.

This theory has a good deal to be said for it, and has seemed to many earnest and reverent minds to alleviate very much the difficulties of the doctrine of eternal suffering. Its advocates do not seek to give any limited meaning to αἰώνιος, but admit eternal punishment, holding that, according to the usage of language, a punishment may be said to be eternal if it is final and its consequences last for ever. The doom of the wicked is frequently called in Scripture, and especially by Paul, θάνατος, ὄλεθρος, ἀπώλεια; and these words are taken on this theory in their most literal sense, as indicating the cessation of conscious existence. Death in general, it is held, denotes the cessation of vital functions and activities: bodily death is the cessation of animal life, and spiritual death is the cessation of the religious life, or fellowship of the soul with God; and so, it is inferred, eternal death, or destruction, is the cessation of all vital functions for ever. This destruction, doubtless, is accompanied with pain more or less intense, as the other kinds of death are; and this explains, on this theory, the many descriptions of suffering as the punishment of the lost.

[1] *Adv. Gent.* ii. 14.

There is much in the analogy of experience to countenance this theory. Sins of sensual indulgence tend to destroy the health and vitality of the body, and lead to disease, and in the end to death. Some kinds of sin also derange the mental powers, and produce imbecility or madness. Indeed, all ungodliness and unspirituality tends to lower the mental powers, and to produce stupidity. Death in sin does really impair the intellectual life of the soul, and tends to reduce a man to the level of a brute. Is it not in accordance with these facts that persistent continuance in sin should issue in the extinction of the soul entirely?

Now, many of the arguments commonly used against this theory do not seem to me conclusive. Thus, it is sometimes said, that we cannot conceive of the annihilation of any existing thing, since in all changes that we know no single particle ceases to exist. But this is really just carping at the word annihilation, for all that is required by the theory is the cessation of consciousness, and that does not involve the metaphysical difficulty of annihilation. Nor am I much impressed with the argument from the natural immortality of the soul. The eternal life of believers is what is most clearly taught by Christ, and no philosophic arguments for the soul's immortality can exclude the possibility of God bringing the existence of the soul to an end. The question cannot be settled by metaphysical arguments either one way or the other, but only by an interpretation of the teaching of Scripture. Now, this theory does really give a fair and natural interpretation of a large number of the passages bearing on the subject, namely, those in Paul's Epistles. I do not think that it is the only possible interpretation of them, though it is the most literal one. On the other hand, there are some, especially in the Book of Revelation, that speak of the sufferings of the wicked as eternal, though it is somewhat precarious to base doctrinal conclusions on the prophetic representations of that book.

We must depart from the literal interpretation of one or other of those sets of passages, and the exegetical question is, which is to be taken in a figurative sense? Our Lord's words are, I think, consistent with either view.

On the whole, it seems to me that the theory of Annihilation is at best only a hypothesis, and that it is impossible to pronounce with any certainty between it and the more common view of the everlasting suffering of the lost. These two views agree in what is most clearly taught in Scripture and is most important, that the punishment of the finally impenitent shall be final, and in that sense eternal, whether it is to involve their eternal existence and suffering or not. They also agree in the belief that the doom of the ungodly shall include awful suffering of unknown character and intensity, but always justly proportioned to their guilt.

Considering this view more generally on its merits as a theory, we may observe (1) that it does not remove the difficulties of reason attaching to the common doctrine. It does not, like the theory of restitution, present us with a unity in the final issue of God's government: there is still a twofold end. God's love and purpose of salvation do not take effect in the case of all men. Nay, so far is this from being so, that He is represented as finally annihilating some of the creatures whom He has made capable of eternal life. This leaves the intellectual problem as unsolved as ever. (2) The burden on our feelings seems to be, to a certain extent, lightened by this theory, since the dreadful idea of never-ending suffering is excluded. But, after all, it is only in degree, and to a limited extent, that this is done. The state of the lost is still represented as a hopeless one; and the time during which their sufferings continue, though not literally endless, must be regarded as of very great and inconceivable duration in order to do justice to the language that seems to assert its absolute eternity. Now, to our minds, there is hardly any practical difference between the one and the other.

This theory, then, while it is not distinctly opposed to Scripture, like that of restitution, is also much less effectual as a relief to the mind and heart from the awfulness of the ordinary doctrine.

## 3. MITIGATIONS OF SUFFERING

Another attempt to evade the difficulty is made by the supposition that there are mitigations or relaxations of the sufferings of the lost, or that they are only mental and not physical. The first of these ideas is said to have been held by many of the Fathers, and has been maintained in a somewhat peculiar form by Mr. T. R. Birks.[1] He believes, indeed, that the punishment of the lost is eternal, but holds that in consequence of Christ's atonement, which he holds to be absolutely universal in its effect, it is not the unrelieved suffering originally threatened as the wages of sin, not the bottomless pit, but the lake of fire, *i.e.*, a bounded and limited place of suffering, surrounded on all sides by the trophies of God's grace and love in the redemption and final blessedness of the saved. In the contemplation of the love of God, and the happiness of their fellow-men, he thinks the lost may obtain some solace even in their penal and eternal sufferings. This theory avowedly rests only on inferences from Scripture, which are precarious and fanciful, and it is open to serious objections. To suppose beings capable of such unselfish and heavenly feelings as to derive comfort from the manifestation of God's love to the saved, and yet to be themselves under condemnation for ever, is a notion that shocks the reason and moral sense even more than the doctrine of eternal punishment does the sensibilities. This theory has, therefore, gained little support.

Dean Farrar's view is somewhat of the same kind though less definite.[2] He objects to the common doctrine in so far as it asserts (1) physical torments, (2) endless duration of these for all the lost, (3) that these are the majority of mankind, and (4) that their doom is irrevocably fixed at death.

The last two of these points are plainly irrelevant to the present question. As to the relative proportion of the lost to the saved, no one can affirm anything, for it has not been revealed; and when asked about it Jesus emphatically

[1] *The Victory of the Divine Goodness*, 1867.
[2] *Eternal Hope.*

declined to answer (Luke 13:23, 24). When we consider the character and conduct of men, we may well lament that so few as yet show signs of faith and holiness; but we are not their judges, and we know not how it shall be at the day of judgment.

And as to the last point, it belongs to a different subject. It seems clear that the doom of some is decided in this life, and any indications of a probation beyond death are inferential and uncertain; but we are certain that whenever it may be fixed, it shall be just and equitable.

Farrar depicts in strong language the agonies of remorse and mental suffering that must be the consequence of unrepented sin; but he contends that there may be a possible purification and conversion of the lost, and that God is ever ready to forgive them if they repent; and also that, even apart from that, there may be certain mitigations of their suffering and a cessation of agonising remorse, without perfect peace, and with the loss, possibly for ever, of the beatific vision of God. Now, in regard to the possibility of repentance for the lost, it is a fact, as he admits, that the soul may become so hardened in sin that repentance is impossible, so that even on his view there may be eternal suffering for such; and whether that is to be only mental or also bodily, is surely a question that involves no principle. We do not know how far the Scripture statements are figurative, and should not dogmatise either one way or other. Then as to the mitigations of suffering, why should we think that there is any need of them? Are we to suppose that God first inflicts a doom that is too terrible to be rigidly enforced, and then in mercy alleviates it? Surely it is far more worthy of God to believe that allowance is made for this from the first, and that nothing is inflicted that is not perfectly just and absolutely necessary.

These theories seem to arise from allowing the feelings to guide and control the judgment; and this, which is dangerous in any case, is specially so in this matter, because the grounds and reasons of the final doom of the ungodly can never be fully known till the Last Judgment, the very purpose of which is to vindicate the justice of God's government. Till then we are speculating on the justice of a supposed punishment before we have heard the trial.

It may be observed that both this notion of mitigations and the theory of annihilation seek to soften the awful severity of eternal punishment simply by lessening its degree, the one in intensity and the other in duration. Now there is, it must be admitted, a natural tendency to shrink from the infliction of suffering; and this is greater the more severe and long continued the suffering is. In the presence of such an infliction we seek something to reconcile our minds and hearts to it. But is it a mere diminution in the amount of the infliction that will really reconcile us to it? I think not. Take the case of any suffering that is warrantably and wisely inflicted by man on his fellow-man, whether it be a painful surgical operation, or the execution of penal justice, or wounds given in self-defence or lawful war. Even for such sufferings we feel sympathy; our heart bleeds for the sufferer, though we cannot disapprove or forbid the infliction. Now what is it that reconciles us to the infliction in such cases? Is it merely that the suffering is comparatively slight or of short duration? Surely not. Such considerations afford an apparent more than a real relief,—a relief that arises from what is defective, not from what is best in our nature. If we had perfect sympathy, the least and briefest suffering inflicted needlessly or unjustly on another would pain us as really as the greatest. On the other hand, we acquiesce, or at least ought to acquiesce, in the greatest and longest suffering when we are satisfied that it is just and necessary, or that it tends to the higher good of the sufferer. It is not the mere slightness or degree that reconciles us to the infliction of suffering, but the justice of the cause and the goodness of the end of the infliction. It is in this direction, accordingly, that we must seek for relief in regard to the final judgments of God, not by attempting to persuade ourselves that they are not so very awful as they seem, but by endeavouring to see how good is their reason and end. The theory of restitution has at least the merit of dealing with the question as one of principle and not of mere degree: it would reconcile us to the severity of future punishment, not merely by representing it as less in degree than eternal, but by holding it to be sent in love and for a gracious end. But it cannot do this without doing violence to the solemn statements of Christ and the fundamental principles of the gospel, and therefore we cannot accept it. But is there not another way in which we may be reconciled to suffering besides the assurance that it is remedial? We acquiesce not only in the pain caused by the surgeon's knife, but also in that inflicted by justice on criminals, for the maintenance of law and the good of society; *i.e.*, the circumstance that suffering is justly deserved and necessarily inflicted satisfies us of its propriety. Now this is precisely what we believe to be the case with the sufferings of the lost. However great or long continued they may be, we are sure that they shall not exceed by a single pang what is deserved by the sinner, and necessary for the vindication of God's law and justice. If they are final and eternal, it is because sinful creatures may become hardened in impenitence, and continue for ever heaping up guilt on themselves. Scripture plainly teaches that in the case of some, at least, it is impossible to renew them again unto repentance (Heb. 6⁶), and we are not at liberty to explain away these solemn words. What can a holy and loving God do with such? He must either terminate their existence after a sufficient manifestation of His holy wrath against sin, or they must be for ever miserable; and in either case their doom is hopeless.

But as to the nature and amount of the sufferings, we may leave that in the hand of God. We, who are ourselves sinners, are very incompetent judges of the desert of sin. We know not what is its exceeding sinfulness in the eyes of holy creatures and a holy God; we know not all the purposes in the universal government of God that the punishment of sinners is designed and needed to accomplish. It is not for us, then, to pronounce dogmatically that any particular degree or kind of suffering would be inconsistent with His justice and goodness. We know that the punishment of each soul will be proportioned to its privileges and to its guilt; there will be varieties in the judgment corresponding to every degree of ill-deserving. We believe that when God's judgment is made manifest we shall have such a sight of the justice, necessity, and great ends served by the punishment of the wicked, that we shall be able to say: "Even so, Lord God Almighty! true and righteous are Thy judgments." If we are satisfied of the general principle, that the vindication of justice may reconcile the most benevolent to the infliction of suffering; then we need not be over solicitous to show positively that the future doom of the wicked shall be just what they deserve: we may leave that in God's hand, knowing that the Judge of all the earth will do right. Let us trust God in this matter; avoid all speculations as to the precise nature of future suffering, whether with a view to show positively its consistency with justice and benevolence, or to heighten its effect on men. The latter tendency has done, perhaps, even more harm than the former. Incalculable damage has been done to the teaching of Scripture by the too literal descriptions by good and earnest men of the sufferings of the lost. The statements of the Bible are all more or less figurative, and are intended to produce the impression of something unspeakably awful: but when men attempt to frame from them an exact conception of the reality, it becomes simply grotesque and horrible. We can form no conception of the other world, and it is far wisest and best to rest content with the general views of Scripture. When we deem it necessary to set before others the awful realities of future punishment, let it be as far as possible in the very language of Scripture, which will produce the most powerful effect; and as we avoid all descriptions of sensual joys in heaven, so let us be very cautious in using sensible pictures of the woes of hell.

Above all, let us handle this solemn subject with tenderness and sympathy. Let there be no appearance of hard insensibility or cruel delight in the sufferings of the wicked, while there is all faithfulness in warning them of their danger. It may not be easy always to combine the two, but it is the thing to be aimed at. And the best way of attaining it will be to keep ever in mind that this solemn doctrine concerns ourselves as well as others. It shows us what even our sin deserves, and therefore ought to humble us; it shows us what, if left to ourselves, must be our doom, and thus should fill us with fear and trembling. If we ever remember this, we shall be able to speak even of this awful subject kindly, though solemnly, as sinful men to brother sinners; and knowing for ourselves the fear of the Lord, we shall persuade men to be reconciled to Him.[1]

### REWARDS AND ACTIVITIES OF THE SAINTS IN HEAVEN

In regard to the rewards and activities of the perfected saints in heaven, besides the statements of their blessed fellowship with God, and exercises of adoration and praise, it is indicated that they shall receive enlarged powers, and opportunities of exercising them in the service of God, in proportion as they have used their gifts here. This is implied in our Lord's parables of the Pounds (Luke 19[12]) and of the Talents (Matt. 25[14]). To be placed over many things, to have authority over cities, must denote to have a position of honourable work for our fellows as well as for God's glory. The same thing would seem to be indicated in Jesus' promise to the Twelve, "that ye may eat and drink with Me in My kingdom, and sit on thrones, judging the twelve tribes of Israel" (Luke 22[30]), though this saying is highly figurative, and may possibly refer to privileges enjoyed in this life. But the promise of sitting on Christ's throne (Rev. 3[20]) seems clearly to refer to the future state. To that also, it would seem, must we apply Paul's mysterious statement that the saints shall judge the world and even angels (1 Cor. 6[2, 3]). The same apostle also speaks of the Church being the means of showing to the principalities and powers in the heavenlies the manifold wisdom of God, and showing in the ages to come the exceeding riches of His grace (Eph. 2[7] 3[10]).

Thus, though generally in the New Testament the outlook to the future extends only to the last judgment and a vision of eternal peace and blessedness beyond, there are various passages that give us a glimpse of activity in that holy and happy state. Can we from any of these glimpses, or the analogy of Scripture, form any notion as to what that activity may probably be?

---
[1] White, *Life in Christ*; Farrar, *Eternal Hope*; Cox, *Salvator Mundi*; Clemance, *Future Punishment*; Salmond, *Doctrine of Immortality*.

The most distinct idea suggested by them is that of kingly rule; and we know that the Christian idea of a king is that he is a minister of God for good to those whom he rules, more especially guiding and helping those whom he rules to obey the will of God and enjoy His blessing. Hence it would seem that the function of the redeemed is to lead other intelligent creatures of God to loyal and loving obedience to Him. Such a task would afford scope for the happy exercise of the highest intellectual and moral powers, and would be altogether worthy of God to intrust to those who have been tried on earth and found faithful.

Now, we may reverently ask, who are those intelligent creatures of God to whom the redeemed in Christ may be supposed thus to minister? Is it likely that they are merely those angels and men who have already lived, and sinned, and been condemned at the universal judgment? Is there any indication in Scripture that points to this? or would the perfected saints in Christ have anything to reveal to such creatures that they did not already know, or any influence more powerful to bring to bear on them than they had already resisted? To me there seems more probability in the idea to which some profound thinkers have been led, that the subjects of the future ministry of the redeemed Church in Christ shall be intelligences yet to be brought into existence in the ages to come, and that the great and everlasting increase of the rational universe and kingdom of God is to take place after the present dispensation has been wound up at the last judgment. This idea enables us to see that the redeemed in Christ may have a special function in relation to the future universe, and that they have been elected and saved, not for their own sakes merely, but to be ministers of holiness and happiness to millions of other souls. That this has not been more generally seen and applied as a key to the understanding of God's purpose is due, I think, to the fact that one or other of two extreme opinions has prevailed as to the relation of God's grace to man's free will, either of which makes the idea just stated impossible or meaningless. One of these opinions is that the will of man must always be free to choose good or evil, and to reject and repel all the influences that the grace of God can bring to bear on it. If this be so, then in any future worlds or ages there must be the same possibility of evil and fall as in the present, and the redeemed Church of Christ would have no special power to train coming races in a sure course of obedience and holiness. Hence Origen, though his wide range of thought extended to ages in the future, could only conceive of them as repetitions of the course of things in this world—freedom, fall, chastisement, and restoration.

The opposite opinion is that God has power in all circumstances, without infringing on the liberty of the will, to prevent sin if He so pleased, and to turn sinners to Himself. In that case the entrance of evil in future worlds might be prevented simply by the gracious will of God; and the employment of Christ and His Church for this end would not be needful, or in any special way efficacious.

Thus, on either of these suppositions, the idea of the finally saved being employed in ministries of grace to other souls, though it might be an interesting speculation, could not form an essential or important part in the general conception of God's government or plan of the universe. But if we take an intermediate position, and say that God can and does secure the conversion of sinners and the perseverance of believers by means of His love and grace manifested in Christ's life and death for sinners, but that for aught we know it may be inconsistent with their free will to keep new created souls from sinning at first and apart from the work of Christ, then we can see how the redeemed Church of Christ may have quite peculiar qualifications for securing, through their testimony of the love of God in Christ, that new created worlds be kept from sin at all, and enabled to serve God freely under the influence of His love alone. They may thus be fitted for a unique and most important function in the universe, and that not by any merit of their own, but by the love and work of Christ that has redeemed them; and the future ages may be neither an endless uniformity nor a mere repetition of the past, but a scene of constant progress, of revealing the grace and glory of God to successive ranks of intelligences to be created, whose nature and history may be endlessly varied, yet without sin.

Thus, too, we can see the cosmical importance of Christ, and His redeemed Church as united to Him; and can meet the difficulty felt by many, in view of modern astronomy, that it is hard to believe that the Son of God became incarnate and died for sin in this earth, so small compared with the vast orbs and systems of the stellar universe. If this divine redemption was destined to be the means not only of redeeming sinners of mankind, but of preventing the entrance of sin and misery in numberless other worlds to be peopled with free and loyal servants of God, could that be said to be unworthy of God? Would it not be entirely in harmony with the Providence that chose the least of all lands as the scene of His revelation here, and the people that were very few and strangers in it to be a blessing to all the families of the earth?

In the discussion carried on in the last generation about the plurality of worlds, it was pointed out, in reply to the argument that it is hard to suppose this globe to be the only seat of rational life in the universe, that for long ages this earth was destitute of living and intelligent creatures while it was in preparation for them, and that so it may be now with other planets even if they have no inhabitants as yet. In like manner the whole long drama of sin, redemption, salvation, and judgment that is running its course in human history, may be but the beginning of the eternal process by which God communicates His holiness and happiness to endless ages of intelligent creatures.

This may, I think, be what is pointed to in Paul's statements about the purpose of God to recapitulate or reconcile to Himself all things in Christ, both things in earth and things in heaven. Christ's redemption extends, as the apostle wrote to the Romans, to the deliverance of the lower creation from the bondage of corruption into the liberty of the glory of the sons of God; it may also include the deliverance of all rational agents that are to be created from the danger of mutability and apostasy from God. It may be conceived to do so because the revelation of all God's attributes in the redeeming work of Christ shows Him to be so transcendently good and lovely as to win and keep the love of free intelligences from ever wandering away from Him.

For this glorious end it may also have been necessary for aught we know that there should be a manifestation of the holiness and justice of God in the just punishment of those who obstinately refuse to obey His will and to accept His offered mercy, and that there should be an everlasting memorial of their righteous doom, though not perhaps that their conscious suffering should endure for ever.

This whole speculation, which is not a mere fancy, but is based on certain New Testament statements, implies a view of the relation of man's will to God's providence and grace which differs from those that have been generally held, but which is, I think, countenanced both by reason and Scripture.

Opinion on this subject has generally been divided between two opposite extremes before referred to, either that the will of man is endowed with such freedom that it can never be certainly determined even by the gracious power of God, but must always have the power of determining itself either for or against it; or that the influence of divine grace is so great that it can always, and in any circumstances, determine the will of man, though not by co-action or necessity, but so as to preserve its freedom. Apart from philosophical considerations, the former view is, I think, disproved by the biblical declarations that God creates in us a new heart, draws us to Christ so that we certainly come, works in us to will and to do, gives faith and repentance,—declarations which have been verified in the experience of many. But it does not follow that because this extreme is not true the opposite is; and there are statements in Scripture that cannot easily or naturally be reconciled with it. Some are described as so hardened that it is impossible to renew them again unto repentance (Heb. $6^{4-6}$); over some Jesus wept, because, though He earnestly desired and sought to save them, they would not (Luke $19^{41}$); and the Lord says by Isaiah, "What could have been done more for My vineyard, that I have not done in it?" (Isa. $5^4$). The most obvious significance of these words is that there are certain conditions in which even divine power cannot certainly turn men's will from evil. This must be, doubtless, because in these cases habit has become as strong as a second nature; and though the physical power of God is infinite, to apply it for this purpose would destroy the essential nature of the will. The power by which He does convert sinners is the spiritual one of love, which does, indeed, work not by mere moral suasion presenting outward motives, but by bringing the constraining influence of the love of Christ to bear on the soul. Thus it may be true that sin has entered the universe because it was not possible at the outset to prevent new-created moral agents from sinning without taking away their freedom; but that through the love revealed in the redemption of Christ, not only can sinners be converted and confirmed in holiness and free obedience, but new orders of rational and moral agents can be created, who, through the story of that love and redemption being brought home to their minds and hearts, may be certainly and for ever kept from sinning without any infringement of their liberty. On the other hand, it may be that none are finally condemned except such as having refused to obey God's law, or to accept His mercy, have finally so hardened themselves that it is impossible to renew them to repentance.

## II. THE DOCTRINE OF CHRIST'S INTERCESSION

IT has been generally held by theologians that our Saviour's work as a Priest includes not only His once offering Himself a sacrifice, but His making continual intercession for us, the latter being that part of His priestly office which He performs in His exaltation as a Priest on His throne. In order, then, to see whether this representation is well founded, and what is its true and essential meaning, let us consider—

1. *The biblical foundation of the doctrine.*—The following are the places in Scripture where the word intercede, or equivalent phrases, are used in reference to Christ:—

(1) In Paul's Epistle to the Romans ($8^{34}$) the verb ἐντυγχάνει is put as the last of four, describing Christ's work as the ground of believers' hope: He died, He rose again, He is at the right hand of God, He makes intercession. Parallel to this is the use of the term μεσίτης, 1 Tim. $2^5$, as describing a still present function of Jesus, in addition to His ransom in the past.

(2) In Heb. $7^{25}$ the same word ἐντυγχάνειν is used of Christ, and further on in the Epistle it is illustrated by the analogy of the high priest entering the holiest of all on behalf of the people. In $9^{24}$ we have ἐμφανισθῆναι, to appear; and in $12^{24}$ we have the title μεσίτης given Him as in 1 Tim.

In Heb. $12^{15}$ and 1 Pet. $2^5$ we have the idea that Christians' worship is acceptable to God only through Christ.

(3) In 1 John $2^1$ Jesus is called our Advocate (παράκλητον) with the Father, *i.e.* one who appears and pleads for us, and through whom we obtain forgiveness.

(4) This points back to the discourses in the Fourth Gospel, where Jesus, while promising to send His disciples another Comforter, virtually claims to be Himself one (John

14[16]), urges them to pray in His name (16[24, 27]), and offers a most solemn prayer for and with them (17).

(5) In the discourses of Jesus recorded by Luke, we find in the parable of the Barren Fig-tree, the vinedresser interceding that it may be spared and get further culture (Luke 13[8]); again, in reference to Peter's approaching fall, Jesus says, "I have prayed for thee" ($\dot{\epsilon}\delta\epsilon\dot{\eta}\theta\eta\nu$), Luke 22[32]; and in 23[34] we have His intercessory prayer for His murderers.

(6) To these must be added the Old Testament passages about the priests' service in the holy place, which the writer to the Hebrews treats as being typical of Christ's priestly work not less really than their offering sacrifice. Also in the great prophecy Isa. 53[12], the servant of Jehovah who makes his soul a guilt-offering is also said to make intercession (יַפְגִּיעַ).

Now, with these passages before us, is there any reason to doubt that Jesus Himself taught that He intercedes for us? The presumption certainly is that He did, and that this is not merely an idea excogitated by His disciples at a later date, but one which they learned from Himself. For it is ascribed to Him, not only in the Fourth Gospel, but in that of Luke also; and is found not in one only, but in at least three distinct lines of apostolic teaching: the Pauline, the Johannine, and the Epistle to the Hebrews.

If it had been only in this last it might possibly be ascribed to Jewish ideas about the priesthood, but this would not account for its appearance in Paul's Epistles where Christ is never called a priest, nor in John's where the form of expression suggests no such ideas. So far as external evidence goes, there is every reason to believe that an idea which appears independently in these different apostolic teachings, and is ascribed to Jesus by two independent evangelists, did really proceed from Him and has His authority.

The only thing that could overcome such evidence would be an inconsistency between the notion of intercession and Christ's teaching as certainly known, or His idea of God. Such inconsistency has been alleged: and if intercession meant an influence used to persuade God to do something which He was else unwilling to do, then this would really be inconsistent with Jesus' teaching and idea of God. But this is not the meaning of intercession any more than it is of prayer in general, which Jesus most earnestly inculcated at the very time that He spoke of God's free bounty and willingness to bestow blessings. If we can form from the biblical representations an idea of Christ's intercession that is in harmony with the Christian conception of God, all reason for refusing to accept it as a part of Jesus' teaching will disappear.

We are thus led to consider—

2. *The nature of Christ's intercession as represented in Scripture.*—As to this, two things may be noticed in the context of the various texts in which it is mentioned.

(1) In most of them there is also mention made, in close connection with it, of the love of God as the source of this and of all saving blessings that come through it. Thus in Rom. 8, both before and after the statement that Christ makes intercession for us, there are emphatic assertions of God's predestination, election, love, as manifested especially in the gift of Christ. So also in 1 Tim. 2, where Christ is called Mediator, God's free and universal grace is also affirmed.

Again, in 1 John, where Jesus Christ is called our Advocate with the Father, there are equally express statements of God's readiness to forgive (1$^9$), and of His love in giving His Son (4$^{10}$).

In His great intercessory prayer (John 17) Jesus is careful to speak of Himself as sent by the Father, and doing His will (vers. $^{2,6}$).

In the Epistle to the Hebrews, intercession appears as an integral part of the priests' functions, and the writer lays great stress on the point of the priest having to be appointed by God (chs. 5$^{4-6}$ 7$^{20-22}$).

These considerations show negatively that the biblical conception of Christ's intercession is not that of persuading an unwilling God to be gracious; but positively, how intercession can find place with God, who is willing to grant it and has Himself appointed it, will appear from another circumstance in the scriptural representations.

(2) In most of the places in which it is mentioned, Christ's intercession is connected with His atoning death on the Cross.

Thus in Rom. 8³¹ the successive acts of the Saviour—died, rose, is at God's right hand, intercedes—are closely connected and form a climax.

In 1 John 2² He who is our Advocate is also described as Himself the propitiation (ἱλασμός) for our sins: that is the ground of His advocacy.

In the intercessory prayer, Jesus refers to His consecrating Himself on behalf of His disciples (John 17¹⁹) as the ground of His petitions; and when He says He had prayed for Peter, He had just before been instituting the sacrament that was to commemorate His death for our sins.

In the Epistle to the Hebrews this, like the other point, is pictorially brought out by the analogy of the priest in the tabernacle entering in before God for the people with the blood of the sacrifice.

From these observations we may gather an idea of our Lord's intercession that might be expressed thus:—Christ's presenting, according to the will and appointment of His Father, His own perfect obedience and sacrifice to God as the ground of the bestowal of forgiveness and all spiritual blessings on men. It is thus a part of Christ's priestly office, and its special purpose is to show, by an actual transaction, the connection between His sacrifice on the Cross and the salvation of His people. That sacrifice was necessary for our forgiveness; and God Himself provided it, giving His Son to die for us. But in the same way it was necessary that it should be made apparent that it is for the sake of Christ's sacrifice that sinners are blessed: hence God has appointed that Christ should appear before Him, presenting His finished work and pleading for the bestowal on His people of the blessings that they need. This argues no unwillingness in God to grant them, but only a determination that it shall be seen that He bestows them on account of the propitiation by which Christ has declared His righteousness in justifying the ungodly. The propriety of Christ's intercession rests ultimately on the same ground as that of His atonement, if that have any objective effect at all. Hence a strong argument for the objective view of the Atonement has been drawn from the Intercession,[1] while those who hold a merely subjective view find it very difficult to explain the Intercession.

In another point of view also Christ's intercession may be seen to be reasonable, inasmuch as it is His requesting as the God-man, the Head and Representative of His people, that His obedience and sacrifice be accepted and the great ends for which He died accomplished, *i.e.*, that He be glorified in the salvation and blessing of the innumerable company whom He has redeemed. This aspect of it is vividly brought out in His farewell discourses and intercessory prayer, in which all His petitions for His disciples are involved in that for Himself, that He may be glorified. Such prayer to God is most suitable to the character and work of Jesus; indeed, we cannot conceive Him as truly and perfectly human without believing that He must have offered such prayers. If, then, He is truly human still, and also acquainted with all our circumstances and wants, we conclude that He must be offering those prayers still, as we have seen Scripture represents Him as doing.

In this aspect Christ's intercession has the same reason and justification as prayer in general. If that is not inconsistent, either with the immutability of the divine purpose or with God's willingness to bestow the things asked for, neither is the intercession of Christ. God will be inquired of by us for what He has promised to bestow in order that our faith and His regard to us may be manifest, and so He says to His Son, "Ask of Me, and I will give Thee the heathen for Thine inheritance."

More particularly, intercessory prayer or petitions offered for others is a practice often enjoined and exemplified in the Bible from the earliest times. We find instances of it in Abraham (Gen. 18 and $20^7$), in Job ($42^8$), in Moses (Ex. $32^{30}$), in Samuel (1 Sam. $12^{23}$), in David (2 Sam. $24^{17}$), in Jeremiah ($7^{16}$), in Daniel (9), and very frequently in the New Testament.

---
[1] See Dr. H. Martin, *On the Atonement*.

In regard to the manner of Christ's intercession, we can say little more than that it is prayer offered on the ground of a perfect, all-prevailing plea. There has been a tendency, on the one hand, to an extreme literalism, and on the other hand to an excessive vagueness in the attempts to conceive of this precious work of Christ. Some have insisted on His intercession being oral or vocal—the actual utterance of articulate prayer as really as on earth. Since our Lord still possesses a body, spiritual and glorified, this is doubtless possible, and we cannot certainly say that it is not really so. But to assert that this must be the manner of Christ's intercession is not warranted in Scripture, and seems to give too much importance to what is material.

Others, again, have held it to be simply His presenting Himself before God as having accomplished the work of our redemption. This, too, has sometimes been represented in a very material way, as presenting His body with the marks of His wounds—nay, with the bleeding wounds themselves—before God. This is even a more gross materialising of a spiritual truth than to insist on actually vocal prayer.

These exaggerations of the material side of Christ's intercession have been chiefly made by the old Lutheran dogmatics. See references in Hase, *Hutterus Redivivus*, § 101.

Doubtless the simple appearance of Christ before God is an intercession in the most literal sense of the word; and in one place it is described as appearing in the presence of God for us (ἐμφανισθῆναι τῷ προσώπῳ τοῦ Θεοῦ ὑπὲρ ἡμῶν, Heb. 9[24]). But there is no reason to limit His intercession to this, or to exclude the offering up of His desires to God in the exercise of that spiritual devotion, aspiration, trust, love, unselfish benevolence, that are implied in intercessory prayer in general, whether merely mental or oral. This seems to be implied in the use of the word ἐντυγχάνειν of Christ, and in itself it is altogether worthy both of God and of Christ.

But Christ's intercession is prayer offered by one who has a just claim for what He desires, and therefore asks with full confidence of success. Hence we find that He uses of Himself not only the verb αἰτεῖν, which commonly describes our prayers, but ἐρωτᾶν (John 14¹⁶ 17⁹· ¹⁵· ²⁰), a word denoting more confidence and assurance of request. Also in John 17²⁴ He uses the word θέλω, " I will."

He who thus pleads for us is the Son, the Father's Fellow, and He asks in the full knowledge that the Father heareth Him always.

It remains now to consider—

3. *The extent of Christ's intercession*, or the persons for whom He pleads, in the way Scripture describes Him as doing; and in this, as under the former heads, we shall follow its guidance.

In His solemn and comprehensive intercessory prayer (John 17), Jesus expressly says that He prays not for the world, but for those whom the Father has given Him (v.⁹), *i.e.* (v.²⁰) for the disciples who had then believed, and for all who should hereafter believe through their word. It is true, as has been pointed out by Alford and others, that this only means that He was not then praying for the world, and also that in v.²¹ He mentions as a consequence or purpose of what he asks for His own, " that the world may believe that Thou hast sent Me"; and so again v.²³. Still the previous statements clearly show that the petitions for the proper blessings of salvation are offered by Christ specially and definitely for His people, those given Him by the Father, who do, or shall, by God's grace believe in Him.

In Rom. 8³⁴ it is said He maketh intercession for us, *i.e.*, unquestionably, according to the context, God's elect, those who are foreordained, called, justified, whom nothing can separate from the love of Christ.

In Heb. 7²⁵ His intercession is said to be for all who come to God through Him, where we see how it is definite indeed, and yet not so as to exclude any who desire an interest in it; for all who desire to approach God, and are willing to have Him as their Mediator.

Probably the same thing is indicated in 1 John 2¹, when it is said, " We have an Advocate with the Father," one who definitely pleads for us who confess our sins, but whom any man, yea the whole world, may have if they will do the same.

It seems clear, therefore, that Christ's intercession, in the full and proper sense, as an authoritative asking of blessings founded upon His redemption, and as set forth in those places where it is most fully described, is offered on behalf of His own people, and has a definite and particular reference to them; while at the same time this special reference need be no barrier to any sinner seeking God's face. Christ's intercession for His own affords hope and encouragement to all, since all are invited to come to Him; and whatever may be said of the secret purpose of God, we have His own assurance, "Him that cometh unto Me I will in nowise cast out."

This view of the extent of Christ's intercession is confirmed by the fact that, as we have before seen, it is always effectual. We cannot suppose that in what He asks of the Father, on the ground of His perfect sacrifice, Christ is ever refused. When, therefore, He asks for salvation for men, it must be for those who are actually saved. But I would not rely on this argument were there not direct Scripture testimony.

Whether there is Scripture evidence also for a universal intercession of Christ for all men is more doubtful. The Lutherans hold that there is, while allowing that the passages just referred to describe a special intercession for the elect. The chief passage on which they found is Christ's prayer on the Cross for His murderers (Luke $23^{34}$). This was an intercession, doubtless, for those who were not then believers in Christ; but many of them certainly became so afterwards on the day of Pentecost and later, and it is best to regard it as a prayer that was answered in the conversion and forgiveness of many who were guilty of His death. In the same way it is generally and justly believed that the prayer of the dying Stephen was answered in the conversion of Saul: "Si Stephanus non orasset, ecclesia Paulum non habuisset."[1]

A more pertinent proof may be urged from Luke $13^8$, where the vinedresser pleads for the barren fig-tree for a year's respite, taken in connection with the references to the world in John $17^{21, 23}$, as showing that Christ prays on behalf of all for a time of forbearance and for the knowledge of

[1] See Hase, *Hutterus Redivivus*, § 101, II.

the gospel; and, as in Rom. 3 the forbearance of God, as well as His complete forgiveness of sins, is represented as grounded on the manifestation of God's righteousness in Christ's propitiation, intercession for that would be grounded on the sacrifice, and would fulfil the conditions as to the nature of Christ's intercession. We might, therefore, hold a twofold reference of Christ's intercession—special, for the blessings of salvation; universal, for a day of grace and means of grace for all men.

Hase says that in the Reformed Dogmatic the intercession of Christ is little regarded, because the salvation of the elect is held to be sure from eternity. But here, I think, he is wrong, both in fact and reason. In point of fact, the doctrine of Christ's intercession has been greatly used by Calvinists in defending their view of the nature and extent of the Atonement, and has been constantly pressed as an argument against universal redemption. Nor have their views of predestination made them think it superfluous, but rather the reverse. Just because in our view salvation depends on the will of God, through the redemption of Christ, the assurance that Christ is presenting that redemption, and pleading its merit for us, has a meaning and a value for us, as I have tried to show. But on any view that makes salvation depend ultimately on the will of man, so as to be hindered by its resistance, it is hard to see how any pleading of Christ before God, or anything that God may do in response to such pleading, can secure salvation, or remove the real obstacle.

PUBLICATIONS OF

# T. & T. CLARK,
## 38 GEORGE STREET, EDINBURGH.
### LONDON: SIMPKIN, MARSHALL, HAMILTON, KENT, & CO. LIMITED.

**Abbott (T. K., B.D., D.Lit.)**—EPHESIANS AND COLOSSIANS. (*International Critical Commentary.*) Post 8vo, 10s. 6d.

**Adam (J., D.D.)**—AN EXPOSITION OF THE EPISTLE OF JAMES. 8vo, 9s.

**Adamson (Rev. T., D.D.)**—STUDIES OF THE MIND IN CHRIST. Post 8vo, 4s. 6d.

——— THE SPIRIT OF POWER. Second Edition. Fcap. 8vo, 1s.

**Ahlfeld (Dr.), etc.**—THE VOICE FROM THE CROSS. Cr. 8vo, price 5s.

**Alcock (Deborah)**—THE SEVEN CHURCHES OF ASIA. 1s.

**Alexander (Prof. W. Lindsay)**—BIBLICAL THEOLOGY. Two vols. 8vo, 21s.

**Allen (Prof. A. V. G., D.D.)**—CHRISTIAN INSTITUTIONS. (*International Theological Library.*) Post 8vo, 12s.

**Ancient Faith in Modern Light, The.** 8vo, 10s. 6d.

**Andrews (S. J.)**—THE LIFE OF OUR LORD. Large post 8vo, 9s.

**Ante-Nicene Christian Library**—A COLLECTION OF ALL THE WORKS OF THE FATHERS OF THE CHRISTIAN CHURCH PRIOR TO THE COUNCIL OF NICÆA. Twenty-four vols. 8vo, Subscription price, £6, 6s. *Additional Volume, containing MSS. discovered since the completion of the Series,* 12s. 6d. net.

**Augustine's Works**—Edited by MARCUS DODS, D.D. Fifteen vols. 8vo, Subscription price, £3, 19s. net.

**Balfour (R. G., D.D.)**—CENTRAL TRUTHS AND SIDE ISSUES. Crown 8vo, 3s. 6d.

**Bannerman (Prof.)**—THE CHURCH OF CHRIST. Two vols. 8vo, 21s.

**Bannerman (D. D., D.D.)**—THE DOCTRINE OF THE CHURCH. 8vo, 12s.

**Baumgarten (Professor)**—APOSTOLIC HISTORY. Three vols. 8vo, 27s.

**Bayne (P., LL.D.)**—THE FREE CHURCH OF SCOTLAND. Post 8vo, 3s. 6d.

**Beck (Dr.)**—OUTLINES OF BIBLICAL PSYCHOLOGY. Crown 8vo, 4s.

——— PASTORAL THEOLOGY OF THE NEW TESTAMENT. Crown 8vo, 6s.

**Bengel**—GNOMON OF THE NEW TESTAMENT. With Original Notes, Explanatory and Illustrative. Five vols. 8vo, Subscription price, 31s. 6d. *Cheaper Edition, the five volumes bound in three,* 24s.

**Besser's** CHRIST THE LIFE OF THE WORLD. Price 6s.

**Beyschlag (W., D.D.)**—NEW TESTAMENT THEOLOGY. Two vols. demy 8vo, 18s. net.

**Bible Dictionary.** Edited by JAS. HASTINGS, D.D. *See page 16. Special Prospectus on application.* Vols. I. and II. now ready.

**Bible-Class Handbooks.** Crown 8vo. Forty-four Volumes, 1s. 3d. to 3s. each. Edited by Prof. MARCUS DODS, D.D., and ALEX. WHYTE, D.D. *Detailed List free on application.*

\*\*\* *Detailed Catalogue free on application.*

**Bible-Class Primers.** Thirty-four now issued in the Series. Edited by Princ. S. D. F. SALMOND, D.D. Paper covers, 6d. each; free by post, 7d. In cloth, 8d.; free by post, 9d. *Detailed List free on application.*

**Blaikie (Prof. W. G., D.D.)**—THE PREACHERS OF SCOTLAND FROM THE 6TH TO THE 19TH CENTURY. Post 8vo, 7s. 6d.

**Blake (Buchanan, B.D.)**—HOW TO READ THE PROPHETS. Part I.— The Pre-Exilian Minor Prophets (with Joel). Second Edition, 4s. Part II.—Isaiah (ch. i.-xxxix.). Second Edition, 2s. 6d. Part III.—Jeremiah, 4s. Part IV.—Ezekiel, 4s. Part V.—Isaiah (ch. xl.-lxvi.), and the Post-Exilian Prophets. *The Series being now complete, Messrs. Clark offer the Set of Five Volumes for 15s.*

**Bleek's** INTRODUCTION TO THE NEW TESTAMENT. Two vols. 8vo, 21s.

**Briggs (Prof. C. A., D.D.)**—GENERAL INTRODUCTION TO THE STUDY OF HOLY SCRIPTURE (*Replacing the Author's* 'Biblical Study,' *entirely re-written and greatly enlarged*). 8vo, 12s. net.

—— MESSIANIC PROPHECY. Post 8vo, 7s. 6d.

—— THE MESSIAH OF THE APOSTLES. Post 8vo, 7s. 6d.

—— THE MESSIAH OF THE GOSPELS. Post 8vo, 6s. 6d.

—— THE BIBLE, THE CHURCH, AND THE REASON. Post 8vo, 6s. 6d.

**Brockelmann (C.)**—LEXICON SYRIACUM. With a Preface by Professor T. NÖLDEKE. Crown 4to, 30s. net.

**Bruce (Prof. A. B., D.D.)**—THE TRAINING OF THE TWELVE; exhibiting the Twelve Disciples under Discipline for the Apostleship. Fifth Edition, 8vo, 10s. 6d.

—— THE HUMILIATION OF CHRIST. 3rd Ed., 8vo, 10s. 6d.

—— THE KINGDOM OF GOD; or, Christ's Teaching according to the Synoptical Gospels. New Edition, 7s. 6d.

—— APOLOGETICS; OR, CHRISTIANITY DEFENSIVELY STATED. (*International Theological Library.*) Post 8vo, 10s. 6d.

—— ST. PAUL'S CONCEPTION OF CHRISTIANITY. Post 8vo, 7s. 6d.

—— THE EPISTLE TO THE HEBREWS: The First Apology for Christianity. Just published. Post 8vo, 7s. 6d.

**Bruce (W. S., D.D.)**—THE ETHICS OF THE OLD TESTAMENT. Cr. 8vo, 4s.

**Buchanan (Professor)**—THE DOCTRINE OF JUSTIFICATION. 8vo, 10s. 6d.

—— ON COMFORT IN AFFLICTION. Crown 8vo, 2s. 6d.

—— ON IMPROVEMENT OF AFFLICTION. Crown 8vo, 2s. 6d.

**Bungener (Felix)**—ROME AND THE COUNCIL IN 19TH CENTURY. Cr. 8vo, 5s.

**Burton (Prof. E.)**—SYNTAX OF THE MOODS AND TENSES IN NEW TESTAMENT GREEK. New Edition. Post 8vo, 5s. 6d. net.

**Calvin's** INSTITUTES OF CHRISTIAN RELIGION. (Translation.) 2 vols. 8vo, 14s.

—— COMMENTARIES. Forty-five Vols.

**Calvini Institutio Christianæ Religionis.** Curavit A. THOLUCK. Two vols. 8vo, Subscription price, 14s.

**Candlish (Prof. J. S., D.D.)**—THE KINGDOM OF GOD, BIBLICALLY AND HISTORICALLY CONSIDERED. 8vo, 10s. 6d.

**Caspari (C. E.)**—A CHRONOLOGICAL AND GEOGRAPHICAL INTRODUCTION TO THE LIFE OF CHRIST. 8vo, 7s. 6d.

**Caspers (A.)**—THE FOOTSTEPS OF CHRIST. Crown 8vo, 7s. 6d.

## T. and T. Clark's Publications. 3

**Cassel (Prof.)**—COMMENTARY ON ESTHER. 8vo, 10s. 6d.
**Cave (Principal A., D.D.)**—THE SCRIPTURAL DOCTRINE OF SACRIFICE AND ATONEMENT. Second Edition, 8vo, 10s. 6d.
—— AN INTRODUCTION TO THEOLOGY. Second Edition, 8vo, 12s.
**Chapman (Principal C., LL.D.)**—PRE-ORGANIC EVOLUTION AND THE BIBLICAL IDEA OF GOD. Crown 8vo, 6s.
**Christlieb (Prof. T., D.D.)**—MODERN DOUBT AND CHRISTIAN BELIEF. 8vo, 10s. 6d.
—— HOMILETIC: Lectures on Preaching. 7s. 6d.
**Clark (Professor W. R., LL.D., D.C.L.)**—THE ANGLICAN REFORMATION. (*Eras of Church History.*) 6s.
**Clarke (Professor W. N., D.D.)**—AN OUTLINE OF CHRISTIAN THEOLOGY. Post 8vo, 7s. 6d.
**Concordance to the Greek Testament**—MOULTON (W. F., D.D.) and GEDEN (A. S., M.A.). Crown 4to, 26s. net.
**Crawford (J. H., M.A.)**—THE BROTHERHOOD OF MANKIND. Crown 8vo, 5s.
**Cremer (Professor)**—BIBLICO-THEOLOGICAL LEXICON OF NEW TESTAMENT GREEK. Third Edition, with Supplement, demy 4to, 38s.
**Crippen (Rev. T. G.)**—A POPULAR INTRODUCTION TO THE HISTORY OF CHRISTIAN DOCTRINE. 8vo, 9s.
**Critical Review** OF THEOLOGICAL AND PHILOSOPHICAL LITERATURE. Edited by Princ. S. D. F. SALMOND, D.D. Quarterly, 1s. 6d.
**Cunningham (Principal)**—HISTORICAL THEOLOGY. Two vols. 8vo, 21s.
**Curtiss (Dr. S. I.)**—THE LEVITICAL PRIESTS. Crown 8vo, 5s.
—— FRANZ DELITZSCH: A Memorial Tribute. *Portrait.* Cr. 8vo, 3s.
**Dabney (Prof. R. L., D.D.)**—THE SENSUALISTIC PHILOSOPHY OF THE NINETEENTH CENTURY CONSIDERED. Crown 8vo, 6s.
**Dahle (Bishop)**—LIFE AFTER DEATH. Demy 8vo, 10s. 6d.
**Davidson (Prof. A.B., D.D., LL.D.)**—AN INTRODUCTORY HEBREW GRAMMAR. With Progressive Exercises in Reading and Writing. 15th Edition, 8vo, 7s. 6d.
—— A SYNTAX OF THE HEBREW LANGUAGE. 2nd Ed., 8vo, 7s. 6d.
**Davidson, Dr. Samuel.** Autobiography and Diary. Edited by his DAUGHTER. 8vo, 7s. 6d.
**Deane (Wm., M.A.)**—PSEUDEPIGRAPHA: An Account of Certain Apocryphal Writings of the Jews and Early Christians. Post 8vo, 7s. 6d.
**Delitzsch (Prof.)**—SYSTEM OF BIBLICAL PSYCHOLOGY, 8vo, 12s.; NEW COMMENTARY ON GENESIS, 2 vols. 8vo, 21s.; PSALMS, 3 vols., 31s. 6d.; PROVERBS, 2 vols., 21s.; SONG OF SOLOMON AND ECCLESIASTES, 10s. 6d.; ISAIAH, Fourth Edition, rewritten, 2 vols., 21s.; HEBREWS, 2 vols., 21s.
**Dictionary of the Bible, A.** (*See page 16.*)
**Dillmann (Prof. A., D.D.)**—GENESIS: Critical and Exegetical Commentary. Two vols., 21s.
**Doedes**—MANUAL OF NEW TESTAMENT HERMENEUTICS. Cr. 8vo, 3s.
**Döllinger (Dr.)**—HIPPOLYTUS AND CALLISTUS. 8vo, 7s. 6d.
—— DECLARATIONS AND LETTERS ON THE VATICAN DECREES, 1869-1887. Authorised Translation. Crown 8vo, 3s. 6d.
**Dorner (Professor)**—HISTORY OF THE DEVELOPMENT OF THE DOCTRINE OF THE PERSON OF CHRIST. Five vols. 8vo, £2, 12s. 6d.
—— SYSTEM OF CHRISTIAN DOCTRINE. 4 vols. 8vo, £2, 2s.

**Dorner (Professor)**—SYSTEM OF CHRISTIAN ETHICS. 8vo, 14s.
**Driver (Prof. S. R., D.D.)**—AN INTRODUCTION TO THE LITERATURE OF THE OLD TESTAMENT. (*International Theological Library.*) 7th Edition, post 8vo, 12s.
—— DEUTERONOMY : A Critical and Exegetical Commentary. (*International Critical Commentary.*) Post 8vo, 12s.
**Du Bose (Prof. W. P., D.D.)**—THE ECUMENICAL COUNCILS. (*Eras of Church History.*) 6s.
**Duff (Prof. David, D.D.)**—THE EARLY CHURCH. 8vo, 12s.
**Dyke (Paul Van)**—THE AGE OF THE RENASCENCE. With an Introduction by HENRY VAN DYKE. (*Eras of Church History.*) 6s.
**Eadie (Professor)**—COMMENTARIES ON ST. PAUL'S EPISTLES TO THE EPHESIANS, PHILIPPIANS, COLOSSIANS. New and Revised Editions, Edited by Rev. WM. YOUNG, M.A. Three vols. 8vo, 10s. 6d. each ; *or set,* 18s. *net.*
**Ebrard (Dr. J. H. A.)**—THE GOSPEL HISTORY. 8vo, 10s. 6d.
—— APOLOGETICS. Three vols. 8vo, 31s. 6d.
—— COMMENTARY ON THE EPISTLES OF ST. JOHN. 8vo, 10s. 6d.
**Edgar (R. M'C., D.D.)**—THE GOSPEL OF A RISEN SAVIOUR. Post 8vo, 7s. 6d.
**Elliott**—ON THE INSPIRATION OF THE HOLY SCRIPTURES. 8vo, 6s.
**Eras of the Christian Church**—
   DU BOSE (Prof. W. P., D.D.)—The Ecumenical Councils. 6s.
   WATERMAN (L., D.D.)—The Post-Apostolic Age. 6s.
   DYKE (PAUL VAN)—The Age of the Renascence. 6s.
   LOCKE (CLINTON, D.D.)—The Age of the Great Western Schism. 6s.
   LUDLOW (J. M., D.D.)—The Age of the Crusades. 6s.
   VINCENT (Prof. M. R., D.D.)—The Age of Hildebrand. 6s.
   CLARK (Prof. W. R., LL.D., D.C.L.)—The Anglican Reformation. 6s.
   WELLS (Prof. C. L.)—The Age of Charlemagne. 6s.
   *The following Two Volumes, completing the Series, are in preparation—*
   BARTLET (J. VERNON, M.A.)—The Apostolic Age.
   WALKER (Prof. W., Ph.D., D.D.)—The Protestant Reformation.
**Ernesti**—BIBLICAL INTERPRETATION OF NEW TESTAMENT. Two vols., 8s.
**Ewald (Heinrich)**—HEBREW SYNTAX. 8vo, 8s. 6d.
—— REVELATION : Its Nature and Record. 8vo, 10s. 6d.
—— OLD AND NEW TESTAMENT THEOLOGY. 8vo, 10s. 6d.
**Expository Times.** Edited by JAMES HASTINGS, D.D. Monthly, 6d.
**Fairbairn (Prin.)**—THE REVELATION OF LAW IN SCRIPTURE, 8vo, 10s. 6d.
—— EZEKIEL AND THE BOOK OF HIS PROPHECY. 4th Ed., 8vo, 10s. 6d.
—— PROPHECY. Second Edition, 8vo, 10s. 6d.
—— PASTORAL THEOLOGY. Crown 8vo, 6s.
**Fisher (Prof. G. P., D.D., LL.D.)**—HISTORY OF CHRISTIAN DOCTRINE. (*International Theological Library.*) Post 8vo, 12s.
**Forbes (Prof.)**—SYMMETRICAL STRUCTURE OF SCRIPTURE. 8vo, 8s. 6d.
—— ANALYTICAL COMMENTARY ON ROMANS. 8vo, 10s. 6d.
—— STUDIES IN THE BOOK OF PSALMS. 8vo, 7s. 6d.
—— THE SERVANT OF THE LORD IN ISAIAH XL.-LXVI. Cr. 8vo, 5s.
**Foreign Theological Library**—*For details see p.* 13.

## T. and T. Clark's Publications. 5

**Forrest (D. W., D.D.)**—THE CHRIST OF HISTORY AND OF EXPERIENCE. 10s. 6d.
**Frank (Prof. F. H.)**—SYSTEM OF CHRISTIAN CERTAINTY. 8vo, 10s. 6d.
**Funcke (Otto)**—THE WORLD OF FAITH AND THE EVERYDAY WORLD, As displayed in the Footsteps of Abraham. Post 8vo, 7s. 6d.
**Gebhardt (H.)**—THE DOCTRINE OF THE APOCALYPSE, AND ITS RELATION TO THE DOCTRINE OF THE GOSPEL AND EPISTLES OF JOHN. 8vo, 10s. 6d.
**Gerlach**—COMMENTARY ON THE PENTATEUCH. 8vo, 10s. 6d.
**Gieseler (Dr. J. C. L.)**—ECCLESIASTICAL HISTORY. Four vols. 8vo, £2, 2s.
**Gifford (Canon)**—VOICES OF THE PROPHETS. Crown 8vo, 3s. 6d.
**Given (Rev. Prof. J. J.)**—THE TRUTH OF SCRIPTURE IN CONNECTION WITH REVELATION, INSPIRATION, AND THE CANON. 8vo, 6s.
**Gladden (Washington, D.D., LL.D.)** THE CHRISTIAN PASTOR AND THE WORKING CHURCH. (*International Theol. Library.*) Post 8vo, 10s. 6d.
**Glasgow (Prof.)**—APOCALYPSE TRANSLATED AND EXPOUNDED. 8vo, 10/6.
**Gloag (Paton J., D.D.)**—THE MESSIANIC PROPHECIES. Crown 8vo, 7s. 6d.
———— INTRODUCTION TO THE CATHOLIC EPISTLES. 8vo, 10s. 6d.
———— EXEGETICAL STUDIES. Crown 8vo, 5s.
———— INTRODUCTION TO THE SYNOPTIC GOSPELS. 8vo, 7s. 6d.
———— THE PRIMEVAL WORLD. Crown 8vo, 3s.
**Godet (Prof. F.)**—AN INTRODUCTION TO THE NEW TESTAMENT: 'The Epistles of St. Paul.' *Authorised Translation.* 8vo, 12s. 6d. net.
———— COMMENTARY ON ST. LUKE'S GOSPEL. Two vols. 8vo, 21s.
———— COMMENTARY ON ST. JOHN'S GOSPEL. Three vols. 8vo, 31s. 6d.
———— COMMENTARY ON EPISTLE TO THE ROMANS. Two vols. 8vo, 21s.
———— COMMENTARY ON 1ST EPISTLE TO CORINTHIANS. 2 vols. 8vo, 21s.
———— DEFENCE OF THE CHRISTIAN FAITH. Crown 8vo, 4s.
**Goebel (Siegfried)**—THE PARABLES OF JESUS. 8vo, 10s. 6d.
**Gotthold's Emblems**; or, INVISIBLE THINGS UNDERSTOOD BY THINGS THAT ARE MADE. Crown 8vo, 5s.
**Gould (Prof. E. P., D.D.)**—ST. MARK. (*International Critical Commentary.*) Post 8vo, 10s. 6d.
**Grimm's** GREEK-ENGLISH LEXICON OF THE NEW TESTAMENT. Translated, Revised, and Enlarged by JOSEPH H. THAYER, D.D. Demy 4to, 36s.
**Guyot (Arnold, LL.D.)**—CREATION; or, The Biblical Cosmogony in the Light of Modern Science. With Illustrations. Crown 8vo, 5s. 6d.
**Hagenbach (Dr. K. R.)**—HISTORY OF DOCTRINES. 3 vols. 8vo, 31s. 6d.
———— HISTORY OF THE REFORMATION. 2 vols. 8vo, 21s.
**Halcombe (Rev. J. J., M.A.)**—WHAT THINK YE OF THE GOSPELS? A Handbook of Gospel Study. 8vo, 3s. 6d.
**Hall (Newman, D.D.)**—THE LORD'S PRAYER. Third Edition, crown 8vo, 4s. 6d.
———— GETHSEMANE; or, Leaves of Healing from the Garden of Grief. Second Edition, crown 8vo, 4s.
———— DIVINE BROTHERHOOD. Crown 8vo, 4s.
**Hamilton (T., D.D.)**—BEYOND THE STARS; or, Heaven, its Inhabitants, Occupations, and Life. Third Edition, crown 8vo, 3s. 6d.
**Harless (Dr. C. A.)**—SYSTEM OF CHRISTIAN ETHICS. 8vo, 10s. 6d.

**Harris (S., D.D.)**—GOD THE CREATOR AND LORD OF ALL. Two vols. post 8vo, 16s.

**Haupt (Erich)**—THE FIRST EPISTLE OF ST. JOHN. 8vo, 10s. 6d.

**Hävernick (H. A. Ch.)**—INTRODUCTION TO OLD TESTAMENT. 10s. 6d.

**Heard (Rev. J. B., M.A.)**—THE TRIPARTITE NATURE OF MAN—SPIRIT, SOUL, AND BODY. Fifth Edition, crown 8vo, 6s.

—— OLD AND NEW THEOLOGY. A Constructive Critique. Cr. 8vo, 6s.

—— ALEXANDRIAN AND CARTHAGINIAN THEOLOGY CONTRASTED. The Hulsean Lectures, 1892-93. Crown 8vo, 6s.

**Hefele (Bishop)**—A HISTORY OF THE COUNCILS OF THE CHURCH. Vol. I., to A.D. 325. Vol. II., A.D. 326 to 429. Vol. III., A.D. 431 to the close of the Council of Chalcedon, 451. Vol. IV., A.D. 451 to 680. Vol. V., A.D. 626 to 787. 8vo, 12s. each.

**Hengstenberg (Professor)**—COMMENTARY ON PSALMS, 3 vols. 8vo, 33s.; ECCLESIASTES, ETC., 8vo, 9s.; EZEKIEL, 8vo, 10s. 6d.; THE GENUINENESS OF DANIEL, ETC., 8vo, 12s.; HISTORY OF THE KINGDOM OF GOD, 2 vols. 8vo, 21s.; CHRISTOLOGY OF THE OLD TESTAMENT, 4 vols. 8vo, £2, 2s.; ST. JOHN'S GOSPEL, 2 vols. 8vo, 21s.

**Herzog**—ENCYCLOPÆDIA OF LIVING DIVINES, ETC., OF ALL DE-NOMINATIONS IN EUROPE AND AMERICA. (*Supplement to Herzog's Encyclopædia.*) Imp. 8vo, 8s.

**Hill (Rev. J. Hamlyn, D.D.)**—THE EARLIEST LIFE OF CHRIST EVER COMPILED FROM THE FOUR GOSPELS: Being 'The Diatessaron of Tatian' Literally Translated from the Arabic Version, and containing the Four Gospels woven into one Story. With an Historical and Critical Introduction, Notes, and Appendix. 8vo, 10s. 6d.

—— ST. EPHRAEM THE SYRIAN. 8vo, 7s. 6d.

**Hodgson (Principal J. M., M.A., D.Sc., D.D.)**—THEOLOGIA PECTORIS: Outlines of Religious Faith and Doctrine. Crown 8vo, 3s. 6d.

**Hutchison (John, D.D.)**—COMMENTARY ON THESSALONIANS. 8vo, 9s.

—— COMMENTARY ON PHILIPPIANS. 8vo, 7s. 6d.

—— OUR LORD'S SIGNS IN ST. JOHN'S GOSPEL. Demy 8vo, 7s. 6d.

**Innes (A. Taylor)**—THE TRIAL OF JESUS CHRIST. In its Legal Aspect. [*In the Press.*

**International Critical Commentary.**
DRIVER (Prof. S. R., D.D.)—Deuteronomy. Post 8vo, 12s.
MOORE (Prof. G. F., D.D.)—Judges. 12s.
SMITH (Prof. H. P., D.D.)—Samuel. 12s.
GOULD (Prof. E. P., D.D.)—St. Mark. 10s. 6d.
PLUMMER (ALFRED, D.D.)—St. Luke. 12s.
SANDAY (Prof. W., D.D.) and HEADLAM (A. C., B.D.)—Romans. 12s.
ABBOTT (Prof. T. K., B.D., D.Lit.)—Ephesians and Colossians. 10s. 6d.
VINCENT (Prof. M. R., D.D.)—Philippians and Philemon. 8s. 6d.
*For List of future Volumes see p. 15.*

**International Theological Library.**
DRIVER (Prof. S. R., D.D.)—An Introduction to the Literature of the Old Testament. Post 8vo, 12s.
SMYTH (NEWMAN, D.D.)—Christian Ethics. Post 8vo, 10s. 6d.
BRUCE (Prof. A. B., D.D.)—Apologetics. 10s. 6d.

## International Theological Library.
FISHER (Prof. G. P., D.D., LL.D.)—History of Christian Doctrine. 12s.
ALLEN (Prof. A. V. G., D.D.)—Christian Institutions. 12s.
McGIFFERT (Prof. A. C., Ph.D.)—The Apostolic Age. 12s.
GLADDEN (Washington, D.D.)—The Christian Pastor. 10s. 6d.
STEVENS (Prof. G. B., D.D.)—The Theology of the New Testament. 12s.
*For List of future Volumes see p. 14.*

**Janet (Paul)**—FINAL CAUSES. Second Edition, demy 8vo, 12s.

——— THE THEORY OF MORALS. Demy 8vo, 10s. 6d.

**Johnstone (Prof. R., D.D.)**—COMMENTARY ON 1ST PETER. 8vo, 10s. 6d.

**Jones (E. E. C.)**—ELEMENTS OF LOGIC. 8vo, 7s. 6d.

**Jouffroy**—PHILOSOPHICAL ESSAYS. Fcap. 8vo, 5s.

**Kaftan (Prof. J., D.D.)**—THE TRUTH OF THE CHRISTIAN RELIGION. *Authorised Translation.* 2 vols. 8vo, 16s. net.

**Kant**—THE METAPHYSIC OF ETHICS. Crown 8vo, 6s.

——— PHILOSOPHY OF LAW. Trans. by W. HASTIE, D.D. Cr. 8vo, 5s.

——— PRINCIPLES OF POLITICS, ETC. Crown 8vo, 2s. 6d.

**Keil (Prof.)**—PENTATEUCH, 3 vols. 8vo, 31s. 6d.; JOSHUA, JUDGES, AND RUTH, 8vo, 10s. 6d.; SAMUEL, 8vo, 10s. 6d.; KINGS, 8vo, 10s. 6d.; CHRONICLES, 8vo, 10s. 6d.; EZRA, NEHEMIAH, ESTHER, 8vo, 10s. 6d.; JEREMIAH, 2 vols. 8vo, 21s.; EZEKIEL, 2 vols. 8vo, 21s.; DANIEL, 8vo, 10s. 6d.; MINOR PROPHETS, 2 vols. 8vo, 21s.; INTRODUCTION TO THE CANONICAL SCRIPTURES OF THE OLD TESTAMENT, 2 vols. 8vo, 21s.; HANDBOOK OF BIBLICAL ARCHÆOLOGY, 2 vols. 8vo, 21s.

**Kennedy (H. A. A., M.A., D.Sc.)**—SOURCES OF NEW TESTAMENT GREEK. Post 8vo, 5s.

**Keymer (Rev. N., M.A.)**—NOTES ON GENESIS. Crown 8vo, 1s. 6d.

**Kidd (James, D.D.)**—MORALITY AND RELIGION. 8vo, 10s. 6d.

**Killen (Prof.)**—THE FRAMEWORK OF THE CHURCH. 8vo, 9s.

——— THE OLD CATHOLIC CHURCH. 8vo, 9s.

——— THE IGNATIAN EPISTLES ENTIRELY SPURIOUS. Cr. 8vo, 2s. 6d.

**König (Dr. Ed.)**—THE EXILES' BOOK OF CONSOLATION (Deutero-Isaiah). [*In the Press.*

**König (Dr. F. E.)**—THE RELIGIOUS HISTORY OF ISRAEL. Cr. 8vo, 3s. 6d.

**Krummacher (Dr. F. W.)**—THE SUFFERING SAVIOUR; or, Meditations on the Last Days of the Sufferings of Christ. Eighth Edition, crown 8vo, 6s.

——— DAVID, THE KING OF ISRAEL. Second Edition, cr. 8vo, 6s.

——— AUTOBIOGRAPHY. Crown 8vo, 6s.

**Kurtz (Prof.)**—HANDBOOK OF CHURCH HISTORY (from 1517). 8vo, 7s. 6d.

——— HISTORY OF THE OLD COVENANT. Three vols. 8vo, 31s. 6d.

**Ladd (Prof. G. T.)**—THE DOCTRINE OF SACRED SCRIPTURE: A Critical, Historical, and Dogmatic Inquiry into the Origin and Nature of the Old and New Testaments. Two vols. 8vo, 1600 pp., 24s.

**Laidlaw (Prof. J., D.D.)**—THE BIBLE DOCTRINE OF MAN; or, The Anthropology and Psychology of Scripture. New Edition Revised and Rearranged, post 8vo, 7s. 6d.

**Lane (Laura M.)**—LIFE OF ALEXANDER VINET. Crown 8vo, 7s. 6d.

**Lange (J. P., D.D.)**—THE LIFE OF OUR LORD JESUS CHRIST. Edited by MARCUS DODS, D.D. 2nd Ed., in 4 vols. 8vo, price 28s. net.

—— COMMENTARIES ON THE OLD AND NEW TESTAMENTS. Edited by PHILIP SCHAFF, D.D. OLD TESTAMENT, 14 vols.; NEW TESTAMENT, 10 vols.; APOCRYPHA, 1 vol. Subscription price, net, 15s. each.

—— ST. MATTHEW AND ST. MARK, 3 vols. 8vo, 31s. 6d.; ST. LUKE, 2 vols. 8vo, 18s.; ST. JOHN, 2 vols. 8vo, 21s.

**Lechler (Prof. G. V., D.D.)**—THE APOSTOLIC AND POST-APOSTOLIC TIMES. Their Diversity and Unity in Life and Doctrine. 2 vols. cr. 8vo, 16s.

**Lehmann (Pastor)**—SCENES FROM THE LIFE OF JESUS. Cr. 8vo, 3s. 6d.

**Lewis (Tayler, LL.D.)**—THE SIX DAYS OF CREATION. Cr. 8vo, 7s. 6d.

**Lichtenberger (F., D.D.)**—HISTORY OF GERMAN THEOLOGY IN THE 19TH CENTURY. 8vo, 14s.

**Lilley (J. P., M.A.)**—THE LORD'S SUPPER: Its Origin, Nature, and Use. Crown 8vo, 5s.

**Lisco (F. G.)**—PARABLES OF JESUS EXPLAINED. Fcap. 8vo, 5s.

**Locke (Clinton, D.D.)**—THE AGE OF THE GREAT WESTERN SCHISM. (*Eras of Church History.*) 6s.

**Lotze (Hermann)**—MICROCOSMUS: An Essay concerning Man and his relation to the World. Cheaper Edition, 2 vols. 8vo (1450 pp), 24s.

**Ludlow (J. M., D.D.)**—THE AGE OF THE CRUSADES. (*Eras of Church History.*) 6s.

**Luthardt, Kahnis, and Brückner**—THE CHURCH. Crown 8vo, 5s.

**Luthardt (Prof.)**—ST. JOHN THE AUTHOR OF THE FOURTH GOSPEL. 7s. 6d.

—— COMMENTARY ON ST. JOHN'S GOSPEL. 3 vols. 8vo, 31s. 6d.

—— HISTORY OF CHRISTIAN ETHICS. 8vo, 10s. 6d.

—— APOLOGETIC LECTURES ON THE FUNDAMENTAL (7 *Ed.*), SAVING (5 *Ed.*), MORAL TRUTHS OF CHRISTIANITY (4 *Ed.*). 3 vols. cr. 8vo, 6s. each.

**Macdonald**—INTRODUCTION TO PENTATEUCH. Two vols. 8vo, 21s.

—— THE CREATION AND FALL. 8vo, 12s.

**Macgregor (Rev. Jas., D.D.)**—THE APOLOGY OF THE CHRISTIAN RELIGION. 8vo, 10s. 6d.

—— THE REVELATION AND THE RECORD: Essays on Matters of Previous Question in the Proof of Christianity. 8vo, 7s. 6d.

—— STUDIES IN THE HISTORY OF NEW TESTAMENT APOLOGETICS. 8vo, 7s. 6d.

**Macgregor (Rev. G. H. C., M.A.)**—SO GREAT SALVATION. Crown 32mo, 1s.

**Macpherson (Rev. John, M.A.)**—COMMENTARY ON THE EPISTLE TO THE EPHESIANS. 8vo, 10s. 6d.

—— CHRISTIAN DOGMATICS. Post 8vo, 9s.

**McCosh (James), Life of.** 8vo, 9s.

**McGiffert (Prof. A. C., Ph.D.)**—HISTORY OF CHRISTIANITY IN THE APOSTOLIC AGE. (*International Theological Library.*) Post 8vo, 12s.

**M'Realsham (E. D.)**—ROMANS DISSECTED. A Critical Analysis of the Epistle to the Romans. Crown 8vo, 2s.

**Mair (A., D.D.)**—STUDIES IN THE CHRISTIAN EVIDENCES. Third Edition, Revised and Enlarged, crown 8vo, 6s.

**Martensen (Bishop)**—CHRISTIAN DOGMATICS. 8vo, 10s. 6d.

—— CHRISTIAN ETHICS. (GENERAL — INDIVIDUAL — SOCIAL.) Three vols. 8vo, 10s. 6d. each.

**Matheson (Geo., D.D.)**—GROWTH OF THE SPIRIT OF CHRISTIANITY, from the First Century to the Dawn of the Lutheran Era. Two vols. 8vo, 21s.

**Meyer (Dr.)**—CRITICAL AND EXEGETICAL COMMENTARIES ON THE NEW TESTAMENT. Twenty vols. 8vo. *Subscription Price*, £5, 5s. *net; Non-Subscription Price*, 10s. 6d. each volume.
ST. MATTHEW, 2 vols.; MARK AND LUKE, 2 vols.; ST. JOHN, 2 vols.; ACTS, 2 vols.; ROMANS, 2 vols.; CORINTHIANS, 2 vols.; GALATIANS, one vol.; EPHESIANS AND PHILEMON, one vol.; PHILIPPIANS AND COLOSSIANS, one vol.; THESSALONIANS (*Dr. Lünemann*), one vol.; THE PASTORAL EPISTLES (*Dr. Huther*), one vol.; HEBREWS (*Dr. Lünemann*), one vol.; ST. JAMES AND ST. JOHN'S EPISTLES (*Huther*), one vol.; PETER AND JUDE (*Dr. Huther*), one vol.

**Michie (Charles, M.A.)**—BIBLE WORDS AND PHRASES. 18mo, 1s.

**Milligan (Prof. W., D.D.)**—THE RESURRECTION OF THE DEAD. Second Edition, crown 8vo, 4s. 6d.

**Milligan (Prof. W., D.D.) and Moulton (W. F., D.D.)** — COMMENTARY ON THE GOSPEL OF ST. JOHN. Imp. 8vo, 9s.

**Monrad (Dr. D. G.)**—THE WORLD OF PRAYER. Crown 8vo, 4s. 6d.

**Moore (Prof. G. F., D.D.)**—JUDGES. (*International Critical Commentary.*) Post 8vo, 12s.

**Morgan (J., D.D.)**—SCRIPTURE TESTIMONY TO THE HOLY SPIRIT. 7s. 6d.

—— EXPOSITION OF THE FIRST EPISTLE OF JOHN. 8vo, 7s. 6d.

**Moulton (W. F., D.D.) and Geden (A. S., M.A.)**—A CONCORDANCE TO THE GREEK TESTAMENT. Crown 4to, 26s. net, and 31s. 6d. net.

**Muir (Sir W.)**—MOHAMMEDAN CONTROVERSY, ETC. 8vo, 7s. 6d.

**Müller (Dr. Julius)**—THE CHRISTIAN DOCTRINE OF SIN. 2 vols. 8vo, 21s.

**Murphy (Professor)**—COMMENTARY ON THE PSALMS. 8vo, 12s.

—— A CRITICAL AND EXEGETICAL COMMENTARY ON EXODUS. 9s.

**Naville (Ernest)**—THE PROBLEM OF EVIL. Crown 8vo, 4s. 6d.

—— THE CHRIST. Translated by Rev. T. J. DESPRÉS. Cr. 8vo, 4s. 6d.

—— MODERN PHYSICS. Crown 8vo, 5s.

**Neander (Dr.)**—CHURCH HISTORY. Eight vols. 8vo, £2, 2s. net.

**Nicoll (W. Robertson, M.A., LL.D.)**—THE INCARNATE SAVIOUR. Cheap Edition, price 3s. 6d.

**Novalis**—HYMNS AND THOUGHTS ON RELIGION. Crown 8vo, 4s.

**Oehler (Prof.)**—THEOLOGY OF THE OLD TESTAMENT. 2 vols. 8vo, 21s.

**Olshausen (Dr. H.)**—BIBLICAL COMMENTARY ON THE GOSPELS AND ACTS. Four vols. 8vo, £2, 2s. *Cheaper Edition*, four vols. crown 8vo, 24s.

—— ROMANS, one vol. 8vo, 10s. 6d.; CORINTHIANS, one vol. 8vo, 9s.; PHILIPPIANS, TITUS, AND FIRST TIMOTHY, one vol. 8vo, 10s. 6d.

**Oosterzee (Dr. Van)**—THE YEAR OF SALVATION. 2 vols. 8vo, 6s. each.

—— MOSES: A Biblical Study. Crown 8vo, 6s.

**Orelli** (Dr. C. von)—OLD TESTAMENT PROPHECY; COMMENTARY ON ISAIAH; JEREMIAH; THE TWELVE MINOR PROPHETS. 4 vols. 8vo, 10s. 6d. each.

**Owen** (Dr. John)—WORKS. *Best and only Complete Edition.* Edited by Rev. Dr. GOOLD. Twenty-four vols. 8vo, Subscription price, £4, 4s. The '*Hebrews*' may be had separately, in seven vols., £2, 2s. net.

**Philippi** (F. A.)—COMMENTARY ON THE ROMANS. Two vols. 8vo, 21s.

**Piper**—LIVES OF LEADERS OF CHURCH UNIVERSAL. Two vols. 8vo, 21s.

**Popular Commentary on the New Testament.** Edited by PHILIP SCHAFF, D.D. With Illustrations and Maps. Vol. I.—THE SYNOPTICAL GOSPELS. Vol. II.—ST. JOHN'S GOSPEL, AND THE ACTS OF THE APOSTLES. Vol. III.—ROMANS TO PHILEMON. Vol. IV.—HEBREWS TO REVELATION. In four vols. imperial 8vo, 12s. 6d. each.

**Plummer** (Alfred, D.D.)—ST. LUKE. (*International Critical Commentary.*) Post 8vo, 12s.

**Pressensé** (Edward de)—THE REDEEMER: Discourses. Crown 8vo, 6s.

**Pünjer** (Bernhard)—HISTORY OF THE CHRISTIAN PHILOSOPHY OF RELIGION FROM THE REFORMATION TO KANT. 8vo, 16s.

**Räbiger** (Prof.)—ENCYCLOPÆDIA OF THEOLOGY. Two vols. 8vo, 21s.

**Rainy** (Principal) — DELIVERY AND DEVELOPMENT OF CHRISTIAN DOCTRINE. 8vo, 10s. 6d.

**Reusch** (Prof.)—NATURE AND THE BIBLE: Lectures on the Mosaic History of Creation in Relation to Natural Science. Two vols. 8vo, 21s.

**Reuss** (Professor)—HISTORY OF THE SACRED SCRIPTURES OF THE NEW TESTAMENT. 640 pp. 8vo, 15s.

**Riehm** (Dr. E.)—MESSIANIC PROPHECY. New Edition. Post 8vo, 7s. 6d.

**Ritter** (Carl)—COMPARATIVE GEOGRAPHY OF PALESTINE. 4 vols. 8vo, 26s.

**Robinson** (Rev. S., D.D.)—DISCOURSES ON REDEMPTION. 8vo, 7s. 6d.

**Robinson** (E., D.D.)—GREEK AND ENG. LEXICON OF THE N. TEST. 8vo, 9s.

**Rooke** (T. G., B.A.)—INSPIRATION, and other Lectures. 8vo, 7s. 6d.

**Ross** (C.)—OUR FATHER'S KINGDOM. Crown 8vo, 2s. 6d.

**Rothe** (Prof.)—SERMONS FOR THE CHRISTIAN YEAR. Cr. 8vo, 4s. 6d.

**Saisset**—MANUAL OF MODERN PANTHEISM. Two vols. 8vo, 10s. 6d.

**Salmond** (Prof. S. D. F., D.D.)—THE CHRISTIAN DOCTRINE OF IMMORTALITY. 8vo, 14s.

**Sanday** (Prof. W., D.D.) and **Headlam** (A. C., B.D.)—ROMANS. (*International Critical Commentary.*) Post 8vo, 12s.

**Sartorius** (Dr. E.)—DOCTRINE OF DIVINE LOVE. 8vo, 10s. 6d.

**Schaff** (Professor)—HISTORY OF THE CHRISTIAN CHURCH. (New Edition, thoroughly Revised and Enlarged.) Six 'Divisions,' in 2 vols. each, extra 8vo.

1. APOSTOLIC CHRISTIANITY, A.D. 1-100, 2 vols. 21s. 2. ANTE-NICENE, A.D. 100-325, 2 vols., 21s. 3. NICENE AND POST-NICENE, A.D. 325-600, 2 vols., 21s. 4. MEDIÆVAL, A.D. 590-1073, 2 vols., 21s. (*Completion of this Period*, 1073-1517, *in preparation*). 5. THE SWISS REFORMATION, 2 vols., extra demy 8vo, 21s. 6. THE GERMAN REFORMATION, 2 vols., extra demy 8vo, 21s.

**Schleiermacher's** CHRISTMAS EVE. Crown 8vo, 2s.

**Schmid's** BIBLICAL THEOLOGY OF THE NEW TESTAMENT. 8vo, 10s. 6d.

**Schubert (Prof. H. Von., D.D.)**—THE GOSPEL OF ST. PETER. Synoptical Tables. With Translation and Critical Apparatus. 8vo, 1s. 6d. net.
**Schultz (Hermann)**—OLD TESTAMENT THEOLOGY. Two vols. 18s. net.
**Schürer (Prof.)**—HISTORY OF THE JEWISH PEOPLE. 5 vols. 8vo, 52/6.
**Schwartzkopff (Dr. P.)**—THE PROPHECIES OF JESUS CHRIST. Crown 8vo, 5s.
**Scott (Jas., M.A., D.D.)**—PRINCIPLES OF NEW TESTAMENT QUOTATION ESTABLISHED AND APPLIED TO BIBLICAL CRITICISM. Cr. 8vo, 2nd Edit., 4s.
**Sell (K., D.D.)**—THE CHURCH IN THE MIRROR OF HISTORY. Cr. 8vo, 3/6.
**Shedd**—HISTORY OF CHRISTIAN DOCTRINE. Two vols. 8vo, 21s.
——— SERMONS TO THE NATURAL MAN. 8vo, 7s. 6d.
——— SERMONS TO THE SPIRITUAL MAN. 8vo, 7s. 6d.
——— DOGMATIC THEOLOGY. Three vols. ex. 8vo, 37s. 6d.
**Simon (Prof.)**—THE BIBLE; An Outgrowth of Theocratic Life. Cr. 8vo, 4/6.
——— THE REDEMPTION OF MAN. 8vo, 10s. 6d.
——— RECONCILIATION BY INCARNATION. Post 8vo, 7s. 6d.
**Skene-Bickell**—THE LORD'S SUPPER & THE PASSOVER RITUAL. 8vo, 5s.
**Smeaton (Professor)**—DOCTRINE OF THE HOLY SPIRIT. 2nd Ed., 8vo, 9s.
**Smith (Prof. H. P., D.D.)**—I. AND II. SAMUEL. (*International Critical Commentary.*) Post 8vo, 12s.
**Smith (Professor Thos., D.D.)**—MEDIÆVAL MISSIONS. Cr. 8vo, 4s. 6d.
**Smyth (Newman, D.D.)**—CHRISTIAN ETHICS. (*International Theological Library.*) Post 8vo, 10s. 6d.
**Somerville (Rev. D., D.D.)**—ST. PAUL'S CONCEPTION OF CHRIST. 9s.
**Stählin (Leonh.)**—KANT, LOTZE, AND RITSCHL. 8vo, 9s.
**Stalker (Jas., D.D.)**—LIFE OF CHRIST. Large Type Ed., cr. 8vo, 3s. 6d.
——— LIFE OF ST. PAUL. Large Type Edition, crown 8vo, 3s. 6d.
**Stanton (V. H., D.D.)**—THE JEWISH AND THE CHRISTIAN MESSIAH. A Study in the Earliest History of Christianity. 8vo, 10s. 6d.
**Stead (F. H.)**—THE KINGDOM OF GOD. 1s. 6d.
**Steinmeyer (Dr. F. L.)**—THE MIRACLES OF OUR LORD. 8vo, 7s. 6d.
**Steinmeyer (Dr. F. L.)**—THE HISTORY OF THE PASSION AND RESURRECTION OF OUR LORD, considered in the Light of Modern Criticism. 8vo, 10s. 6d.
**Stevens (Prof. G. B., D.D.)**—THE THEOLOGY OF THE NEW TESTAMENT. (*International Theological Library.*) Post 8vo.
**Stevenson (Mrs.)**—THE SYMBOLIC PARABLES. Crown 8vo, 3s. 6d.
**Steward (Rev. G.)**—MEDIATORIAL SOVEREIGNTY. Two vols. 8vo, 21s.
——— THE ARGUMENT OF THE EPISTLE TO THE HEBREWS. 8vo, 10s. 6d.
**Stier (Dr. Rudolph)**—ON THE WORDS OF THE LORD JESUS. Eight vols. 8vo, Subscription price of £2, 2s. Separate volumes, price 10s. 6d.
——— THE WORDS OF THE RISEN SAVIOUR, AND COMMENTARY ON THE EPISTLE OF ST. JAMES. 8vo, 10s. 6d.
——— THE WORDS OF THE APOSTLES EXPOUNDED. 8vo, 10s. 6d.
**Stirling (Dr. J. Hutchison)**—PHILOSOPHY AND THEOLOGY. Post 8vo, 9s.
——— DARWINIANISM: Workmen and Work. Post 8vo, 10s. 6d.
**Tholuck (Prof.)**—THE EPISTLE TO THE ROMANS. Two vols. fcap. 8vo, 8s.

**Thomson (J. E. H., B.D.)**—BOOKS WHICH INFLUENCED OUR LORD AND HIS APOSTLES. 8vo, 10s. 6d.
**Thomson (Rev. E. A.)**—MEMORIALS OF A MINISTRY. Crown 8vo, 5s.
**Tophel (Pastor G.)**—THE WORK OF THE HOLY SPIRIT. Cr. 8vo, 2s. 6d.
**Troup (Rev. G. Elmslie, M.A.)**—WORDS TO YOUNG CHRISTIANS: Being Addresses to Young Communicants. On antique laid paper, chaste binding, fcap. 8vo, 4s. 6d.
**Uhlhorn (G.)**—CHRISTIAN CHARITY IN THE ANCIENT CHURCH. Cr. 8vo, 6s.
**Ullmann (Dr. Carl)**—REFORMERS BEFORE THE REFORMATION, principally in Germany and the Netherlands. Two vols. 8vo, 21s.
**Urwick (W., M.A.)**—THE SERVANT OF JEHOVAH: A Commentary upon Isaiah lii. 13–liii. 12; with Dissertations upon Isaiah xl.–lxvi. 8vo, 3s.
**Vinet** (Life and Writings of). By L. M. LANE. Crown 8vo, 7s. 6d.
**Vincent (Prof. M. R., D.D.)**—THE AGE OF HILDEBRAND. (*Eras of Church History.*) 6s.
—— PHILIPPIANS AND PHILEMON. (*International Critical Commentary.*) Post 8vo, 8s. 6d.
**Walker (James, of Carnwath)**—ESSAYS, PAPERS, AND SERMONS. Post 8vo, 6s.
**Walker (J., D.D.)**—THEOLOGY AND THEOLOGIANS OF SCOTLAND. New Edition, crown 8vo, 3s. 6d.
**Warfield (B. B.)**—THE RIGHT OF SYSTEMATIC THEOLOGY. Crown 8vo, 2s.
**Waterman (L., D.D.)**—THE POST-APOSTOLIC AGE. (*Eras of Church History.*) 6s.
**Watt (W. A.)**—THE THEORY OF CONTRACT IN ITS SOCIAL LIGHT. 8vo, 3s.
**Watts (Professor)**—THE NEWER CRITICISM AND THE ANALOGY OF THE FAITH. Third Edition, crown 8vo, 5s.
—— THE REIGN OF CAUSALITY: A Vindication of the Scientific Principle of Telic Causal Efficiency. Crown 8vo, 6s.
—— THE NEW APOLOGETIC. Crown 8vo, 6s.
**Weir (J. F., M.A.)**—THE WAY: THE NATURE AND MEANS OF SALVATION. Ex. crown 8vo, 6s. 6d.
**Weiss (Prof.)**—BIBLICAL THEOLOGY OF NEW TESTAMENT. 2 vols. 8vo, 21s.
—— LIFE OF CHRIST. Three vols. 8vo, 31s. 6d.
**Wells (Prof. C. L.)**—THE AGE OF CHARLEMAGNE. (*Eras of the Christian Church.*) 6s.
**Wendt (H. H., D.D.)**—THE TEACHING OF JESUS. 2 vols. 8vo, 21s.
**Wenley (R. M.)**—CONTEMPORARY THEOLOGY AND THEISM. Crown 8vo, 4s. 6d.
**White (Rev. M.)**—SYMBOLICAL NUMBERS OF SCRIPTURE. Cr. 8vo, 4s.
**Williams (E. F., D.D.)**—CHRISTIAN LIFE IN GERMANY. Crown 8vo, 5s.
**Winer (Dr. G. B.)**—A TREATISE ON THE GRAMMAR OF NEW TESTAMENT GREEK, regarded as the Basis of New Testament Exegesis. Third Edition, edited by W. F. MOULTON, D.D. Ninth English Edition, 8vo, 15s.
—— THE DOCTRINES AND CONFESSIONS OF CHRISTENDOM. 8vo, 10s. 6d.
**Witherow (Prof. T., D.D.)**—THE FORM OF THE CHRISTIAN TEMPLE. 8vo, 10/6.
**Woods (F. H., B.D.)**—THE HOPE OF ISRAEL. Crown 8vo, 3s. 6d.
**Workman (Prof. G. C.)**—THE TEXT OF JEREMIAH; or, A Critical Investigation of the Greek and Hebrew, etc. Post 8vo, 9s.
**Wright (C. H., D.D.)**—BIBLICAL ESSAYS. Crown 8vo, 5s.

## T. and T. Clark's Publications. 13

### THE FOREIGN THEOLOGICAL LIBRARY.

The following are the Works from which a Selection of EIGHT VOLUMES for £2, 2s. (or more at the same ratio) may be made. (Non-subscription Price within brackets):—

**Baumgarten**—The History of the Church in the Apostolic Ago. Three Vols. (27s.)
**Bleek**—Introduction to the New Testament. Two Vols. (21s.)
**Cassel**—Commentary on Esther. One Vol. (10s. 6d.)
**Christlieb**—Modern Doubt and Christian Belief. One Vol. (10s. 6d.)
**Delitzsch**—New Commentary on Genesis. Two Vols. (21s.)
—— Commentary on the Psalms. Three Vols. (31s. 6d.)
—— Commentary on the Proverbs of Solomon. Two Vols. (21s.)
—— Commentary on Song of Solomon and Ecclesiastes. One Vol. (10s. 6d.)
—— Commentary on the Prophecies of Isaiah. *Last Edition.* Two Vols. (21s.)
—— Commentary on Epistle to the Hebrews. Two Vols. (21s.)
—— A System of Biblical Psychology. One Vol. (12s.)
**Döllinger**—Hippolytus and Callistus; or, The Church of Rome: A.D. 200-250. One Vol. (7s. 6d.)
**Dorner**—A System of Christian Doctrine. Four Vols. (42s.)
—— History of the Development of the Doctrine of the Person of Christ. Five Vols. (52s. 6d.)
**Ebrard**—Commentary on the Epistles of St. John. One Vol. (10s. 6d.)
—— The Gospel History. One Vol. (10s. 6d.) Apologetics. Three Vols. (31s. 6d.)
**Ewald**—Revelation: Its Nature and Record. One Vol. (10s. 6d.)
—— Old and New Testament Theology. One Vol. (10s. 6d.)
**Frank**—System of Christian Certainty. One Vol. (10s. 6d.)
**Gebhardt**—Doctrine of the Apocalypse. One Vol. (10s. 6d.)
**Gerlach**—Commentary on the Pentateuch. One Vol. (10s. 6d.)
**Gieseler**—Compendium of Ecclesiastical History: A.D. 451-1409. Three Vols. (31s. 6d.)
**Godet**—Commentary on St. Luke's Gospel. Two Vols. (21s.)
—— Commentary on St. John's Gospel. Three Vols. (31s. 6d.)
—— Commentary on the Epistle to the Romans. Two Vols. (21s.)
—— Commentary on 1st Corinthians. Two Vols. (21s.)
**Goebel**—On the Parables. One Vol. (10s. 6d.)
**Hagenbach**—History of the Reformation. Two Vols. (21s.)
—— History of Christian Doctrines. Three Vols. (31s. 6d.)
**Harless**—A System of Christian Ethics. One Vol. (10s. 6d.)
**Haupt**—Commentary on the First Epistle of St. John. One Vol. (10s. 6d.)
**Hävernick**—General Introduction to the Old Testament. One Vol. (10s. 6d.)
**Hengstenberg**—Christology of the Old Testament. Four Vols. (42s.)
—— Commentary on the Psalms. Three Vols. (33s.)
—— On the Book of Ecclesiastes, etc. etc. One Vol. (9s.)
—— Commentary on the Gospel of St. John. Two Vols. (21s.)
—— Commentary on Ezekiel. One Vol. (10s. 6d.)
—— Dissertations on the Genuineness of Daniel, etc. One Vol. (12s.)
—— The Kingdom of God under the Old Covenant. Two Vols. (21s.)
**Keil**—Introduction to the Old Testament. Two Vols. (21s.)
—— Commentary on the Pentateuch. Three Vols. (31s. 6d.)
—— Commentary on Joshua, Judges, and Ruth. One Vol. (10s. 6d.)
—— Commentary on the Books of Samuel. One Vol. (10s. 6d.)
—— Commentary on the Books of Kings. One Vol. (10s. 6d.)
—— Commentary on the Books of Chronicles. One Vol. (10s. 6d.)
—— Commentary on Ezra, Nehemiah, and Esther. One Vol. (10s. 6d.)
—— Commentary on Jeremiah and Lamentations. Two Vols. (21s.)
—— Commentary on Ezekiel. Two Vols. (21s.) Book of Daniel. One Vol. (10s. 6d.)
—— Commentary on the Minor Prophets. Two Vols. (21s.)
—— Biblical Archæology. Two Vols. (21s.)
**Kurtz**—History of the Old Covenant; or, Old Testament Dispensation. Three Vols. (31s. 6d.)
**Lange**—Commentary on the Gospels of St. Matthew and St. Mark. Three Vols. (31s. 6d.)
—— Commentary on the Gospel of St. Luke. Two Vols. (18s.) St. John. Two Vols. (21s.)
**Luthardt**—Commentary on the Gospel of St. John. Three Vols. (31s. 6d.)
—— History of Christian Ethics to the Reformation. One Vol. (10s. 6d.)
**Macdonald**—Introduction to the Pentateuch. Two Vols. (21s.)
**Martensen**—Christian Dogmatics. One Vol. (10s. 6d.)
—— Christian Ethics, General—Social—Individual. Three Vols. (31s. 6d.)
**Müller**—The Christian Doctrine of Sin. Two Vols. (21s.)
**Murphy**—Commentary on the Psalms. *To count as Two Volumes.* One Vol. (12s.)
**Neander**—General History of the Christian Religion and Church. Vols. I. to VIII. (60s.)
**Oehler**—Biblical Theology of the Old Testament. Two Vols. (21s.)
**Olshausen**—Commentary on the Gospels and Acts. Four Vols. (42s.)
—— Commentary on Epistle to the Romans. One Vol. (10s. 6d.) Corinthians. One Vol. (9s.)
—— Commentary on Philippians, Titus, and 1st Timothy. One Vol. (10s. 6d.)
**Orelli**—Prophecy regarding Consummation of God's Kingdom. One Vol. (10s. 6d.)
—— Commentary on Isaiah. One Vol. (10s. 6d.) Jeremiah. One Vol. (10s. 6d.)
**Philippi**—Commentary on Epistle to Romans. Two Vols. (21s.)
**Räbiger**—Encyclopædia of Theology. Two Vols. (21s.)
**Ritter**—Comparative Geography of Palestine. Four Vols. (26s.)
**Sartorius**—The Doctrine of Divine Love. One Vol. (10s. 6d.)
**Schürer**—The Jewish People in the Time of Christ. Five Vols. (10s. 6d. each.)
**Shedd**—History of Christian Doctrine. Two Vols. (21s.)
**Steinmeyer**—History of the Passion and Resurrection of our Lord. One Vol. (10s. 6d.)
—— The Miracles of our Lord in relation to Modern Criticism. One Vol. (7s. 6d.)
**Stier**—The Words of the Lord Jesus. Eight Vols. (10s. 6d. per vol.)
—— The Words of the Risen Saviour, and Commentary on Epistle of St. James. One Vol. (10s. 6d.)
—— The Words of the Apostles Expounded. One Vol. (10s. 6d.)
**Ullmann**—Reformers before the Reformation. Two Vols. (21s.)
**Weiss**—Biblical Theology of the New Testament. 2 Vols. (21s.) The Life of Christ. 3 Vols. (31s. 6d.)

# THE INTERNATIONAL THEOLOGICAL LIBRARY.

The following eminent Scholars have contributed, or are engaged upon, the Volumes named:—

| | |
|---|---|
| An Introduction to the Literature of the Old Testament. | By S. R. DRIVER, D.D., Regius Professor of Hebrew, and Canon of Christ Church, Oxford. [*Seventh Edition.* 12s. |
| Christian Ethics. | By NEWMAN SMYTH, D.D., Pastor of the First Congregational Church, New Haven, Conn. [*Third Edition.* 10s. 6d. |
| Apologetics. | By A. B. BRUCE, D.D., Professor of New Testament Exegesis, Free Church College, Glasgow. [*Third Edition.* 10s. 6d. |
| History of Christian Doctrine. | By G. P. FISHER, D.D., LL.D., Professor of Ecclesiastical History, Yale University, New Haven, Conn. [*Second Edition.* 12s. |
| A History of Christianity in the Apostolic Age. | By ARTHUR CUSHMAN MCGIFFERT, Ph.D., D.D., Professor of Church History, Union Theological Seminary, New York. [12s. |
| Christian Institutions. | By A. V. G. ALLEN, D.D., Professor of Ecclesiastical History, Episcopal Theological School, Cambridge, Mass. [12s. |
| The Christian Pastor. | By WASHINGTON GLADDEN, D.D., Pastor of Congregational Church, Columbus, Ohio. [10s. 6d. |
| Theology of the New Testament. | By GEORGE B. STEVENS, Ph.D., D.D., Professor of Systematic Theology in Yale University, U.S.A. [*Just published.* 12s. |
| Theology of the Old Testament. | By A. B. DAVIDSON, D.D., LL.D., Professor of Hebrew, New College, Edinburgh. |
| An Introduction to the Literature of the New Testament. | By S. D. F. SALMOND, D.D., Principal, and Professor of Systematic Theology and New Testament Exegesis, Free Church College, Aberdeen. |
| Old Testament History. | By H. P. SMITH, D.D., late Professor of Biblical History and Interpretation, Amherst College, U.S.A. |
| Canon and Text of the New Testament. | By CASPAR RENÉ GREGORY, Ph.D., Professor in the University of Leipzig. |
| The Latin Church. | By ARCHIBALD ROBERTSON, D.D., Principal of King's College, London. |
| The Ancient Catholic Church. | By ROBERT RAINY, D.D., Principal of the New College, Edinburgh. |
| Encyclopædia. | By C. A. BRIGGS, D.D., Professor of Biblical Theology, Union Theological Seminary, New York. |
| Contemporary History of the Old Testament. | By FRANCIS BROWN, D.D., Professor of Hebrew and Cognate Languages, Union Theological Seminary, New York. |
| Contemporary History of the New Testament. | By FRANK C. PORTER, Ph.D., Yale University, New Haven, Conn. |
| Philosophy of Religion. | By ROBERT FLINT, D.D., LL.D., Professor of Divinity in the University of Edinburgh. |
| The Study of the Old Testament. | By HERBERT E. RYLE, D.D., President of Queens' College, Cambridge. |
| Rabbinical Literature. | By S. SCHECHTER, M.A., Reader in Talmudic in the University of Cambridge. |
| The Life of Christ. | By WILLIAM SANDAY, D.D., LL.D., Lady Margaret Professor of Divinity, and Canon of Christ Church, Oxford. |
| The Christian Preacher. | By JOHN WATSON, D.D. ('IAN MACLAREN'), Sefton Park Presbyterian Church of England, Liverpool. |

EDINBURGH: T. & T. CLARK, 38 GEORGE STREET.

*T. and T. Clark's Publications.* 15

# THE INTERNATIONAL CRITICAL COMMENTARY.

EIGHT VOLUMES NOW READY, VIZ. :—

**Deuteronomy** (Dr. Driver), 12s. ; **Judges** (Dr. Moore), 12s. ; **Samuel** (Dr. H. P. Smith), 12s. ; **S. Mark** (Dr. Gould), 10s. 6d. ; **S. Luke** (Dr. Plummer), 12s. ; **Romans** (Dr. Sanday and Mr. Headlam), 12s. ; **Ephesians and Colossians** (Dr. T. K. Abbott), 10s. 6d. ; **Philippians and Philemon** (Dr. Vincent), 8s. 6d.

The following other Volumes are in course of preparation :—

## THE OLD TESTAMENT.

| | |
|---|---|
| **Genesis.** | T. K. CHEYNE, D.D., Oriel Professor of the Interpretation of Holy Scripture, Oxford. |
| **Exodus.** | A. R. S. KENNEDY, D.D., Professor of Hebrew, University of Edinburgh. |
| **Leviticus.** | Rev. H. A. WHITE, M.A., Fellow of New College, Oxford, and Theological Tutor in the University of Durham. |
| **Numbers.** | G. BUCHANAN GRAY, M.A., Lecturer in Hebrew, Mansfield College, Oxford. |
| **Joshua.** | GEORGE ADAM SMITH, D.D., Professor of Hebrew, Free Church College, Glasgow. |
| **Kings.** | FRANCIS BROWN, D.D., Professor of Hebrew and Cognate Languages, Union Theological Seminary, New York. |
| **Isaiah.** | A. B. DAVIDSON, D.D., LL.D., Professor of Hebrew, Free Church College, Edinburgh. |
| **Jeremiah.** | A. F. KIRKPATRICK, D.D., Regius Professor of Hebrew, and Fellow of Trinity College, Cambridge. |
| **Minor Prophets.** | W. R. HARPER, Ph.D., President of Chicago University. |
| **Psalms.** | C. A. BRIGGS, D.D., Edward Robinson Professor of Biblical Theology, Union Theological Seminary, New York. |
| **Proverbs.** | C. H. TOY, D.D., Professor of Hebrew, Harvard University, Cambridge, Massachusets. |
| **Job.** | S. R. DRIVER, D.D., Regius Professor of Hebrew, Oxford. |
| **Daniel.** | Rev. JOHN P. PETERS, Ph.D., late Professor of Hebrew, P. E. Divinity School, Philadelphia, now Rector of St. Michael's Church, New York City. |
| **Ezra and Nehemiah.** | Rev. L. W. BATTEN, Ph.D., Professor of Hebrew, P. E. Divinity School, Philadelphia. |
| **Chronicles.** | EDWARD L. CURTIS, D.D., Professor of Hebrew, Yale University, New Haven, Conn. |

## THE NEW TESTAMENT.

| | |
|---|---|
| **Acts.** | FREDERICK H. CHASE, D.D., Christ's College, Cambridge. |
| **Corinthians.** | ARCH. ROBERTSON, D.D., Principal of King's College, London. |
| **Galatians.** | Rev. ERNEST D. BURTON, A.B., Professor of New Testament Literature, University of Chicago. |
| **The Pastoral Epistles.** | Rev. WALTER LOCK, M.A., Dean Ireland's Professor of Exegesis, Oxford. |
| **Hebrews.** | T. C. EDWARDS, D.D., Principal of the Theological College, Bala ; late Principal of University College of Wales, Aberystwyth. |
| **James.** | Rev. JAMES H. ROPES, A.B., Instructor in New Testament Criticism in Harvard University. |
| **Peter and Jude.** | CHARLES BIGG, D.D., Rector of Fenny Compton, Leamington ; Bampton Lecturer, 1886. |
| **Revelation.** | Rev. ROBERT H. CHARLES, M.A., Trinity College, Dublin, and Exeter College, Oxford. |

*Other engagements will be announced shortly.*

EDINBURGH: T. & T. CLARK, 38 GEORGE STREET.
LONDON: SIMPKIN, MARSHALL, HAMILTON, KENT, & CO. LTD.

## A GREAT BIBLICAL ENCYCLOPÆDIA.

*To be completed in Four Volumes, Imperial 8vo.*

### NOW READY—VOLUMES I. and II.

**The Times.**—'*If the other volumes come up to the standard of the first, this Dictionary seems likely to take its place as the standard authority for biblical students of the present generation.*'

**The Guardian.**—'*The work promises to be, when completed, the best biblical encyclopædia in English.*'

**The Academy.**—'*Both the editors and the publishers are to be congratulated upon the appearance of the first volume of this most excellent work. . . . If the other volumes keep up to the high level of this one, the editors will have produced the best biblical Dictionary which has yet appeared.*'

A

# Dictionary of the Bible

### DEALING WITH ITS LANGUAGE, LITERATURE, & CONTENTS, INCLUDING THE BIBLICAL THEOLOGY.

Edited by JAMES HASTINGS, M.A., D.D.,

With the Assistance of J. A. SELBIE, M.A., and, chiefly in the Revision of Proofs, of
A. B. DAVIDSON, D.D., LL.D., Edinburgh; S. R. DRIVER, D.D., Litt.D.,
Oxford; H. B. SWETE, D.D., Litt.D., Cambridge.

*Full Prospectus, with Specimen Pages, from all Booksellers, or from the Publishers.*

VOLUME I.—A TO FEASTS.
VOLUME II.—FEIGN TO KINSMAN.

*Published Price per Volume—*

**In Cloth, 28s.**
   **In Half-Morocco, 34s.**

www.ingramcontent.com/pod-product-compliance
Lightning Source LLC
Chambersburg PA
CBHW032105220426
43664CB00008B/1139